SURVIVING
YOUR
ACADEMIC JOB
HUNT

ADVICE FOR
HUMANITIES PHDS

D1535596

Kathryn Hume

palgrave
macmillan

For Rob Hume,
who taught me all I know about academic politics

SURVIVING YOUR ACADEMIC JOB HUNT
© Kathryn Hume, 2005.

All rights reserved. No part of this book may be used or reproduced in any manner whatsoever without written permission except in the case of brief quotations embodied in critical articles or reviews.

First published in 2005 by
PALGRAVE MACMILLAN™
175 Fifth Avenue, New York, N.Y. 10010 and
Houndmills, Basingstoke, Hampshire, England RG21 6XS
Companies and representatives throughout the world.

PALGRAVE MACMILLAN is the global academic imprint of the Palgrave Macmillan division of St. Martin's Press, LLC and of Palgrave Macmillan Ltd. Macmillan® is a registered trademark in the United States, United Kingdom and other countries. Palgrave is a registered trademark in the European Union and other countries.

ISBN 1–4039–6728–8 hardback
ISBN 1–4039–6729–6 paperback

Library of Congress Cataloging-in-Publication Data

Hume, Kathryn, 1945–
    Surviving your academic job hunt : advice for humanities PhDs / by Kathryn Hume.
        p. cm.
    Includes bibliographical references (p.) and index.
    ISBN 1–4039–6728–8 (alk. paper)
    ISBN 1–4039–6729–6 (pbk.: alk. paper)
        1. College teachers—Employment—United States. 2. Universities and colleges—Faculty—Employment—United States. 3. Job hunting—United States. I. Title.
LB2331.72.H86 2005
650.14'04372—dc22   2004050855

A catalogue record for this book is available from the British Library.

Design by Newgen Imaging Systems (P) Ltd., Chennai, India.

First edition: January 2005

10 9 8 7 6 5 4 3 2 1

Printed in the United States of America.

Contents

Preface

As a humanities PhD, you have devoted five to ten years to getting your degree, and almost everyone in that position wants an assistant professorship. How, though, can you hope to get one when states are slashing their universities' budgets by ten percent and more? You hear rumors that a prestigious Ivy program placed less than a third of its English PhDs, and indeed the figure bandied about is that only something like forty percent of humanities PhDs get tenure-track jobs eventually. Or a friend at a medium-ranked state university gloomily tells you, "we have one hundred and twenty in the PhD program; sixty will actually get their degrees, and maybe a dozen will get tenure-track jobs, but ten of those jobs will be 4–4 or 5–5." Is this all one can hope for at the end of the rainbow?

If you prepare yourself properly—or if your departmental program prepares you—you can improve considerably on those odds. In 2003, Penn State's English department job hunters surpassed their previous records: Those who did full searches—not limiting themselves to one location or to only the best schools—all got tenure-track jobs. One hundred percent. More ordinary patterns prevailed in the previous few years, but even those are noteworthy. In 2002, eleven job hunters from that department landed eight faculty positions. Four of them got 2–2 or 2–3 loads, one a 3–3 with very short semesters. The other three obtained 4–4 jobs, though one has very good research facilities nearby, one has tiny classes, and the third has very good pay and benefits. Of the fourteen hunting the previous year, eight got jobs at schools that value their research as well as their teaching, while others got teaching-oriented jobs at attractive and collegial schools, or became technical writers, or searched again in 2002 and mostly succeeded. In the year prior to that, nine out of fifteen got jobs, and five of those who went jobless got good positions in 2001 or 2002. So far, almost everyone from this program who truly wanted to be a teacher and researcher and who was able to bear the stress of hunting three years in a row found tenure-track employment. What, then, do you need beside luck and determination?

You need knowledge and planning. This handbook can inform you about the process, and it will help you lay out a timeline so that you accomplish all you need to at each stage in the process. Your department can use this framework to give you rigorous training to face the challenges ahead of you. Even if your department does nothing to train job hunters, you can train yourself, or—better yet—you can band together with other hunters and help each other. The basics are all here. Three chapters cover the hunt procedure: the timeline and documents, the conference interview, and the campus interview and negotiations. The last two chapters introduce you to some less-than-obvious information about conditions of employment and departments. The economics and politics of being an assistant professor will not just come into play down the road; they are relevant to getting the job as well. You need to understand some of the problems of being a faculty member if you are to be able to project yourself as a colleague rather than as a student. Additionally, these chapters will help you understand better what questions to ask when you get to a campus, what perquisites to bargain for, and what to look for when trying to determine how satisfactory the job might be.

Why another book on job-hunting? Several with real virtues are available. Heiberger and Vick's *The Academic Job Search Handbook* (1996) seems to me the best overall, though for people in the humanities, the rhetorical approach used in Formo and Reed's *Job Search in Academe* (1999) should let you put the problems in terms with which you are very familiar. I recommend these, but since they counsel job hunters in a broad range of disciplines, they generalize their advice until it more or less applies to Engineering and Sociology as well as Humanities. I have chosen to concentrate on closely allied humanities fields that follow nearly the same pattern and schedule and whose basic expectations are practically interchangeable. These include English, History, Philosophy, modern languages and Comparative Literature, Linguistics, Classics, Art History, the rhetorical side of Speech Communication, African American Studies, American Studies, Women's Studies, Film Studies, Religious Studies, and Jewish Studies. This approach permits me to be much more field-specific. If one tries to extract the most generally applicable pattern from fields that are too disparate, the result is necessarily lifeless and artificial; vividness usually lies in specifics. Whatever the faults of this little book, it will try not to bore you with abstractions.

Like the two handbooks mentioned earlier, *The MLA Guide to the Job Search* (1996) and *The Chicago Guide to your Academic Career* (2001) assume a somewhat idealized world. At times they seem to work on the assumption that you can afford to be picky about the jobs you apply for

or accept. Such assumptions may derive from some of their writers' connections to elite institutions; such assumptions may also reflect conditions
in nonhumanities fields. I am writing for people who do not come from
elite institutions. If your degree says Chicago or Berkeley, your application is usually taken seriously at a research-oriented school, and you
might indeed have some choice. If you come from a middle-ranked state
university or less-distinguished private university, your CV may not carry
much weight unless your record itself can command respect. This book
will show you what you need to make it stand out.

For information about how to adapt to the assistant professorial
duties, you also have good books to turn to: Boice's *Advice for New
Faculty Members* (2000), Goldsmith et al.'s *The Chicago Guide to your
Academic Career*, Menges et al.'s *Faculty in New Jobs* (1999), Deneef and
Goodwin's *The Academic's Handbook* (1995), Schoenfeld and Magnan's
Mentor in a Manual (2nd ed., 1994), and Toth's *Ms. Mentor's Impeccable
Advice for Women in Academia* (1997). All of these may help you learn
to apply for grants or develop a relationship with a mentor or build networks at conferences. Only Toth gets into the dynamics of departmental
politics—wittily and cannily—but she does stress their gendered aspects
at the expense of other possible perspectives. Although my book is much
briefer than these tomes, I will give you some facts about the economic
underpinnings of your career and the basic principles of how and why
institutions work as they do, and what the implications are for you as a
junior member of such an institution.

This is a survival manual for humanities PhDs, not an idealized or gen-
eralized description of a process, and not a book of etiquette. It reflects
one person's sardonic and intensely practical view of how to survive and
thrive in academe.

I owe many of the anecdotes to friends in other universities, and to the
job hunters whom I have helped prepare for the market. Amy Smith
designed the thesis description document; Don-John Dugas and Matt
Kinservik originated the concept of the cheat sheet; Greg Colón Semenza
developed a good check list for keeping application documents straight
and supplied me with an entire portfolio of all documents used for a
search. I owe particular thanks to them and to those job hunters who
have generously let me use their job documents, both for their successors
and now for a larger audience. Special thanks for anecdotes and documents to Marco Abel, Dana Anderson, Elizabeth Archuleta, Adam Banks,
Paul Cannan, Beth Capo, Marianne Cotugno, Rich Cunningham,
Mark Decker, Amy Elias, Jess Enoch, Pat Gehrke, Susan Searls Giroux,
Anne Fisher Gossage, Sean Grass, Debra Hawhee, Heather Hayton,

Elisabeth Heard, Brent Henze, Ylce Irizarry, Jeff Karnicky, Janet Cooper LayPort, Lara Lomicka, Mark Longaker, Gillian Lord, Kelly Marsh, Jennifer Merriman, John Muckelbauer, Vorris Nunley, Harvey Quamen, Howard Rambsy II, Catherine Reed, Lisa Roney, Umeeta Sadarangani, Wendy Sharer, Andrew Slap, Jillian Smith, Michael Svoboda, Srividhya Swaminathan, Julie Vedder, and many others. Colleagues and friends who read the manuscript, supplied information, or who collaborated in training job hunters are also owed my heart-felt thanks: Bob Blue, Barbara Bullock, Deb Clarke, Keith Gilyard, Liz Jenkins, Philip Jenkins, Vincent Lankiewish, Janet Lyon, Jeffrey Partridge, John Protevi, Ralph Rodriguez, Marie Secor, Jack Selzer, Garrett Sullivan, John Whalen-Bridge, and Ed Williams.

One

How to Plan Your Job Hunt: Timeline and Documents

If you were to make a list of everything you need to do for a job hunt, you might well feel daunted. By breaking the process down into monthly steps, I hope to help you apportion your time and reduce chaos to manageable clusters of activity. First, note the date of your field's national convention where preliminary interviews take place. The American Academy of Religion (AAR) meeting takes place in late November. Speech Communication interviews also take place in November, and some preliminary screening interviews for History take place at autumn regional or specialty meetings. Philosophy, English, and the various languages hold their meeting at the very end of December. History and Linguistics meet at the beginning of January. Preparations for interviewing can start four months in advance, so toward the end of July (for Religious Studies, Speech Com, and some History) and late August (for the rest). Women's Studies, African American Studies, Jewish Studies, and American Studies candidates will hunt at one or more of those meetings, depending on the emphasis of their work.

If you are lucky enough to get campus interviews, the worst of the scramble will probably be over in March; late jobs do open up, though, so you might be going through some of this process in April, May, or even later. August through April constitutes the basic job hunting cycle for academic jobs in the humanities. During that cycle, most of your waking hours will be devoted to preparations and drill, to asking questions or digging for information on schools, to jittery high hopes or unproductive laments over things you think you might have done better. Along with all this, you will be finishing or revising your dissertation, and probably teaching as well.

When Should You Go on the Job Market?

Advice will vary, and so will the conventions of your field. If you belong to a data-driven field and your thesis mostly consists of writing up the results, you can finish it very quickly, so job hunting when you have just started writing the dissertation is reasonable. If you are in a field in which you might reasonably apply for only five jobs, you should still have time to do some work, so again, you might start hunting when several chapters remain to be written. If, however, you are in a field in which you can apply for sixty or more jobs, you will be frantically trying to find enough hours in the day just for that. Humanities dissertations tend to take much longer than their authors expect. Very few writers can hope to finish by August if the thesis is only half-written when the job list appears. Given the intensely consuming nature of a search, you will get little or nothing written between the appearance of that first job list in September and the end of the cycle in March or April. Ideally, therefore, you should not hunt until your dissertation is drafted, but you may not be afforded that luxury unless your department needs lots of warm bodies to teach its elementary courses. If you have any choice in the matter, I suggest going on the market for the first time when your dissertation is done and can be defended just before or just after the interview conference.

Some students have found it valuable to do a partial search somewhat earlier than this ideal starting point. The need for a green card, for instance, might make you wish to search early to maximize your window of opportunity. In a selective, early search, you apply only for the most attractive jobs. From this, you can hope at least to get the experience of a real interview, and if you get one of these prime jobs, you will probably work like crazy to defend in August before taking off for the new horizons. By limiting yourself to jobs that truly attract you in an early search, you avoid having to turn down a job you find unappealing, or you avoid accepting it, knowing that your finished record one year later might have helped you secure a job you liked better. A partial search still takes great amounts of time and energy, but it has worked well for candidates who could afford the cost of an extra trip to the conference. Its benefits for most candidates, though, came in confidence and effectiveness during their searches the next year. Few actually get a job during the partial search unless their field is very hot.

The decision regarding when to search must be individual, but figure that you start with a heavy black mark against you if you turn up for a research-oriented job without degree. Indeed, some research-oriented jobs are contingent upon your having defended, since you cannot properly teach the graduate seminars without the degree. Schools happy to hire you as an ABD (all but dissertation) tend to be teaching-intensive, and may demand so much time for students and collegial activities as actually to prevent you from finishing. Better, therefore, if you can do so, to hunt when you are finished or very nearly finished. Your having defended definitely makes your application more attractive.

What to Do during the Year prior to Going on the Market

Here are some things you should try very hard to do during the year prior to your search. I have classified them as institutional, expository, professional, and practical.

A. Institutional Things to Do

- Sit in on your department's job-hunt training program, if it has one, so you know more than a year in advance what will be expected of you.
- Take steps to add useful credentials to your CV. For most fields these will be technological and web-related, but a language or an editing course might help in some fields.
- If your department lets graduate students serve on search committees, try to get such an assignment. You will see a search from the other side, and might observe or even participate from the hiring side if you attend the conference.

B. Expository Things to Do

- Make preliminary drafts of your CV and letter of application.
- Assemble material for a teaching portfolio.
- Polish the chapter or article(s) that will serve as your writing sample(s).
- Push yourself hard on your dissertation. If that is finished, then work on articles and on turning your dissertation into a book.
- If you are in Comparative Literature or a language department, practice talking about your research and work in your languages as well as in English. Your interview may be partly or wholly in the other language(s), and you must be as fluent as possible. The longer you practice

talking on predictable topics, the more easily you will handle any linguistic challenges.

C. Professional Things to Do

• Join your field's professional organization. Study its job list, both printed and electronic versions, just to get a feel for the process.
• Read the *Chronicle of Higher Education* faithfully throughout the year. You may well be asked your opinion on hot issues, and will want to know any problems relating to the schools you are considering.

D. Practical Things to Do

• Buy good interview clothes at the winter sales the year before you hunt.
• Get credit cards. You will need to charge multiple air travel tickets in the same month. A popular candidate may have to put more than $5,000 for travel on a credit card, and schools can be slow to reimburse you.
• If you do not know how to drive, take lessons and get a license. You may be expected to rent a car and drive in from a distant airport—and should you get the job, you may need a car in your new town.
• Start putting aside every scrap of money you can. A job hunt costs a few thousand dollars if you include copying, dossiers, postage, tickets, conference costs, hotels, food in restaurants, interview clothing, a return to hunt for housing, car rentals, and rent deposits. On top of that, of course, you may need to be able to pay some or all of your moving costs; you may need to cover medical insurance for the period between jobs; and if you do not finish your degree in time, you will owe more tuition.

You may be wondering, "Is there any way around all of this?" Not really. The days when a supervisor could get you a job by calling a few friends are long gone, at least in the humanities. You have to make your own way in the market. International students sometimes make the mistake of assuming that their thesis director will get them a job. They may even feel that attending job-hunt training would show a lack of faith in their supervisor, a lack of loyalty. That feeling is misplaced.

The Job Hunt Cycle: August through April

Here is a checklist to help you plan your time. Each item will be explained in greater detail later.

August and September

(for History and Speech Communication, start in June or July, and move up the other activities accordingly)

1) Take care of any of the preliminaries you failed to do the prior year.
2) Design the various versions of your job application documents—research versus teaching jobs is the chief division, but you may be able to apply for two or more periods, or two fields, so you need separate documents for each.
3) Provide your departmental or university dossier center with your materials.
4) Ask your faculty recommenders to write their letters.
5) See your department's placement officers, if any, and talk to your supervisor and other friendly faculty about the process.

October and November

6) Collect information from the web on schools to which you are applying.
7) Apply for jobs.
8) Register for your professional conference.
9) Practice answering interview questions daily.
10) Do a mock interview; videotape it if possible.
11) Get a flu shot in November if you can; if not, get it in December.

December

12) Do more mock interviews.
13) Gather information on the schools and people interviewing you.
14) Prepare syllabi tailored to the schools interviewing you.
15) Go to your profession's conference and interview.

January and February

16) Send e-mail thank you notes for interviews and follow up on any references or materials you may have promised to send.
17) Do a mock campus presentation.
18) Travel to your campus interviews.

March and April

19) Make decisions and negotiate job terms.
20) If necessary, continue applying to late-opening jobs and add to your credentials for the next cycle of applications.

Since new jobs continue to appear, you may in fact be applying to new jobs in March and doing campus interviews in May, but if you are lucky, your life will start returning to normal in April, except that you may be planning to relocate on the opposite side of the country. This will involve reading a large packet of information so you can choose your retirement plan, reading yet more confusing forms to choose a medical plan, preparing book orders, designing syllabi, dealing with a mover, finding housing, and finishing up at your current school. No matter how prepared and professional you are, you will feel overwhelmed by the amount of information and the number of forms you have to fill out. Be sure to start informing yourself about your new location. Read some novels set there, and if you can squeeze it in, read a regional history.

Timeline Analysis

1) Take Care of Any of the Preliminaries You Failed to do the Prior Year

The year before you go on the market is the time to add credentials to your CV. Take every opportunity to gain technological skills. Join a pilot program using technology in the classroom. Get a webmaster certification. Build a course website. Learn about software that might be useful to you for teaching grammar, languages, or symbolic logic. Take a course in pedagogy from your university's center for improving teaching. Improve your skills with a language. If you teach technical or business writing, try to put your class onto doing a real-life assignment for a local company. All of these will provide you with extra qualifications and skills to talk about in an interview. If you hunt more than one year, continue to add to your credentials throughout the process.

This is also the time to deal with practical matters. Make plain to family and friends that you will not be free to join in holiday festivities this year. Make sure you know how or where to get airline tickets; some schools will arrange those for you, but others will expect you to handle that nuisance. Remove from your telephone answering machine all humorous noises or jocular comments and be sure it works well. Remove whimsical quotations from the signature of your e-mail.

August and September

2) Design Various Versions of Your Job Application Documents

The documents you need for applications consist of CV, letter of application tailored to different kinds of jobs and schools, shorter and longer teaching portfolio, dissertation description, writing sample, and syllabi.

CV *(see examples, pp. 130–178)*

Your CV documents your *past*. You will need at least two versions, one aimed at research schools, another at teaching institutions. This will be true for History, Philosophy, Linguistics, Speech Communication, and any literature degree. If you apply for literature and composition/rhetoric jobs, you will need different versions (research vs. teaching) for each, so four versions in all. If you are in a language department, you will need four versions aimed toward literature or language pedagogy as well as research and teaching. The differences reside principally in the order you follow to present the credentials and the amount of detail in any one section. For research schools, your research credentials come before teaching, and for teaching schools, the opposite. The amount of detail is governed by your emphasis. Presentations you have made at brown-bag lunches or workshops you have attended may be relevant to a teaching-oriented job, but would seem trivial as research credentials.

Think about your audience and how your CV will be used. Search committee members will sit around a large table, asking each other for this or that person's documents. Having your name in fairly large letters across the top makes it possible for someone across the table to spot your CV, whereas having "Curriculum Vitae" across the top is useless. Remember that material in the left margin is visually most gripping. Place information you do not wish to emphasize near the right margin and toward the end of a unit or section. Break your information up into logical units and make these units visually separate from each other.

Consider the function of each section. You need your name, personal web page address, and where you can be reached in the month before the conference by e-mail, phone, and mail. After that contact material, you need your professional credentials, including education, description of dissertation, publications, research interests, significant honors, and indications of teaching interests and effectiveness in the classroom. The final information for most fields will be the names of your recommenders, information on how to reach them, and a statement on how a school can obtain your complete dossier. (Dossiers ordinarily cannot be sent out to anyone who asks; you have to give permission, since it costs you money. Hence, you say that upon request, you will arrange to have it sent.) Do not give your office phone number if your graduate status only entitles you to a shared desk in a warren of cubicles. You do not want an interview message to go astray there, so just list your home phone. Remember, too, that some schools close a few days before Christmas; you do not want a document sent to school, where it might languish ten days before becoming available to you.

Here are other ways you need to tailor your data to its intended audience. Particularly when applying to a research-oriented school, separate refereed articles, chapters, and essays in collections from book reviews and encyclopedia entries. Hard-line scholars will not be favorably impressed by students who lump these together either because the students naïvely think the projects equivalent or because they want to make their publication list look longer. You should list articles sent out, but only give the journal name if you have received a "revise-and-resubmit." After all, anyone can send to the best journals in the field, but that does not mean the article is of that caliber. Your teaching interests and abilities should aim to show how useful you could be in a department. When you list recommenders, give their e-mail address and their phone numbers. Particularly over the winter break, their home phones (if they permit) could make the difference between your getting a campus interview or not. Following up on a conference interview, I had to phone referees for further information. Lack of home phone number made finding the right Sullivan in the greater Boston area a nightmare, but because of term break, none of the referees was to be found at the office, and the university website listed office phones only.

What else helps? Many job hunters list the societies to which they belong. Memberships do not prove professional activity, but no memberships can suggest lack of professionalism. Any honors prior to the major college honors (e.g., Phi Beta Kappa, *summa cum laude*) are irrelevant. If you boast of high school glories, readers will recoil with disdainful pity at your having nothing more worthwhile to claim for yourself. One article in a top-ranked journal is worth more to a research-oriented school than all the fellowships and travel grants you can list. Teaching prizes as a graduate student will count heavily in your favor with any employer.

The CV is only a piece of paper, but it represents you, so take trouble over its appearance. If you are doing new kinds of work, use a modern-looking font, not something designed in the eighteenth century. If you do historical scholarship in one of the older periods, a conservative font nicely reflects that orientation. If you are working on Native American literature or history, you might use small appropriate tribal symbols to ornament the top of the first page or to indicate section breaks. A Renaissance specialist might use something from an emblem book or antique printers' symbols. Study examples of CVs and decide where boldface, italics, large or small capitals, underscoring, change of font, and change of font size will help make information stand out. Such typographical styling is crucial to making information easy to retrieve and pleasant to look at. Do not get too flashy, though, or run wild with graphics. Make sure you supply enough white space to relieve the eye. Remember also not to shrink your font below eleven in size; many search committee members are old enough that tiny fonts cause eye strain, which will prejudice them against your documents. You will need time to play with your options and find what you like best, so start early. You can enjoy making the CV something you are proud to have represent you.

Letter of Application

Whereas the CV documented your past, the letter of application represents your *future*. You are trying to make a department see that you would be a useful and productive member, a colleague in every sense. Each letter must be adapted so as to make clear why your credentials fit their job description. Tweaking the appropriate form of your letter to fit the job is time-consuming but necessary. Because you may find yourself trying to do thirty to eighty such letters at once, establish your priorities and get the applications to your preferred jobs out first, since the first hundred applications to arrive get read by more members of a search committee than the last three hundred. Every member who is at all conscientious looks at the first fifty to one hundred, but many later ones are seen by only the most diligent member of the committee and its chair.

Rhetorically, the trouble spots in the letter are

a) Making yourself appear to be the right candidate for their job;
b) Saying something that shows you have done research on that department; and
c) Saying that you hope to see them at the conference.

Tone is very important at these three points. Being too pushy or too sure of your welcome may irritate some readers, but so will your being smarmy or servile.

Your tactic for the first trouble spot is to *show* them that you are suitable and desirable; you cannot simply *tell* them that you are the candidate they are looking for. To begin with, you do not know what they really want. Beyond the official description, they may want a peacemaker between clashing personalities in the period, or they may silently prefer a male or female or minority candidate, or someone on the committee may be hostile to approaches based on Deleuze and Guattari. If you are a Deleuzian theorist, your telling them that you are the right person for the job will provoke an irritated snort. Irritation is a reaction you wish to avoid. When a tired committee meets late at night to whittle four hundred applications down to the twenty-five for which they will seek writing samples, members will eagerly seize on any reason for discarding a candidate. Your basic tactic is to mention the specifications in their job ad and present your qualifications in a way that makes you seem a good fit for those needs. You also try to make plain how your methodology is widely applicable in different sorts of courses and engages the students in unexpected ways.

Your tactic for the second should be to show awareness of the kind of school (university, liberal arts college, community college, sectarian school) and some knowledge of the department, but avoid fulsome praise ("your well known program"). Sometimes a quote from their department mission statement can be put to good use. If you are applying to a sectarian school, you may wish to comment on your interest in working in a Christian or Latter Day Saints community, but you should get advice beforehand on what that school expects, and not waste your time or theirs by applying if your beliefs and lifestyle are not suitable to theirs. If a school is located somewhere with an extreme climate and you happen to know that you like that climate, you can make that plain. If you have lived in a dangerous part of a big city, you can indicate that the school's having such a location does not faze you. "I'm a Chicagoan, and grew up across the street from the projects, so I can deal with urban environments and would love to get back to a big city" addresses an issue without labeling it a problem.

Another way to prove that you have tried to visualize yourself in their department is to talk about their courses, using their course numbers. You can mention those courses in their list that you could teach with little or no lead-time, and also mention some you would be happy to work up if given a bit of warning. In the folder you are building on each school you apply to, you will, of course, keep their course descriptions, since you will need to be able to refer to them when preparing for an interview.

To handle the third rhetorical trouble-spot, you need to indicate that you will be at the national conference, but do not write as if you assume you are getting the interview, and do not sound servile. Just state that you will be attending the conference and would enjoy a chance to learn more about the job from them, and be sure to give information on where you can be reached in the days just before the conference, in case they put off scheduling an interview until very late.

Beyond these trouble spots, the letter should present your credentials with an eye to how they can make you look useful. What can you do for that school? What research do you intend to move on to next? Your answer will depend on the job. If you are marketing yourself as either "nineteenth century" or "poetry," you would pursue another nineteenth-century topic for your second book if the job were Victorian, but you might pursue a poetry book that ranged into another century if you secured a poetry-genre job. How much will you have to do to your thesis to turn it into a book manuscript? You should comment on that if you are serious about doing research. If your thesis topic takes you outside of specialist arguments into some cultural topic of wider interest, you might indicate your awareness that you could present some of your findings in nonscholarly lectures for alumni. Some schools are eager to acquire faculty who will help woo donors in that and other fashions. Intelligently chosen comments that go beyond strict formula will make the reader remember your application.

Here is a final piece of advice on adapting your letter to your audience. Students specializing in highly theorized topics often feel they must show off their membership in such a community by loading their letters with its jargon. They may, indeed, have become so acclimated to the vocabulary that they no longer realize just how opaque it is to anyone even slightly outside their specialty. I have known brilliant students—good teachers and promising writers—who seemed primed for success but did not get any conference interviews. They saw simplifying their letters as dumbing their research down, and resisted presenting themselves as cheerful and collegial rather than as intellectually formidable. In your thesis description, you can afford to show a bit of that theoretical engagement, but keep the letter as approachable, friendly, and collegial as possible.

Keep electronic and hard copies of every letter you send. Do not just change the address and addressee and fail to keep the original saved separate from the next version. Each letter should be just individual enough that you need the true form, not an approximation. If you get an interview, you will want to know *exactly* how you represented yourself.

Syllabi

You might or might not wish to include selected syllabi in your application, but you will definitely want many versions of syllabi worked up prior to the interview. These should include a course description, book list, and reserve list, but not the day-by-day lesson plan. The earlier you write the basic syllabi that can be adapted to specific departmental courses, the better, since once you are truly involved in applying and gathering information on schools you will not have time for syllabus design. Do those now and then adapt them to particular schools later, making sure you know the length of their semester. Job hunters have often been told that they got the campus interview because the conference interview committee was impressed by individualized syllabi. Most candidates do little research on the school and spend no effort trying to picture how they might fit in or contribute to a school's mission, so candidates with tailored syllabi stand out.

Working up syllabi takes time, and if you have never taught anything but your department's elementary service courses, you may wish to browse course syllabi to get ideas. The web offers useful sites for this. Try the following as starting points.

- African American literature syllabi:
  http://www.georgetown.edu/tamlit/teaching/af-am_syl.html
- American Lit syllabi:
  http://www.millikin.edu/aci/crow/syllabi.html
- History syllabi:
  http://www.ceu.hu/crc/Syllabi/west-syllabi/documents/History
- Literature syllabi (mostly British):
  http://www.english.upenn.edu/~jlynch/syllabi.html
- Religious Studies syllabi:
  http://www.aarweb.org/syllabus
- Philosophy syllabi:
  http://www.earlham.edu/~peters/gpi/teaching.htm
- Women and Gender related syllabi:
  http://www.umbc.edu/cwit/syl_lit.html

You will doubtless feel very short of time to work on syllabi, but that time will pay for itself when you are asked, two weeks before your new job starts, to teach an unexpected course. You may be able to pull one of these out, and know exactly what books to order and what materials to put on reserve.

Teaching Portfolio

You may want two versions of this document, a two- to four-page version to include with your application, and a longer one to hand out at interviews. The shorter might include a brief statement of teaching philosophy, a description of the courses you have taught, and a digest of your numeric scores on class evaluations. (You will find models among the documents at the back of this book.) The longer form would include expanded discussions of your courses in addition to student comments (with carefully chosen negative remarks among the positive), and possibly a letter from the professor who supervised your teaching composition, an elementary language course, or a more advanced section or course in your subject area. You might wish to include (or carry separately, as handouts in interviews) photocopies of student papers that you have commented upon and marked. Some people present an eighty-page portfolio; this tends to make interviewers grumble because they do not wish to wade through it. Keep even your longer version reasonable in length, not more than twenty sheets of paper, say, unless you also include a couple of marked-up student papers.

Dissertation Description

You will have to write an abstract to satisfy Dissertation Abstracts International and various thesis requirements. You can just use that abstract in the application, or you can produce a somewhat different document. One Penn State PhD designed a brilliantly effective thesis description that other job hunters have imitated since. For the one-page version, see that of Madeleine Maxwell (p. 195); for the two-page form, see Jorge Colón (pp. 196–97). Abstracts are usually unreadable, thanks to their compression of complex arguments; single spacing; and their lack of paragraphing, subheads, and other aids to comprehension. This document offers comments under five headings: Value of research specialization, argument of the dissertation, contribution of the dissertation, teaching applications, and relevance to future research. The single-page presentation answers many of the questions that search committees will be asking about your thesis, and the clear headings make both reading and remembering very easy. The two-page version follows the original format for the first page, and adds chapter descriptions on the second.

Writing Sample

Some schools demand a writing sample with your application; others request it if you seem promising. If you decide to send an offprint with the application, do not be surprised if you later receive a request for a writing sample. Such requests are dispatched to everyone who made the first cut without a check to see if anything is in the file. You can send another copy, send a different sample, or just tell them to check their files. Such a situation might give you an excuse to make e-mail or phone contact with the head of the search committee in a fashion that could help make your name known to him or her.

Depending on your interests, you may need more than one writing sample. A self-contained article will work better than a long chapter, and if already printed, it will look finished in ways that a typescript cannot. A partial chapter leaves your skills at building an argument incompletely demonstrated. Most schools specify a twenty-page sample, so a fifty-page chapter does not win you favor, and it will cost a lot to photocopy and send. If what you send is a draft, be extra careful with your spelling and punctuation. You may prefer a loose form of punctuation and flexible grammar, but many of your readers will count against you every split infinitive, and some of them will mark such errors in red for their fellow search committee members to contemplate. Have several friends and mentors read your sample. You may feel you need to send two samples: your printed article might be a medieval seminar paper worked up, but the job is nineteenth century. You might send the article to illustrate your skills at building a complete argument, and you send a portion of a nineteenth-century chapter to illustrate your thinking in the desired field. Explain your logic for sending both in your cover letter. You can always offer to send a complete chapter or the whole dissertation if they wish to see more.

You might like to put your CV, teaching portfolio, and writing sample or samples on a web page. Be warned, however, that many members of your search committee will be inexpert with the Internet, and might well not bother to look at you further if they cannot have your paper record on the table in front of them. Furthermore, poor schools have little or no computer support, so faculty forced to look for information on the web might have to eat up their own personal access time to do so.

3) Provide Your Departmental or University Dossier Center with Your Materials

Go to your university dossier service or to the department secretary responsible for doing this chore and establish a file. Learn the names of the staff members who will be handling material and carry out all of your future dealings in person. Your orders for instant dispatch of desperately needed items are less likely to fall through the cracks if you are known as a polite, friendly client than if you are merely the sender of imperious e-mails. After the first few free dossiers, you will probably have to pay several dollars each for subsequent sendings. Some such services let you put down $100 in advance so that they can send things out without waiting for you to come in and pay. Up-to-date career centers permit credit cards.

4) Ask Your Faculty Recommenders to Write Their Letters

Ask three to five faculty members to write letters of recommendation for you, and be sure that each one is genuinely willing. Do not wait until the last minute. Some professors notoriously take forever to do this chore. You can make it easier for them by providing a fact sheet on yourself, on your aims and qualifications, on whatever it is that might make you stand out as interesting and different. Remind them of your seminar paper topic. Talk extensively with any who are willing, and feed them information that you think would be helpful in the letters of recommendation. Do remind them not to use your actual phrases, because if two recommenders use the same words, their doing so undermines your letters' credibility. Ask them to look over your CV and application letters. You will need a complete dossier by mid-October, so ask for letters the first week in September.

5) See Your Department's Placement Officers, if Any, and Talk to Your Supervisor and Other Friendly Faculty about the Process

If your department has faculty who oversee job hunters, consult these placement officers. Supply them with an information sheet about yourself, your interests, your dissertation, and the kind of job you are most eager to get. Also, bring CVs, sample letters, dissertation descriptions, and any other documents you expect to use. They can start a file on you with this material, and refresh their memories about your needs and aims. The more they know about you, the better they can ferret out information that might be useful to you. You should run your CVs and letters by them at least twice, as well as get feedback from your thesis supervisor and any other mentors on whom you can impose for useful criticism.

When your dossier is complete, you can arrange for a copy to be sent to a placement officer (or to your supervisor) so that someone can make sure that all the letters are effective. While they can ask a colleague to fix a few typos, they should not ask someone to rewrite to make a letter more positive, though they can ask if the colleague was aware of the ambiguity or negative impact of some particular phrase. If the letter really is not positive enough, the placement officer can advise you to have it removed from the dossier. Letters from specialists outside your department and university may pose problems. Any recommender trained in a British university will write a much more balanced, assessing, critical letter than is customary now in America, and such a letter would be read as totally damning, even by those who understand intellectually the cultural difference in the rhetoric. Someone in France may produce two lines of handwritten recommendation that will do little to help you in this country. Such culturally different letters scream at the reader in the American context of puffery, in which everyone is the next superstar. Such letters are often better removed, but you will need field-specific advice on that decision.

October and November

6) Collect Information from the Web on Schools to Which You are Applying

This you need to do as you write the individually tailored letters of application. The web makes turning up the needed information relatively easy. Here are sources for department web pages.

- African American:
  http://www.pressroom.com/~afrimale/aaud.htm
- Classics (for graduate and undergraduate programs, respectively):
  http://www.williams.edu:803/Classics/Grad_programs.html
  http://www.humanities.uci.edu/classics/departments.html
- Comparative Literature:
  http://www.swan.ac.uk/german/bcla/clusa.htm
- English (for 1,300 sites in the United States alone, and even more, worldwide):
  http://www.nyu.edu/gsas/dept/english/links/engdpts.html
- French:
  http://www.french-at-a-touch.com/Schools_and_Universities/american_universities_for_the_states_a_-_i.htm
- History:
  http://chnm.gmu.edu/assets/historydepts/departments.php?function=find

(for 1,200 around the world) For North American history departments, http://www.historycooperative.org/elibrary/hw/depts.html
- Jewish Studies (academic programs): http://jewishstudies.virtualave.net/Jewish_Studies_at_Universities/USA/index.shtml
- Latin American Studies, also helpful for Spanish: http://socrates.berkeley.edu:7001/Research/links.html (North American programs come far down the list.)
- Philosophy: http://www.apa.udel.edu/apa/asp/departments.asp
- Religious Studies: http://www.clas.ufl.edu/users/gthursby/rel/depts-na.htm
- Russian: http://ash.swarthmore.edu/slavic/rusweb.html
- Speech Communication: http://www.natcom.org/ComProg/deptlist.htm
- Women's Studies and Gender Studies programs: http://research.umbc.edu/~korenman/wmst/programs.html

If I haven't listed one for you, ask around in your department; an equivalent probably exists. Keep all the information you glean from such a site in a file devoted to your application to that school.

Design a check sheet that lists the school, the kind of job, whether they requested writing sample or dossier up front, and whether they requested it later. Make places for yourself to list information about anything special sent to them, and the date it was sent—this will protect you from the anguished attempt to remember whether you really did send a writing sample. Note down any communication you receive from them, with the date. You may do this as a series of columns, or as a variety of listed entries with places for check marks (see sample, p. 207).

7) Apply for Jobs

Everyone in a humanities field can look for job ads in the *Chronicle of Higher Education*. For literature jobs, you search the on-line job information list (JIL) of the Modern Language Association (MLA), which has been appearing in mid- to late September, the printed version in the second week of October. Use both. The electronic search process is clumsy, and you could well miss attractive jobs if you rely solely on that.

In history, the job list is found in the American Historical Association's *Perspectives* and on line at the Association's website, http://www. theaha.org. Those in linguistics should watch http://www.linguistlist.org as well as the MLA list and the *CHE*, and some languages have job lists, such as the American Association of Teachers of German, where jobs sometimes appear before the MLA list comes out. Philosophers can use the job ads at the American Philosophical Association site, http://www. apa.udel.edu/apa. Religious Studies jobs get listed at http://www. aarweb.org/openings/default.asp. New websites posting jobs in higher education appear and disappear too frequently to list them all here, but look for current ones and share information with your job-hunting friends. Special sites exist for looking outside of the United States. Each field has its own places where jobs are advertised, so ask around. Some jobs are advertised in specialist journals, too. Apply for all the jobs for which your qualifications are adequate and applicable, but do not waste effort and money on unsuitable jobs. Legally, a school cannot afford to hire someone who does not fit the ad reasonably closely. Get your applications in the mail within two weeks of the job list's appearance, if possible, and send first the applications to the most attractive jobs.

8) Register for the Professional Conference

Register promptly. Whereas the advice would once have been to stay away from conference hotels because their elevators and switchboards were inadequate to full occupancy, that seems no longer to be a problem. Hence, although the conference hotels are pricier, you will find it very convenient if most of your interviews are in the hotel where you are staying. If you are not going to be accompanied by a partner, make arrangements to share the room with a job-hunting friend. You will be able to practice for interviews together, and having someone to talk to over meals will make the process much more enjoyable and less lonely. If the conference does not secure good rates for the conference hotels, browse the web for cheaper lodgings in the general vicinity. Beware of cheap lodgings a long way off; public transportation during the holiday season or on a Sunday morning can be sporadic or nonexistent. To help pay for this, you may wish to apply to a funding source in your university for graduate students attending conferences. Some professional bodies also make small amounts ($100 for MLA) available to successful graduate applicants, but such subventions must be applied for.

9) Practice Answering Interview Questions Daily

While you wash the dishes, stand in line at the grocery store, or shower, you should be asking yourself and answering questions from the list in chapter 2. Whenever you are alone, do this out loud. Different parts of the brain are involved with silent and spoken answering. No matter how well practiced you are at silent answers, you still might go blank when trying to talk aloud to people. Only if you practice endlessly aloud can you guarantee yourself the fluency you will need when under pressure.

Decide which three or four points you want to make about yourself in your interviews and practice ways of inserting them into the imagined questions and conversations.

10) Do a Mock Interview; Videotape it if Possible

Some universities have an interview room in their job center with a video camera. You can also borrow a camera. Watching yourself on tape afterward is excruciating, but it may alert you to mannerisms that you can work to curb. Wear your interview clothes and seriously consider changes if they are urged upon you. Your style may not seem fitting to older interviewers. If your mock interviewers consider something seriously inappropriate, the chances are that your real interviewers will also. Do not approach the first mock interview as a chance to dip your toe in and see what it's like, planning to get serious for the second. You will be wasting everyone's time and damaging your own chances if you have not been practicing earnestly for a month on your answers to interview questions.

11) Get a Flu Shot in November if You Can; if not, Get it in December

Some students fail to follow this advice, and regret their insouciance later on. One athletic job hunter, who felt it would be immoral to get a shot during a year when serum was in short supply, returned from his final campus interview with a temperature of 105° F. He ended up in the emergency room and heard a nurse say blithely to his wife that brain damage only started at 106°. You may be healthy when you start this procedure, but the incredible stress, particularly during campus interviews, has the potential to deplete your energy and your immune system. If your mind has enough control over your body, you may avoid getting sick until the end of the last interview, but if you lose that control, you could be sick during campus interviews and blow one or more of them. Colds are bad enough, but an acute case of flu can set your career back an entire year.

December

12) Do More Mock Interviews

A total of two official mock interviews is about as much as you can hope for from the faculty of your department. If you are lucky, your supervisor may do one or two more for you. Do not just wait for faculty to pitch in, though. Job hunters should interview each other frequently and relentlessly. Indeed, you can turn it into a game and bonding ritual. In groups of three and four, meet every week over beer and try to stump your fellows with new variations on the basic questions. A departmental graduate student association could arrange student-run practice interviews. Throughout December, keep rehearsing answers to the questions, aloud when possible. Students have thought my insistence on practicing aloud silly, only to find themselves unable to formulate answers in the mock interviews, even though they knew that they "had" a good answer. One hunter ignored practicing aloud until after she froze in both of the mock interviews, so she taped the questions and played them to herself as she drove to the conference, and answered aloud in the car. By the end of the trip, she had gained in fluency, and in interviews, she no longer blanked.

13) Gather Information on the Schools and People Interviewing You

Invitations to interview start coming at the end of November and during the first week of December, with the rest drifting in during the second and third weeks if your field's conference is held between Christmas and the New Year. You may get invitations as late as the twenty-second. That means you have less than a month and sometimes barely a week to collect information from the web on the schools that wish to see you, and learn about the people who will be present in the interview. Useful material to collect or at least make notes on includes the mission statements for university and department, strategic plans, courses offered, the professional interests of the interviewers, those of that school's people in your field and adjacent periods, and an article or book by each interviewer. Download or photocopy those articles and read them; skim parts of the books. If you are interviewing with three schools, this is feasible, but less so if you are lucky enough to have fifteen interviews—and if you are favored with too many interviews, it behooves you to cancel those with the schools that attract you least as early as possible, thus permitting them to seek another interviewee. Save one less favored school and schedule it early so you get interview practice, but cancel a few others. Twelve to fifteen interviews are the maximum anyone can handle. Just telephone the department of one you decide to cancel and tell the secretary who answers that you would like to withdraw your name from their Art Historian or their Spanish Golden Age search, and thank them for their time and trouble. Do not expect to get much sleep between the early days of December and the holidays. Not only are you collecting data on your interview schools, you also have to extract the major points and write them up, and then crunch them down to the essentials that you semimemorize just before the interview.

14) Prepare Syllabi Tailored to the Schools Interviewing You

Syllabi tailored to the interviewing school are extremely effective. Do up one-or-two page syllabi with the books and assignments that you would use for three or four of their courses that you could be expected to teach. In addition, you need syllabi from courses that you have already taught and you should do up three or four "dream" courses, one each for various levels from introductory lecture course to graduate seminar. These courses should be imaginative and designed to attract students, and some may not correspond to any in the department's current course list. Draw on any special background you have to individualize your courses. Can you join science and technology to your humanities field? Do you have military training that could give spin to a course? International experience? An ethnic background? Try to individualize some of these dream courses, or give an unconventional flavor to a standard historical course.

15) Go to Your Profession's Conference and Interview

You should be developing a folder for each interview. Make them different colors. Label them clearly. In the folder goes information on the school, on your interviewers, the tailored syllabi, the syllabi for courses you have actually taught, your dream courses, and a teaching portfolio. Taped inside the front of the folder should go a "cheat sheet." This piece of paper includes the job description, points in your letter tailored to this job, names and basic professional interests of your interviewers, basic information on the department (number of faculty, number of majors, number of graduate students), the three or four points you wish to make about yourself, and a few questions you wish to ask them. It also includes the hotel, room number, and phone number of the interview suite. You can go over this sheet one more time just before knocking on the door of the suite.

If a fellow PhD trained with the same thesis supervisor on topics similar enough that you will be competing for the same jobs, get together beforehand and figure out how to differentiate your presentations of your training and interests and plans to teach courses so that you do not sound indistinguishable.

Be sure to have a sheet with phone numbers for your job placement officers, your supervisor, and any friendly faculty mentors. If a problem comes up in an interview, you want to be able to get advice quickly.

Travel lightly. If possible, limit yourself to carry-on luggage—holiday travel increases the likelihood that airlines will lose your suitcase. Be sure that your basic interview clothes and folders of information are in a carry-on. To make sure that you have all that you need, start a list of things to take with you and check them off as you pack them. In your general anxiety, you will find it all too easy to overlook socks, the necktie that goes with the conference suit, or an alarm clock (hotel wake-up service is not always reliable, especially when the hotels are fully occupied and the staff harried).

January and February

16) Send E-mail Thank You Notes for Interviews and Follow Up on Any References or Materials You May Have Promised to Send

This is your chance to remind them which candidate you are. If, for instance, you feel you answered one question badly, you can say you realized later what had been behind one of their questions, so you can now offer an answer more to the point, and then give it. If you promised another chapter, or in the course of discussion promised to send a reference to an article, be sure to send the reference. You need thank only the head of the search committee, but if one of the committee members was particularly friendly or professionally interesting, you might follow up with a note. Do not be pushy, but send an e-mail if it seems reasonable.

If they invited you during the interview to address them by first name, then use a first name salutation in your note.

17) Do a Mock Campus Presentation

If you can gather a few sympathetic faculty and some fellow job hunters, give the presentation you expect to make at your first campus interview and get feedback on its effectiveness. If your own school is interviewing candidates, attend one or two of their presentations to learn what works and what does not.

18) Travel to Your Campus Interviews

You need to have made arrangements well in advance for a non-job-hunting friend to teach your classes while you are away at campus interviews. Travel will be grueling; sometimes you may be back for no more than a day or two before you take off at dawn again. Blizzards will force last-minute changes. Travel food will undermine your morale and digestion. Being on show every minute of a campus interview wears you down. A badly run school can make the visit a frustrating hassle. Take your vitamins. Get as much sleep as you can. Some students report nightmares after a string of campus visits. On the positive side, you will meet many interesting and friendly people, and some will seem really attractive as potential colleagues. Many will go out of their way to be helpful, informative, and entertaining. Enjoy what you can.

March and April

19) Make Decisions and Negotiate Job Terms

Consult freely. Schools that know their offers are not very competitive are cleverly setting up campus interviews as early as possible, in hopes of forcing you to accept rather than risk going jobless. Given the vagaries of academic calendars, the schools you want to hear from may be on vacation until the very end of January and doing nothing to contact their preferred candidates. When arranging your earliest campus interviews, you can claim other commitments and try to put the interview off a week.

You may well face the unpleasant possibility of taking a job with a low salary, a heavy teaching load, no research facilities at all, and a very isolated, snow-bound location because you have not yet heard from a school that attracts you more. In the present market, no one can lightly turn down any job; nothing guarantees that you will be offered a better one, even if your book finds a press miraculously fast. Those of you with partners may face heavy pressure to take an unattractive job for geographical reasons. Ask yourself how you will feel in a dozen years if the marriage has ended and you are stuck in a job you dislike. If the work conditions have not let you do enough publishing to be a plausible candidate on the market, you could be stuck there. Indeed, a job you hate could bring the end of that marriage, leaving you personally worse off in this unsatisfactory job than in one you liked better.

20) If Necessary, Continue Applying to Late-opening Jobs and Add to Your Credentials for the Next Cycle of Applications

Because you are up against a pool of second- and third-time job hunters who got no jobs their previous tries or got jobs they do not like, you are competing with some people who have amassed more impressive CVs, some even with books accepted. You gain nothing by repining. Instead, note what you have to do to join that more attractive group with books accepted, and start working on yours. If you can't beat 'em, join 'em.

Two

Conference Interviews

You approach a hotel door. You turn off your cell phone so it will not interrupt the interview. You hear voices inside and wonder whether to knock or not. You take one last glance at your cheat sheet for this university, and rap boldly on the door at the appointed hour. You shake hands with two or six people, and note the coffee urn and the awkwardly placed chairs. Your heart beats faster as you sit down.

Conference interviews can be frightening because four to ten years of graduate study and preparation get judged during a twenty or forty-five minute conversation. Moreover, your knowledge is not the only issue; your manner, your fluency, your intensity, your political savvy, your winsomeness and charm are also important. Those who are shy dread the conference interview, but even they need not do so. Remarkably, you can produce fluent, cogent answers if you prepare in the right fashion. Moreover, as you go through several interviews, producing those answers without freezing, you will gain an immense sense of competence and confidence. You may even find it fun. One does not need a divine gift, just practice. Here are a variety of things you need to do to prepare yourself to do well in this highly artificial situation.

Image

Look natural. Oddly, you have to practice this. Look at least somewhat dressed up and thoroughly professional. Make sure your clothes look good when you sit as well as when you stand. By that I mean something pretty specific. A short skirt, no matter how stylish when you stand, will ride halfway up to your crotch when you sit in a low armchair. That sends the wrong signal to male interviewers, and is likely to irritate female interviewers as well. If your skirt exposes your knees, wear very opaque panty hose, or your knees will flare white if you sit in a low chair and look like a pair of headlights, drawing attention. Slacks pose no such problems. Men, make sure your socks stay up, and show no skin if you cross your legs. Suits are not necessary unless you have heard that a particular school is very formal and "gentlemanly"; a tweed jacket and good-quality slacks (not chinos) are fine. You may wish your outfit to reflect ethnic or cultural background, but avoid appearing too exotic. Give thought to your accessories: Interview committees after their tenth interview of the day will wax extravagantly sarcastic and giggly over a candidate's ill-chosen necktie. Completely bland clothes, however, are no help to their remembering you, so you should wear at least one unusual bright color. Wear your outfit several times before the interview so the new-clothing stiffness disappears. Because you may have to do a lot of walking and standing, make sure the new shoes are well broken-in and comfortable, and avoid high heels. Quite apart from the discomfort, you will look wobbly if you do not wear them regularly.

Present yourself as a colleague, not a student. Make this a conversation, and get them involved in it by asking questions. You should not just sit and wait for their probes. Do not just react; be active as well. You may find it difficult to overcome student deference or shyness. You may come from a background where modesty is prized and bragging abhorred. While you do not wish to boast here, you must continually and thoroughly demonstrate why you are good. If you are shy, remember that you have learned to overcome that in the classroom. Draw on your classroom persona. Work to transform yourself into a colleague before you have actually been given the job. Try to see things from a faculty point of view and project that view, which will differ considerably from a student perspective. Study chapters 4 and 5 of this book in order to understand some faculty concerns.

A school wants to know what you can do for it, so you need to think about the kind of school it is and the kind of programs it runs. If it is a community college, think about the needs of nontraditional students and international students working to improve their English. If the institution is a small liberal arts college, you will want to know how much emphasis it puts on training its majors for graduate school as opposed to other kinds of employment. Also, remember to refer to both such schools as colleges, not universities. If the school has a religious identity, is that identity largely a historical phenomenon or is it essential to that school's profile? If the department has many missions, you need to think about the needs of programs and majors and emphases. Ponder running a program—composition, Irish Studies, a postcolonial reading group, a business minor attached to a language department. What would that involve? If you are concerned with computers in the classroom or elaborate websites for courses, be sure you know what software would be appropriate and have an idea of what kind of support personnel are needed to keep a classroom system working smoothly.

Your manner must be reasonably energetic and forceful. A Canadian job-hunter warned me that being too energetic would not go over well if you interview with Canadian schools, and Midwesterners may find New York-style high-speed talk bothersome, so fine-tune your manner to the actual school. Some dynamism is necessary for most American schools because people extrapolate from your personal behavior to your probable performance in a class. If you are too low-key, they may conclude that students would find you boring and dreary. If you seem low-energy and tired, they will hypothesize that you will be unable to take the pressures of teaching, scholarship, and service.

Avoid looking awkward. For example, do not walk into the room with your briefcase in your right hand. That will cause a clumsy shuffle when you shake hands. If they offer you a glass of water, accept it. Adrenaline will dry your throat out, and your coughing and croaking for water in the middle of the interview calls attention to your extreme nervousness and makes you seem inept. Be sure beforehand that your cell phone has been turned off so it doesn't jangle everyone's nerves and force you to grope frantically in an inner pocket or the bottom of your purse. Anticipate the end of the interview. The indication that things are over may be abrupt: "I guess that's it, then." You should have an exit line or a pleasantry prepared to avoid awkwardness. One very practical response is "May I make two points about my interests that didn't come up? The first is . . . the second. . . ." Then thank your interviewers, and ask them when they will be making their decision.

Some schools prefer not to spend their budgets on interview suites and so use an interview center—usually a hotel ballroom divided into hundreds of cubicles. Some fields do all their interviewing in this fashion; if not in a ballroom, their interviewers will talk to you in a coffee shop or bar. Ask your supervisor what you are likely to face in this respect. Most of the advice for nonsuite interviews applies in such other locations. Beware of letting the questions in the next cubicle or booth distract you. Block out the noise and concentrate fiercely, even while striving to look relaxed.

Try to look as if you are enjoying this. If you are confident and can make them feel your love for your subject and your enthusiasm for teaching, that is worth more than carefully polished answers. The more fluent you are, the more you can simply project personality; if you are shy, though, or not quick at repartee, then hone those answers. If you are in the groove and answering well, you will find the process exhilarating and exciting. Enjoy the high and let that enjoyment show.

Attitude

Be positive. Be optimistic. Can do! If you learn that the school with which you are interviewing really needs someone to teach the intellectual prose course in your historical period, say cheerfully that you would have from January to September to work up a new course. If a school hired you and wanted that course, you would get to work right away. Your school has a useful database that would be an ideal resource, and Professor Diogenes has taught the course, so you will consult both and could start working on texts and a syllabus immediately. You must show similar willingness toward almost any courses you might be offered. You may have specialized in something esoteric, but the smaller the department to which you are applying, the more they will need you to be a generalist in your teaching.

Indeed, generalist versus specialist issues will often cause you to walk a fine line. Say you specialize in francophone (but not French) literature; or Caribbean literature in English; or Asian American or African American but not canonical American literature. A department may say it wants such a specialist, but you will nonetheless find that they probe to make sure you can comfortably teach outside your narrow research area. You may even be asked in a campus visit to teach something very mainstream, despite its not being your field, simply to allay this fear of the alien. The same will be true if you take your first job outside of the United States: When you try to get back into the country after three or ten years, you will have to strain to prove your ability to fit normal American academic expectations, even though lip service may be given to multicultural experience. By contrast, if your credentials are very standard, you must make yourself stand out as unusual and desirable for other abilities, often by adding technological experience.

Let your interviewers know that you can imagine yourself at their school. Sound positive about their school. Do not play hard to get and do not voice any dissatisfaction or even minor worries at this stage about finding work for a partner or schools for your kids. All the larger worries—partner's job, benefits for same-sex partner, need for special schooling for a child—should be saved until after the job offer has been made. For now, just be positive.

Be positive about your graduate experience, though you need not go overboard in feigned rapture. Keep statements about your graduate school specific: "The French department has modified its culture program in the following fashion. . . ." "My advisor gave me a great deal of training in that." "The rhetoric courses I took gave me better tools for linking literature to current events than most PhDs get from traditional literature programs." If you badmouth your current school, they will figure that you will badmouth them when you leave, or worse, while you are there. People do not want a rotten apple in their barrel.

From the beginning, stress your ability to balance research, teaching, and service. Your graduate years have probably exposed you to all three at the same time, so your role as assistant professor will not be that strange to you. Draw assurance from that. You need to exude confidence and thoughtfulness in equal measure.

Be yourself. Do not just try to guess what they want to hear. Some people really want to meet a new person with a fresh perspective. If they begin what sounds like an argument, they may just be challenging you to state your position even in the face of opposition, and may like you better if you can do so. You can always hedge slightly. "On the basis of my experience so far, I would choose your first option for the following reasons. . . . What are the considerations that make you prefer the alternative?"

Be courteous, even if someone is rude and aggressive. You may be faced with a confident assertion about something in your field that you know to be wrong, yet find your interviewer belligerently unwilling to entertain an alternative view. Plenty of loons inhabit academe, and some get on search committees. Never lose your temper, even if you dislike a question. I observed an interview committee cross off its list a candidate who blustered angrily when asked the standard business interview question, "Why should we hire you?" This common question offers an opening for you to present your virtues, but the interviewee somehow felt threatened or demeaned and his truculence turned everyone against him.

If something goes wrong, do your best to pull yourself together and carry on. One candidate broke into a profuse nosebleed just as she was knocking on the suite door. She had to start her interview by running to their bathroom and washing off blood while wadding up tissues to hold to her nose. This proved, in fact, to be a remarkably successful ice breaker, and her carrying on without going to pieces put her in very good standing with that committee. Interviewers have responded positively to someone who burst into tears out of sheer nervousness but who explained it was just nervousness, got herself in hand, and answered the questions well. If you trip on a rug and fall flat, do your best to laugh it off. Gallantry under fire used to be admired on battlefields, and its modern equivalent might just get you your job.

Preparation

Memorize a ninety-second description of your dissertation. Time yourself and be able to recite it without hesitation if awakened at three o'clock in the morning. Once you have delivered this description to your interviewers, you can offer to expand on any part of it they wish to learn more about. This is much safer than talking for five minutes and having their eyes glaze over, and it lets you ask them what they want to hear about. You may be asked for such a description only once or twice, but you will slip bits of it into all of your discussions. This ninety-second description is invaluable.

If you are in Comparative Literature or a language department, you should memorize versions of this ninety-second spiel in all of the languages that might be relevant to your job hunt. You should also practice answers to the questions in your language as well as in English, or—if you are, say, a native speaker of Spanish—practice the questions in English as well as Spanish, even though you expect to get a job in a Spanish department. Remember, too, that if you are being interviewed for a generalist position by a multilanguage department or an all-literatures or humanities department, most of your interviewers will know nothing at all about your specialty. Do not use jargon. In the simplest language you can, stress the originality and importance and applications of what you have done.

Crucial to an effective interview is making sure you tell your interviewers what you think they most need to know. Hence, you must memorize a list of three or four points that you will make during any interview, and prepare ways of working them into the conversation. Start out the interview determined to present them and use them to guide the conversation where you want it to go. Otherwise, you will drift in any direction that the chance concerns of individual interviewers happen to push the conversation. These three or four points are the details that make you stand out, your particular virtues, the things that should make them want to hire you. You may have to work them in individually, or may get a question like "Why should we hire you?" or "What should we know about you?" That would let you trot those points out all together. If you have not managed to get a couple in, you may be able to do so when they ask if you have questions or when they are about to close. Just say you want to make a couple of points first, do so, and then thank them for the interview.

Brainstorm with friends and fellow job hunters. Generate variations on the questions and answer them. Ask yourself questions and answer them as you walk, work out, sit in the car, shower, sit on the toilet, or stand in line at the cash register.

Whenever possible, answer the questions you are asking yourself out loud. You need to get used to the sound of your own voice, and you need to engage the part of your brain involved in speaking—a different part from one that silently compiles answers. If your credentials involve more than one language, you will need this fluency in all of them, so practicing aloud is crucial. Work to vary your tone and expression. Use your hands.

Construct a profile of your strengths and rehearse them. Think about your weaknesses and prepare for questions about them. If there is an unusual gap in your preparation—you are a medievalist but you cannot read German, or you did not work with a big-shot professor at your school in your field—have a well-considered answer to a question on the subject. Do not say negative things about the famous professor; he or she may be a bosom buddy of someone interviewing you, or the interviewer may enjoy needling the professor by passing on such a negative comment (with your name attached) at the next professional conference.

Prepare for the interview as if it were the most important exam in your life, but do not let the interview be an exam unless that is clearly what the interviewers intend it to be. You can try to turn the interview into a conversation by asking them as many questions as they ask you. You can answer a question and then ask one. "When I teach rhetoric, I think three main things are important: A, B, and C. Is this consistent with the philosophy of your course?" After all, you really do want to know the answer. It will help you frame answers to subsequent questions that should make you more suitable to your interviewers.

Bring materials with you, such as sample syllabi of past courses, courses you would like to teach, and—best of all—syllabi for courses they offer. Bring a teaching portfolio; if you have two versions, you will have sent the shorter with your application, but bring the longer one to the interview and leave one copy with them.

Be informed. Follow the relevant controversies in the *Chronicle of Higher Education* for the previous year, and be able to describe your thoughts on some. The *Chronicle* will alert you to any hot issues at that particular school and will let you show your professionalism. If your own school has undergone some publicized crisis, work out tactful answers to probes. Interviewers may question you about recent racial upheavals or a dean's resignation or a faculty member's having been fired for sexual harassment. Discretion is best; say the minimum. Particularly if your department's politics have been stormy, point out that such matters are not shared with graduate students and that you know no details of what happened.

Hunters attending the MLA tell me that their advice is to ignore the job information center. You can stand in line for four hours only to be told (erroneously) that your interviewers have not registered their suite information, or to be given the wrong information. Instead, call the interviewing chairperson; do it the night before, but if you cannot connect then, call from the hotel lobby fifteen minutes or half an hour before the interview and get the suite number. One candidate found the suite's line constantly busy and the desk mulishly unwilling to hand out the suite number. Since the department had not made the information available in a timely fashion, the enterprising and desperate job hunter was reduced to getting it by bribing a bell captain with a twenty-dollar bill. Most departments are more responsible and helpful, and not all job centers produce the frustration that so many hunters have felt at the MLA on account of the number of job candidates the center has to serve. Such centers at smaller conferences may offer a very different experience: e-mail facilities, the chance to see old friends and meet rivals for your jobs, and a good opportunity to network. Ask people in your field what its job center might be good for.

The Contents of Your Briefcase

You should have a color-coded folder for each school with which you are interviewing in a given part of the day. In this folder is the cheat sheet attached to the inside cover, the copy of the letter you sent, the syllabi tailored to the school, your syllabi for previously taught courses and dream courses, your teaching portfolio, and the table of contents of your dissertation, just to remind you of the chapter titles. Bring your longer teaching portfolio if you have two versions. Be sure to make a conversational opening that will allow you to present it to your interviewers. Also, bring photocopies of student papers that you have marked up and commented upon. These might be separate, or might be part of the larger teaching portfolio.

If your thesis is well along but not defended, bring a copy of the whole manuscript with you so you can prove that it exists. To reduce weight, you could print it single space and on both sides, but you can tell them the real number of pages. People lie about the state of their dissertation, and sometimes even supervisors do. You need to be able to prove that yours is as you say it is. A diskette cannot inspire the same confidence, however much more convenient to carry.

Plan for emergencies. Have with you a few kleenex, a few cough drops, a small bottle of cough syrup, and a headache remedy.

Talking about Your Teaching

Even when you interview with research-oriented schools, you will find that a lot of an interview will concern teaching. You need to have given a lot of thought to every aspect of pedagogy.

First, you need syllabi of at least some of the following sorts:

- a survey for your historical period (e.g., Spanish Golden Age, Victorian, Renaissance art)
- a broad survey (modern European history, post-Renaissance philosophy, world religions, world literature, British literature from Beowulf through the Romantics, History of Film)
- your dream courses for various levels of student, including graduate— these should reflect knowledge beyond the dissertation and should not be too highly specialized in topic
- a writing or language-acquisition course
- a rhetoric or pedagogy course
- a genre course
- a theory or methods course

If you are in applied linguistics and language acquisition, Philosophy, Gender Studies, Art History, or Speech Communication, you will have to adapt some elements in this list, but you can see the principles involved. Be sure you have material for an honors seminar, a senior-level course, a graduate seminar, and a sophomore survey. Be clear in your own mind what differentiates a sophomore from a senior course, and a senior from a graduate seminar. How would readings and assignments differ? Do not skimp on preparing these syllabi; draw up the book list, the reserve list, and do all the basic thinking for running the course in earnest. One successful job hunter was given two weeks' notice to teach a graduate seminar that had to be different from the one he was scheduled to teach the following spring. He simply looked over the syllabi he had created for job hunting and smoothly activated one. His quick readiness impressed his new school enormously.

For period courses, prepare a traditional syllabus and a more radical version. Be prepared for questions (some hostile) on which canonical author you mean to discard to make space for someone noncanonical. Know arguments about breadth versus depth and know what you are trying to accomplish with your chosen texts. You might be asked how you would approach teaching one particular author, either well known or obscure. You should also have given thought to how you would teach any of the standard period courses. Know the prices of the standard anthologies. If you have to choose between one and another for teaching an anthology course, price might be a factor. You should also know the canon politics behind each relevant anthology and be able to defend your choice of one over another.

Check the school's catalogue, and prepare syllabi with some of their courses in mind. Be able to say that you could teach English 15, 30, 232, 436, and 577 (their course numbers) with little or no preparation, and would be able to take on 200 and 457 with a bit of warning. If you cannot memorize the course numbers, at least have their titles or subject matter clearly in mind.

When asked about your dream course, do not describe something very esoteric and specialized; try to ensure some general appeal. Specify the level you are aiming for, and if the first one you describe is a senior honors seminar, then balance that with a course you would thoroughly enjoy as an introductory lecture course. Emphasize undergraduate teaching, even lower-level teaching; most of your students will be lower-level undergraduates, and a school will not want someone who is obviously hoping to avoid that sort of teaching. The more the school emphasizes teaching, the more lower-level syllabi you should present.

Talking about Your Research

Be able to talk about your methodological positioning. Step back and think through your stance with regard to predecessors, influences, and schools of thought. Do not make claims for your method that will not stand up, and be candid about its limitations, but never speak dismissively or disparagingly of your work, even in jest. With regard to the limitations of your argument, you can make the point that you intend to fix them when you turn your dissertation into a book.

Know your dissertation backwards and forwards. Have your ninety-second description ready, but be prepared to discuss any part of your work at greater length. When describing your arguments, remember to use textual examples. This is extremely important. The most common mistake made by inexperienced interviewees is talking in abstract generalities. *Be sure to anchor each and every one of your general statements with references to specific texts or evidence or examples.* Make sure the central texts are clear in your mind. Refer in detail to them to make all of your points.

The Interviewers

When a school calls you to set up an interview, you will usually be told the names of your interviewers; if not, ask. Write the names down, and then look the people up either on their home pages or in a professional bibliography to find out what they have published. Read a bit of their work if you can; at least read an article by the person whose interests come closest to yours. Make reference to this article if you get a reasonable opening, but do not force it and do not challenge its author on some point of disagreement. Instead, call attention to overlaps or compatibilities between his or her work and yours, and talk about how much you would enjoy having colleagues with such interests. If this person's work is genuinely of interest to you, you can, when shaking hands as you leave, say something to the effect that you know this is an interview situation and you can't ask some questions you'd like to about his or her work, but could you keep in touch by e-mail? Establishing yourself as a professional colleague with related interests rather than just as a suppliant graduate student can improve your profile, and you can indeed make a real professional contact there.

Be aware of cultural differences. If an interviewer for a German department job is a native German, for instance, your having read some of his publication or having informed yourself about the department may seem sycophantic to his German sensibilities. Get advice from your mentors on this issue. All American interviewers know that you have done homework especially for the interview—and in that sense you are apple-polishing and you all know it—but most would interpret such a reference as an indication that you are interested in the job and school. They will welcome proof that you have taken some trouble to learn about them. Interviewees who show no such interest in the school rarely come across as attractive candidates.

Be prepared for interruptions of the interview and possibly for inattentiveness of the part of some interviewers. You may be the ninth candidate seen that day, or one of the interviewers may be coming down with the flu. Someone may come back late from lunch, or be too upset by having had a wallet stolen to concentrate on you.

An Array of Questions

Here are the kinds of questions you might meet and for which you must prepare. These have been gleaned from many sources, some of them anonymous handouts circulated from school to school; a few are so old they were mimeographed. Some were contributed by colleagues. Most were reported by Penn State job hunters as actual questions they had faced, and a few came from business magazines. Sometimes I have cast them in field-specific terms to stir up your imagination. Don't just skip over those outside your field. Work out what the equivalent problem is in your own field, and then recast them for yourself. Interviews follow no set structure, but figure on some opening remarks, some questions about your current and future research, questions about your teaching experience, and then a chance for you to ask a few questions.

Preliminaries

The committee members will probably base their opening questions on the letter of application you sent, so go over your letter to this school just before the interview. Frequently, an interviewer will underline a term or two in the letter and ask you to explain what you mean by "authenticity" or "thesis nearly done" or "challenging Adorno." You may be asked what brand of feminist you are or what methodology informs your work or what your intervention is. Remember that their questions about "posthumanist" or "judgment" will come from their definition of the term, which may differ from yours. Try to catch such differences before they develop into misunderstandings. You can say, "I define historicism as follows [brief definition]; therefore, I consider thus-and-such to be the case."

If you do not know the answer to a question, avoid saying "That's a good question." That phrase is meant to flatter students while you scramble to think of an answer; your interviewers are not students in need of your praise, and this reply will sound condescending or saccharine. Try "I haven't thought about that before. Thinking out loud, I find myself preferring your first alternative." Another formula: "I don't know. I would approach thinking about the topic in this way and maybe this and that." You might then ask what they think and why.

Someone may say, "Before we start, can you tell me how you became interested in the eighteenth century?" or "Why did you go into Russian?" or "What drew you to Religious Studies?" Nothing, however, is off the record or "before" the interview. Everything you say may be used against you. The interviewer is probably just trying to throw you an easy question to help you relax.

They may ask about your next book, meaning what you will turn to after the dissertation book. You *must* have a well-thought-out project, and preferably have two or three possibilities in mind. One might be more attractive in terms of a particular job than another. Say that your thesis was on eighteenth-century history of science. If you are hired as an eighteenth-century historian, a project on some other aspect of eighteenth-century culture might make sense, but if you were wanted specifically for history of science, then you might well follow that interest forward or back into a different century. If you are job hunting in two periods or two areas (film and literature, for example), you would expect to answer with the book project that better fits the particular job.

Questions They May Ask

Testing You

- Why should we hire you?
- Teach me something new!
- What motivates you?
- Two of us went to the production of *Richard II* last night. Tell us why we as modernists should care about this play (this, to a Renaissance candidate).
- Why do you rely so heavily on your thesis supervisor's work? Did he make you? Was it just to save you time? What does it do for you?

- What do you know about the argument that theory has exhausted its appeal and usefulness?

In-your-face questions may be used to see if you can think quickly, handle being surprised, and come up with something interesting.

Teaching Questions

You must be able to comment on all aspects of teaching in your field. The entire interview will not consist of questions as difficult as some of these, but you may get one or two per interview.

- Which courses are you most comfortable teaching?
- You have two teaching awards. Which of your techniques do you think makes you such a good teacher?
- What pedagogical theory do you prefer for teaching a language (or a composition) course?
- Could you teach the language (or composition) course along pedagogically different lines?
- What was the best class you ever taught? What was the worst, and why was it so bad? How did you handle the problems?
- What is your favorite or most effective "active" assignment for a course?
- What is your dream course? What are your dream courses?
- Suppose you design both an upper-level undergraduate course and a graduate seminar on the same topic. What would differ in your two versions? How would you handle the material differently for those two audiences?
- How does your teaching philosophy influence your teaching?
- Do you share your own writing with students?
- What texts would you most like to teach?
- If you taught the Civil War history course, what books would you use?
- How would you introduce your students to using original documents?
- What have the students you taught been like?
- How do you make students care about classical philosophy? about Milton? about Chinese art?
- What do you find most difficult about teaching and how have you worked to overcome that difficulty?
- How would you approach in a classroom an extremely controversial topic or text in your field—*American Psycho*, *Satanic Verses*, holocaust

art by non-Jews that seems exploitive, Mel Gibson's *The Passion of the Christ*, someone's art forgeries as having artistic value in their own right?

- Given the job description and what you have learned about us from the website, how do you see yourself fitting into our program?
- What do you see as some of the more pressing contemporary issues in technical communication? in language acquisition pedagogy?
- What do you think are the most important aspects of teacher training?
- How would you teach a group of TAs from different programs?
- Could you teach a service-learning program?
- What do you see as the role of freshman writing in addressing the needs of nontraditional communities?
- In what ways might technology expand and/or limit your teaching?
- What web resources would you use with your class in Art History/Renaissance Philosophy/Religious Studies/Japanese History?
- When you show film in the classroom, do you show clips? ask students to watch the films outside class? How do you ensure that films will be available so they can watch them?
- What particular kind of student do you find it hardest to deal with?
- In your diversity class, what students are hardest to deal with and how do you handle the problem?
- What would you do if a student asked you your religious affiliation when you are teaching a world religions course? [a good answer: If I'm doing my job right, you shouldn't be able to tell.]
- What do you think of Women's Studies courses that are only open to women students?
- What was your most embarrassing experience in a classroom?
- How do you reconcile the conflict between teaching and research?
- Which types of interactions with students do you feel are most productive, from both your perspective and that of your students?
- How do you balance lecturing and discussion?
- Would you comment on the controversy over composition courses being used to instill political correctness?
- What theoretical assumptions inform your composition teaching? Your teaching of a language?
- How do you introduce and address difficult topics such as race, gender, and identity in your course?
- How far should you go toward challenging people's beliefs without destroying them? How do you distinguish between beliefs and prejudices?
- Ever since September 11th, the connection between religion and violence has been an issue. If you taught a course on this subject, what texts, films, and other materials would you use?

- Our department has not managed to build contacts with such programs as Women's Studies and African and African American Studies. Do you have ideas or interests that might help us make connections with other programs?
- Are there cross-listable courses that you could teach?
- Many people are concerned with identity and "authenticity"; how do you handle the problems of being a white American teaching minority American literature? a Westerner teaching non-Western religions?
- What problems do you see with your teaching Spanish when you are not a native speaker?
- If you had to teach an entire course centered on one book written in the last fifty years, what would you use? If on one author, which one?
- If you had to teach only one book for the rest of your life, what would you choose?
- How do you approach survey courses?
- Suppose you enter your eight A.M. survey class for the first time and the students all look bored and resentful. What would you do?
- We teach our introductory class with an enrollment of 300. Some feel that teaching anything to a group that large is pointless. Is there any way to give examinations other than multiple choice in such a class?
- Which textbook would you use for a course in your historical period? (Job hunters must know the major texts, histories, and anthologies.)
- What texts would you use for teaching World Literature or World Religions or World Philosophy or World History?
- Many texts exist for your field: What is the biggest gap that they do not cover and how do you bring that material into the classroom?
- Many people who teach Religious Studies focus on texts and scriptures, but much of what matters is everyday outlook and rituals. How do you try to articulate such experience?
- When teaching any European literature, how do you convey to American students the assumptions about class?
- Which software would you use to teach symbolic logic?
- Why in your syllabus did you use a particular obscure (or popular) novel rather than a canonical text?
- How do you deal with defiant or apathetic students?
- How do you handle students who militantly take refuge in the fundamentals of their scriptural belief and deny what you teach or refuse to learn it?
- Teaching literature from militantly nonreligious writers like Shaw and Ibsen or radical contemporary writers like Kathy Acker often offends religious American undergraduates; how do you handle that?

- What would you do if you find that a student has plagiarized his final paper, and has gone home for the break so you can't discuss it with him?
- Isn't using film in a drama class just a way to dumb it down?
- If you taught a course in religion (or violence or race) and popular culture, which films would you use? which novels? Supposing this were a diversity course, how would you give fair representation to non-Western religions and cultures?
- What are the similarities, do you think, between your students and ours?
- What films would you use in a course on twentieth-century French culture? on Latin America? on postcolonial Africa?
- You're used to a big school; how are you going to adjust to giving our liberal arts college students the amount of attention and feedback that they have a right to expect? (You must prepare for questions reflecting this anxiety on a small teaching college's part. One thing you might do is photocopy some student papers you have marked up and commented upon; you could pull these out in such an interview and show the kind of attention you pay to student work.)
- You specialize in Latino/a (or African American) literature, but can you teach the usual anthology course survey of American literature?
- Can you teach German (or French, Spanish, Italian) Culture as well as language and literature courses?
- Can you teach business writing in French (or Russian or Portuguese)?
- Can you teach a course in technical translation?
- Can you teach World Literature in translation? What texts would you use?
- Can you teach Western Civilization? What texts would you use?
- Given that your philosophical specialty is classical Greek philosophy, can you teach applied ethics (Medical, Business, Engineering)?
- Everyone is crying out that students in Business and Law need to take ethics courses. If you were teaching one, how would you put it together? What materials would you use?
- What texts would you use in a Philosophy for scientists course? In a Literature for scientists course?
- Can you mount a webcam movie on a website?
- How do you define the role of a thesis supervisor?
- What role should thesis-committee members play?
- If you were asked to supervise a dissertation immediately upon arrival, could you do it?
- Are you ready to supervise graduate students writing dissertations?

- Given the number of students who enter a PhD program and the much smaller number that leave with degrees, what do you think the role of a supervisor should be?
- Minority candidates who specialize in Renaissance drama or nineteenth-century British poetry may well be asked, "Can you teach African American (or Latino/a or Asian-American) literature?" however irrelevant that may be to their specialty.

Questions about a Secondary Interest

If you have a secondary interest, you will have to prepare to answer questions about it. Most secondary fields are intellectually similar to main fields, so the main field questions will tell you what to prepare. If you got an MFA before switching to a PhD track, you may be hoping that a teaching-oriented institution can use your skills both in research and creative writing. If this is the case, you may need to prepare additional answers for creative writing questions as well as for those found above.

- How do you incorporate instruction in grammar, usage, and style into your creative writing classes?
- How do you select texts for your creative writing courses, and can you give us several examples of texts you've used successfully?
- How do you grade creative writing? Is it different for beginning and advanced courses?
- In your opinion, what is the proper relationship between a creative writing program and the literature program?
- Describe your current project/s and current efforts at publication.
- How do you employ peer review and individualized instruction in the teaching of creative writing?
- Writers often end up teaching composition and freshman seminars on our campus, so if you had to teach a freshman seminar, what theme would you choose? If you were teaching a beginning composition course, how would you organize it and what texts would you select?
- We know that creative writing courses are popular, but they tend to draw students from our survey and other literature courses. We also know that our students want to get jobs when they graduate, not just publish the great American novel. How would you make the case for creative writing instruction at the undergraduate level?
- Can you teach business, technical, or basic writing?

• We're a small program in the middle of nowhere. How will you manage without a community of writers around?

Curricular Questions

• What goals should a degree in your field have in the twenty-first century?
• What do you think needs to be done to keep from ghettoizing various "studies" programs under the broader department umbrella?
• Does the very existence of an African American concentration ghettoize that topic?
• Should a student in Native American Studies or Asian American Studies have to know at least one language relevant to the studies area?
• How is your work on linguistics/ancient Greek rhetoric/Punk music/advertising relevant to a literature department?
• You do Cultural Studies. Are you really leaving literature behind? What literature will you deal with in your classes, and how do you approach it? Do you see yourself as trying to change the nature of literature departments? If so, why?
• What courses do you think you would like to develop and offer that we don't already have?
• What is the role of composition in an English department?
• How would you justify using literature in a composition course?
• How would you define the curricular paradigm in your field?
• How do you justify a whole course on Nietzsche? Picasso? García Márquez? Victor Hugo? Toni Morrison? C. S. Lewis?
• We have a required Shakespeare course. I believe we should keep that, but John here thinks we should get rid of all such requirements. What do you think?
• Which courses should be required of majors in our department, and why?
• A student of mine is thinking of specializing in your area. Why should she?
• What do you think is the most difficult course to teach in a French department?
• Should literature in translation be taught in an English department?
• Have you had any experience in distance learning, and could you help us set up a distance learning program?
• Our course in research techniques for entering graduate students has been a disaster; what should one do in such a course to teach them the basics of research and whatever else they need to thrive in the field?

- We're trying to start a _____ program or concentration in our department; what courses and support systems do you think such a program needs? (Cultural Studies, Gender Studies, Film Studies, Women's Studies, Irish Studies, Rhetorical Studies, American Studies, Postcolonial Studies, Studies in the Americas, African and African American Studies, Chicano/Latino Studies, Asian American Studies, Civil War Studies, integrated Business minor, and the like.) If you are applying to a language department, you may be asked about setting up or altering their offerings in culture or in business writing in that language. If you are in any of these recognized subfields, you *must* have a thoughtful answer in mind.

Research-oriented Questions

- What presses might be interested in your thesis book once it has been revised? Why do you think so? (Be able to list a couple of books the press has published that are similar to yours. Be sure you understand the relative prestige of the various presses you think might be approached. You do not sound professional if you think you should approach a minor state university press first and University of Chicago Press second. If you cannot answer this question effectively, an interviewer who values professional competence will cross you off the list right then and there. Six out of nine candidates in one search snickered nervously and said they had never thought about presses before. Functionally, their interviews terminated at that point, five minutes in.)
- In what journals do you hope to land your work? (Know the major journals in your specialty and in the larger departmental range of journals. An answer that has nothing but specialty journals will be a black mark against you because most members of the department will never have had reason to look at them. You need to know the relative prestige of journals.)
- We have to worry about department members landing research in the "top twenty" journals on the Dean's approved list; while we're interested in someone with an off-beat focus like yours, we want to know how readily your work might fit into basic departmental outlets.
- How does your research influence your teaching?
- What does your dissertation contribute to its field?
- Why did you write the dissertation you did?
- How do you negotiate aesthetics and its commodity status (film, art)?

- What do you mean when you say that you are "putting Foucault aside" to build your argument?
- Why do you build your argument on Freud when his work is so thoroughly exploded?
- Is your thesis just theory, or does it have any practical application?
- Why do you use Foucault to define your intellectual universe? Historians have pretty well shot holes in many of his claims. He creates fascinating theories but the facts contradict them.
- Isn't your work rather antiquarian/esoteric/philosophical? How does what you do matter? Or how does it expand our historic understanding/literary knowledge/humanistic horizons?
- Do you really think a posthumanist approach is a good thing for a humanities department?
- You mention reforming the rhetorical conventions of male political practice. What do you mean by that?
- What was the most interesting primary document you found during your research and how did you use it?
- Where would you go looking for other primary documents that have not been previously used?
- What is your intervention in the field?
- Who in the field most influenced you?
- How far along is your dissertation right now?
- What conclusions did you reach in your dissertation?
- What's a hot book in that field right now?
- How would you map the current scholarship in Cultural Studies, specifically in the areas of critical race theory and postcolonialism, and what aspects of these discourses engage you most as a scholar?
- What do you think of Caldofreddo's new book? (If you have not read it, be honest and say so.)
- What is the cutting edge in your field and how does your work extend it?
- Who else is working in your area?
- Who are the leading active scholars in your field?
- What do you need to do to revise your thesis as a book?
- How did your research interest evolve?
- Do you see yourself as applying someone's theory to your material, or are you constructing your own theoretical framework?
- Do you think you can get any outside grants to support your research?
- What is the relevance of so non-literary a Cultural Studies topic to a literature department?
- How will you handle research with a 4–4 load?

- How are you going to balance our teaching load with research and service? (The best answer to this kind of question is to draw a parallel between the demands on an assistant professor over six years and those on a graduate student during the PhD over a similar period. The courses you teach and take add up to a similar number, you write a book plus a number of term-papers/articles, and you do a certain amount of service. If you have not strung your PhD out over too many years, you have perfect proof that you can handle the demands of the job.)
- You have watched junior faculty succeed or fail during the time you got your degree; what did you learn from watching them try to establish a career?
- I see you have written an article on Schiller/Spinoza/Monet. Can you tell me about it?
- In your writing sample, you talk about a recent return to empiricism. Will you explain what you mean by that?
- What are the two most important political films/novels in the last five years?
- Which film/novel of the last ten years will be valued one hundred years from now?
- What websites do you recommend to your students for their research?
- What kind of African American intellectual are you?
- How do you situate yourself in the discourse of African American/ Latino/a intellectuals? Who are your models?
- How do you define membership in a Native American tribe and what is your stand on the blood quantum arguments?
- Why should you call an author Native American if he or she has never lived on a reservation?
- Does your argument apply to all African American (or other minority) writers? Does it apply to some white writers as well? (This kind of crossover question is common, thus forcing race-based or ethnic comparisons, even if you did not have that in mind in your research. The underlying anxiety derives from essentializing or anti-essentializing concerns.)
- Does what you are identifying as a women's technique in fiction apply to all female writers? Does it apply to any male writers? (Again, the issue relates to essentializing, and you need good answers.)

Questions about You or Your Training and Background

- What are your strengths and what are your weaknesses? (Claiming perfectionism as your weakness is worn out. Find something different.)

- What were the strengths of your graduate training, and what were the weaknesses?
- You're doing both film and literature. Are you really interested in literature at all?
- You're doing Cultural Studies and literature. Are you really interested in literature at all, and if so, why spend time on popular music or TV legislation?
- Why did you become a German or History or Linguistics major and go on to a PhD?
- What's your agenda for the next five years?
- What do you expect to have accomplished in the next ten years?
- Where do you see yourself professionally in ten years' time?
- What are your hobbies?
- Who taught you how to write?
- What is your personal relationship with your work?
- Will you need a green card? (If you do need one, you should do some homework if your field rarely hires foreign nationals. Find out from their website and by phoning around exactly what person in what office at what phone number handles green card matters at that school. Be able to tell the interview committee what forms the department will have to file and what these forms entail. Their part is actually pretty easy, so avoid making it sound difficult. Giving them the information on the relevant administrator and office at their school will demonstrate your competence and helpfulness.)
- What administrative experience have you had?
- What is your administrative style?
- How do you feel about administration?
- How would you run a first-year writing program?
- How did you train/coordinate the TAs for the multisection class?
- What was your year in Germany like and how did it improve your grasp of the language? (If you are applying to a language department, you will get questions about your experience living in the country where that language is spoken unless you are a native speaker.)
- What do you think of Professor Brockengespenst? (Someone interviewing you may know someone in your graduate school department and may ask about that person. If you have had a good experience with the professor mentioned, you can say something about it, but if your experience was not good, be bland. You do not want enmity, and you do not wish to feed negative information to help along someone else's vendetta.)
- Why do you want to become a history professor?
- It's cold outside, isn't it? I bet State College has cold winters. How do you like living in State College? (Avoid negativity, and remember that if

their school is in a cold region or their school isolated, your disparaging the cold or a rural location will make you seem unlikely to be happy in their university.)

Problem Questions

Schools are not supposed to ask about your marital status, sexual orientation, family, or the like. However, some may ask anyway in order to establish how well you would fit into their institutional or department culture. You will need to think about how to handle this. "You're not supposed to ask me that" will not be well received. One of the anonymous sets of questions in the department's files has the following suggested line. "I have the sense that you are concerned that my personal life might somehow affect my work in your department. Can you be more specific about your concerns so I can put them to rest?"

Interesting questions, some of them problematical, can emerge when you deal with religiously affiliated institutions. If you apply for such a job, start by doing your homework. Is the religious association historical only? The older the school, the more likely it is to have been founded by a particular religious group, but many such institutions are secular now. Does a religious association show itself as a preference for faculty who are people of faith who will view the world from a position of faith, but all faiths (not just all versions of Christianity) are welcome? Or is one particular form of faith central to life and thought on the campus? If the connection is only historical, you may find little or nothing to differentiate it from a state university. If faith of some sort is the key, you may find the give and take within shared assumptions invigorating. If the school holds to a particular doctrine and if you share their doctrinal views, you may find theirs to be the perfect job: Many such schools have smart, disciplined students, and you and your colleagues would have something in common aside from a love of literature. Given the current renewal of religious fervor, you may find deeply rewarding such campus experiments in how to make religion an abiding part of everyday life.

Do not assume a monolithic outlook on campus, or uniformity within a type of school; some Catholic schools are very liberal, others conservative. Even at a seriously committed institution, you may find some startling diversity, whether in a critical probing of religion or in student activities: a Women's Studies group carrying prochoice placards or a gay/lesbian/bisexual group celebrating gay pride week. If issues such as these have arisen on a campus at which you are interviewing, you may find yourself being asked how and where you draw the line when it comes to free speech in a sectarian institution. You will be asked how you teach your subject so as to accommodate religious sensibilities, and to what extent do you try to do so. You may be asked how you would comment on a religiously controversial film or art exhibit, or how you would handle students' queries about *The DaVinci Code*, or the currently popular apocryphal gospels containing what are being called lost truths of Christianity. The situation may be put to you as follows: "As you may know, our school comes from a particular tradition, which is especially reflected in its teaching mission and in the quality of the educational experience we offer our students. Do you feel that you would be comfortable with that mission and that tradition? If we hired you, could we be confident that your teaching and your approach would not run contrary to this mission?"

Some sectarian schools may pose problems for the nonreligious applicant, or the applicant from another religious tradition. From the perspective of faith, religious commandments supercede rules about inappropriate questions issued by a professional society. If you know in advance of such a clash between your lifestyle or beliefs and theirs—and schools that care about this usually provide you with a document to sign and send back before they set up an interview—you would do better to save your time and trouble and not apply, no matter how perfectly the job description suits you. One strict evangelical school insists that you sign a document promising not to drink, dance, or play cards, and that you would take the stance that homosexuality and nonmarital sex are sins whenever they come up in your literature courses. Another asks you to compare the theology of your church with theirs; a job candidate for this school was told that if she had children, they would have to attend that particular sect's church school. If you are going to apply to a Latter Day Saints (Mormon) school, you must accept the limitations that it will put on the books you can teach and the subjects you can discuss in class, and for Brigham Young University, you will have to pass the interrogation on your faith by an Elder of the church. A feminist Milton specialist found the attitudes of one small Jesuit school toward both her feminism and Milton rather distressing, but this does not mean that she would have found similar attitudes at another Jesuit institution. If the fit between you and a particular school's tradition is good, you will have no trouble with their questions, but be prepared for queries and attitudes that you would not expect from secular schools.

Questions Regarding Their Department and School

- Why are you interested in working for our department?
- Why are you interested in our school specifically?
- You're from a big university. How will you handle the demands of a small liberal arts college like ours?
- Say you get offers from both a top liberal arts college and a major research university. Salary is about the same. Which would you choose and why?
- How would you feel about living in Pocatello? Stockton? The Bronx? (Schools may be isolated or they may perch precariously in a dangerous part of a city; you can get probes into how you will feel about dealing with the problems specific to that particular location.)
- You're from the East. How will you adapt to living in the Texas panhandle? Alternatively—you're from San Francisco; how will you cope with living in rural Pennsylvania? Or you're from Michigan; how do you feel about living in Alabama? You're from Georgia; how will you manage a Minnesota winter?
- What do you know about our school?
- What do you know about our school's doctrinal positions?
- What do you know about North Carolina? Idaho?
- What can we tell you about our department/school?
- From what you've seen on our website, which faculty have interests that might mesh with yours? (This one is important, and you need to have done your homework.)

Questions You Might Wish to Ask

People unprepared to ask serious questions sometimes blunder into asking "How many books does your library have?" or "How many students attend your university?" Given the dire market, answers to those questions are unlikely to determine your decision, and your asking them strongly suggests that you have not researched the school. You want to know as much about job conditions as you can learn, but you also want to be careful not to sound too concerned about yourself alone. Here are some much more productive questions. Obviously, not all of these issues will concern you; ask only about those that do.

- How would you like to use someone with my credentials?
- Which courses do you see me teaching?

- What areas would you hope that I might develop for you?
- What are you hoping that this hire can do for your department? (The point to this nexus of questions is to make your interviewers identify what they want to acquire, and if they reveal any hitherto hidden needs—such as teaching a particular course—you can present your credentials for doing that job for them. If other candidates do not winkle out that hidden item, then they will end up looking less useful than you.)
- Are you interested in department members doing outreach as part of their service? (Many departments need to entertain alumni and also get requests from the Rotary Club or the local historical society, which want free lecturers. If your research has some popular appeal, this would make you a good lecturer to alumni or to the public, and you might do your school some useful service.)
- What kinds of computer support and technological training does your university/college offer? Is there a workshop, for instance, that would train faculty to create websites for their courses?
- What kinds of travel and research money do your faculty get?
- What opportunities do you offer for faculty development (e.g., learn a new language, attend an NEH seminar, attend a seminar on bibliography or administration)?
- What kind of relationship exists between this regional campus and the main campus? What kinds of control does the main campus exert locally?
- What kind of sabbatical policy does the school have?
- Does your school have a study-abroad program or summer course abroad, and do members of the department ever participate as group leader or teacher?
- What is the teaching load? What sort of mix of courses might I be expected to teach?
- What is the intellectual community like? Is there a faculty and graduate reading group in Cultural Studies? Is there an interdepartmental medieval group? Is there a forum in which department members present their research?
- What are recent developments in the department or school?
- Is the department expanding or contracting?
- Is the school investing in technology for language acquisition or remedial grammar practice?
- What new areas of curriculum has the department been developing?
- How easy is it to design new courses and get them on the books?
- Are team teaching or interdisciplinary team-taught courses easy to set up, or are there problems with funding them?

- Does the library acquire databases routinely and easily, or is the budget pinched for such research tools? If the school is part of a state system, does it have problems such that one campus acquiring the database means that others cannot? Is the library good at working out piggy-back license arrangements with that other campus? (If you are a historical scholar and the school is isolated, the answer to this question might be very important to your future.)
- What's the cultural life like in the town? (Usually you will have more urgent questions to ask, but this is a good one to end on if the interview seems to have run out of steam. It lets them talk positively, and if they shrug and change the subject, that also tells you something.)

When you leave, ask when you might expect to hear from them, and when they are planning to make their decision. The moment you leave the room, jot down their answer. When you get home, e-mail a follow-up thank you note to the search chair. Send any offprints or references promised.

Note that this may not be the best stage at which to query them about tenure requirements, although if they bring it up, by all means learn what you can. Make sure that you do not appear to be trying to find out what the bare minimum may be. Interviewers who publish heavily will turn hostile if you sound as if you are hoping to scrape by with as little publication as possible. Instead, ask what the records of people who recently received tenure looked like when they came up for consideration.

Logistics of the Conference

Arrive the day before the conference starts and get oriented. Stay at the conference hotel (in which most of your interviews will take place) if you can afford to. Share your hotel room (to cut costs and give you someone to talk to). A partner is ideal if that partner understands the nature of your obligations and anxieties, but you can also share with a fellow job hunter. You want someone with whom you can relax, go out to a tasty supper, share anecdotes, and practice interview questions. The partner must understand that nothing matters to you during this conference but your hunt; if your partner is nonacademic and views this as a vacation, he or she must be reconciled to doing the sightseeing and even some of the dining alone. Better to come on your own than damage a relationship with a serious clash of interests. Here is some good advice from one job hunter: Although you may have no money, do not stint during the conference. Stay at the conference hotel, eat at an interesting restaurant rather than Macdonald's, and use phones freely to call your partner and unload whatever is on your mind. The money will be well spent in ameliorating your experience.

Take everything you need for interviews (including interview clothing) in carry-on luggage. You should bring with you a dictionary of your field's terms (literary, philosophical, theoretical) and copies of any articles you have written, as well as your writing sample. You can expect to get questions on the older work, and by now you may nearly have forgotten what it was about. Review it a bit when you are tired of drilling yourself on questions and definitions of your terms.

If you have an understanding partner, try to scrape up the money for the two of you to go together. That partner can help you carry the afternoon's folders, help you talk your impressions aloud, supply advice, and be unobtrusively supportive. Your partner can carry a snack, a spare pair of panty hose, even a spare shirt or blouse (in case you drop tomato sauce on your front at lunch). The partner should not appear at the door of the interview suite with you, but can sit in the lobby. Your partner might carry a few medicines—painkiller, cough syrup, or antidiarrhea medication. You never know what you might want urgently! The partner might also carry a cheap tape recorder into which you can speak your impressions and information after each interview. Record when you can hope to hear from the school, what further information you have promised, and any questions on which you wish to follow up by e-mail.

When scheduling interviews, try to schedule your preferred schools after the first interview, since you gain immensely more fluency with that bit of experience. While I advise trying to keep two hours between interviews to allow for note taking and getting to another hotel, some job seekers strongly prefer cramming interviews closely together so that their adrenaline stays up and they ride the crest of the wave from one interview to the next. The letdown during a wait can be irritating beyond belief to these personality types. Judge this decision by your own psychology. If you meditate, figure on finding a comfy chair and meditating for twenty minutes to recharge your batteries. You do need notes on each interview, but hasty talk into a small tape recorder could cover the main points in ten minutes.

When your time slot has come, knock on the door, even if you can hear interview activities going on inside. Some schools figure they will talk to one candidate until the next makes his or her presence known, so do not hold back.

Do not trust your impression of the interview. Many interviews that seemed like love feasts never produce further contact, and some that seem failures do get you to the next stage. Do not grizzle over washouts or lost opportunities. Keep thinking positively of what is to come, not negatively about what you cannot change. Remember that some very decent jobs get listed after the major conference. If you feel you flopped on your only two interviews, this is bad, but it is not the end of the world. Furthermore, if you feel that you did not answer a question well, you can make that the excuse for a follow-up e-mail, giving your considered answer and saying something enthusiastic about the interview.

Avoid social arrangements with family or old friends; stay focused on job hunting. It helps to have a cell phone with you, since if you are running late for an interview, you can call to say that you are on your way, but keep it off most of the time. You want to be able to reach others, not have friends trying to invite you to a party.

The MLA says you must have two weeks to accept or reject an offer, and other professional organizations have similar guidelines. You can refuse to give a decision on the spot, citing your society's rules. Know what your professional organization recommends on this point. Most schools would not try to get you to say yes on the spot, but it helps to know your rights.

Never, never, never promise you will go to a particular school until you have the offer in writing. If the school in question is your dream school, you can certainly give every encouragement, and say that if the written offer is along the lines discussed, you certainly expect to accept, but your supervisor told you never to commit yourself until you have it in writing. Blame the supervisor, blame the placement officer, but never let yourself be bullied or sweet-talked into making an absolute commitment before you have done what you can to boost the terms and before you have received the letter. Once a written offer has been made, improving your terms is much more difficult, so work your requests into the dickering early. If you really want a particular job, you can say, "This is the job I want and I expect to accept the offer, but let's talk about some of the terms." That is conditional enough that you can still withdraw if you need to for some reason. Some departments try to pressure you into an oral commitment and do not wish to offer writing until you have committed, in part because they lose face with the dean if you turn them down; some also wish to avoid their cumbersome paperwork unless they are sure of a positive outcome. This pressure, however, should be resisted, especially if it is a school you do not want and you are waiting to hear from one you do. You want to see the actual terms. You also lose negotiating room if you have simply said yes. For the possible bargains you can drive, see the next chapter.

Telephone Interviews

Some telephone interviews screen candidates to decide which ones will be interviewed at the conference; some telephone interviews replace the conference interview, and determine who will be brought to campus; some are the only interview that school can afford, and might result in an offer directly. Some will be conducted by one person; others may be conference calls. A polite school calls and arranges for a good time to talk to you; you certainly can ask for them to call at a time more convenient to you, which will let you review your notes on that school. Your standard preparations for conference interviews will not be as much help as you might wish in a telephone situation. However, you can pin up notes to yourself, which is a distinct advantage. You can also ask at the outset that speakers identify themselves each time they ask a question. Here are a few things to do or remember.

Unlike face-to-face situations, telephone interviews give you no visual feedback. At a conference interview, you can see facial expressions, indications that you have babbled too long, signs of disagreement. You have no such prompts in a telephone interview.

Keep a cheat sheet taped to the wall by the phone and a bottle of water and box of kleenex nearby. Be sure the cheat sheet lists the three or four points you wish to make about yourself for this job, and check them off as you make them. Print the names of your interlocutors on a sheet of paper with bits of information about the person's interests under the name. Download their pictures from the web if there are any and paste them above the names. If you have no web pictures, look through an old magazine and cut out a few male and female faces of the right general age and paste those up. Pretend that those people are your interviewers and direct your eyes to the right one for the answer. Try to "persuade" the person whose picture you are looking at. This is a technique used by people in business school, and corny though it sounds, job hunters who have tried it said that it genuinely helped them.

Work hard to vary your vocal production; use more range of voice than you might otherwise. They will extrapolate from your speaking voice to possible classroom effectiveness, so you must show variety and vigor and emotions. You can improve your vocal manners by having a friend give you a mock-interview by phone. This friend can tell you if you let your intonation fall off too much toward the end of your sentences. Possibly you leave many sentences unfinished, or your tone is flat and unvaried. Such problems leave a worse impression over the phone than face to face, so work on them.

If you are an international student, the point of such a call may well be to make sure your English is good, so be sure to speak clearly and do not let natural exuberance push you into high-speed talk. If you have any accent, speed will vastly reduce your comprehensibility.

Although unannounced phone interviews are rare for people in most fields, departments with language jobs may designate a professor to call you out of the blue and talk in the target language, expecting to assess your basic fluency that way. Surprise is thus a deliberate tactic. You might even get a call from two professors, alternating questions in your two non-English languages and expecting you to answer in the appropriate language. Because you might get a call with no warning, you may wish to have a general cheat sheet (in all relevant languages) pinned up by the phone. That will help keep you from blanking on crucial terms.

The Problems Caused by Inept Interviewers

One of the most difficult problems you may have to deal with will be inexperienced interviewers. They may be very bad at asking questions that will let them judge you or let you show off your paces. If you realize that you are not being allowed to make a good presentation, you must do everything you can to take the interview into your own hands. Look for opportunities to say, "Let me tell you about my teaching." Do not let yourself get drawn into protracted arguments over some point of interpretation or matter of ideology. You can be blunt: "I will be happy to discuss this at greater length if it is a central concern to the committee, but if not, could I tell you a bit more about some of my other qualifications?" If one person is yammering on about this irrelevant issue, the rest of the committee will probably chime in then on your side, and help you push toward a more useful set of topics. They will, in fact, appreciate your effort to steer the conversation in a more useful direction. Getting an interview back on track when it has been derailed takes skill; you are unlikely to get to the next stage if you fail to make that interview work, so you have nothing to lose by trying blunt measures, and you might gain significantly in respect from some members of the committee. If the head of the search committee is inexperienced and does not remember to tell you when to expect to hear from that school, you can prompt her or him with a question.

The Aftermath

The weeks following the conference are in some ways worse than the interview process. For that, you had adrenaline to carry you through. While waiting for the invitations to campus, though, you relive every question and awkward moment, and second-guess your every answer. The best thing you can do to get your mind off such profitless speculation is to work on possible campus presentations.

Three

Campus Interviews and Negotiating Terms

You must have done well in your conference interviews, because now you are facing campus interviews. In the former, your chances were probably one in ten; now they are usually one in three. Campus interviews cost schools so much that they do not like bringing in more people than necessary. Whereas the brief hotel interview demanded intensity and the ability to answer any question instantly and effectively, the campus interview demands sustained energy and unflagging enthusiasm. Moreover, while your answers are important, your collegiality is more significant. People want to be sure that you will fit in and contribute your share to a joint enterprise. You will be on display for a day or two, talking with individuals, committees, and larger audiences. The trick is to stay eager, engaged, and happy to talk to anyone. You must be as enthusiastic when you trot out some comment on your work the fifteenth time as you were the first. You must not give briefer answers late in the visit. You may feel that everyone has heard your explanation and that it sounds sillier each time you say the words, but in fact everyone has not heard it, and the perceived silliness just results from the repetitions.

Beyond your energy, you will need many copies of the syllabi worked up for this school, one or more presentations (the most usual being a talk and a class), and a lively sensitivity to your different audiences (so you can tailor your comments appropriately). Review your answers to all the conference questions. As at that first interview, most of the campus questions and discussion will concern teaching rather than research, even at research-oriented institutions, so be ready to talk about all aspects of teaching. You will notice one major difference from the conference interview: Now the school is trying to make a pitch for itself to you, so while you are still being judged, you are also being wooed. Part of that is being treated as an equal, and that demands that you call people by their first names if that is the pattern they follow. For some job hunters, this familiarity can be as difficult as anything else in this phase of the process, but you have got truly to believe that you are an adult, a polished professional, and not an apprentice any more. Enjoy this leap forward in your status, enjoy the wining and dining, and stay alert. Turn your cell phone off for most of the day, so your attention remains focused on your interlocutors.

First, you need information in order to set up your interview smoothly; then you need to understand the audiences before whom you will be performing. This chapter will list the groups you will meet in one form or another, and will try to sketch their interests and concerns. Your knowing what they are looking for will let you vary your answers to suit their interests. My list is based on the most complex institutional form you are likely to deal with: the large state university. Smaller and less wealthy schools will run you through a less elaborate set of hoops, though they will probably supply plenty of one-on-one contact. You are on your own for that kind of conversation; the agendas of individuals cannot be foreseen.

Setting Up the Interview

First, a warning: If your least-favored school tries to set up a campus interview in early January, do all you can to delay your visit a week or two. They may well be trying to get you in early and make an offer, and then you will have a maximum of two weeks in which to say yes or no. Your other schools may not even have arranged interview dates by the time this two-week deadline arrives. You would need courage, lunacy, or both to turn down a real job in hopes of something better, knowing that you may get nothing else. If humanly possible, avoid getting into this situation. You may wonder, "Why go at all? Why not cancel?" First, the conditions might prove more attractive than you had realized. Second, this may be the only institution that actually makes you an offer. You cannot truly know that you would rather have your wisdom teeth extracted through your ears than go to a particular school until you have visited it, so do not hasten to expunge it from your list. Only if you pile up so many campus trips that you cannot survive them all do you eliminate possible jobs.

When you are telephoned about setting up a campus interview, here are some of the things you need to ask for or enquire about.

Your Schedule

Any well-run school will present you with your schedule ahead of time, or when meeting you at the airport. If you prefer it sent to you before you take off, ask for that. Specify early in the discussion of your visit that you would like a half hour before your talk if possible in which to be alone and get your head together.

Meetings with Certain Groups

If you wish to meet with undergraduates or graduate students, say so in advance so you can be sure that they will be worked in to the schedule. You might, for instance, ask to eat breakfast with a few undergraduate majors. Student reactions to you will be particularly influential if you are interviewed at a liberal arts college, where teaching is stressed; this will probably also be the case if you are a minority job candidate, for the department will almost certainly set up a chance for you to talk to local minority students. As one such job hunter remarked, he was aware that minority student input on minority candidates was taken far more seriously than white student input on white candidates, in part because of the need for inspiring and approachable role models. Be sure you learn what any students you talk with are hoping to see from this hire.

The Nature of Your Talk

You need preliminary information about your job talk. How long should it be? Who will be attending? Specifically, will students be there as well as faculty? These questions let you show your rhetorical awareness of pitching the presentation to the right audience or audiences. While a few elite institutions may wish an intellectually formidable, conference-style presentation, you are vastly more likely to be told that this should be a talk, not an article read aloud. However, most places realize that you will have a written form (or at least notes) in front of you. What "talk" means is a presentation that is accessible and lively. Do not use theoretical jargon. Use short sentences. Emphasize your main points rhetorically. Use your classroom techniques, not your article-writing skills. Your ability to wow a class with a rousing performance is what will be assessed. Department members will judge your scholarly skills from your writing sample. Those in your particular discipline may ask more scholarly or theoretical questions, but most of your audience will be pleased by something that is easy to understand and rewarding to ponder.

The Nature of Your Teaching Demonstration

If you are to teach a class, find out as much as possible in advance about what you should cover. Also, ask what will be covered in that course's next class. If you are delayed by a blizzard, you want to have done a bit of preliminary planning for that later class so you do not have to take it over with no preparation.

Who Will Pick You Up at the Airport?

Find out and read some of that person's work. This may be your longest stint one-on-one with a member of that school, more than an hour if the school is situated in a major city. You do not wish the ride to be punctuated by awkward silences. Remember, though, that anything you say will probably be reported upon, so think before speaking. Language departments often detail the job of picking you up to a native speaker of your language to test your fluency, so be prepared to chat in that language.

What Days of the Week are Involved?

If you stay over a Saturday night to save money on airfare, you may well have a Sunday blank. Be sure to have work with you to do if the weather is inclement; if possible, though, see something of the town or city, and ask if some member of the department can show you around a bit. If they offer you the choice of time on your own or with someone, choose the more sociable option.

Special Needs

If you are vegetarian, or allergic to shellfish, or cannot eat pork, mention this in advance so that your hosts do not plan social events based on something you cannot consume. A vegetarian who forgot to issue this warning found himself at a faculty member's house for supper being presented with a fancy, much-talked-up lamb dish that he had to refuse; this caused bad feelings. Another kind of special need might be video equipment to make your presentation. If you have broken your leg and are on crutches, you should mention this, lest you be expected to trek long distances, especially outside on icy surfaces.

Your Audiences and Their Interests

In the course of meeting people and committees, you will probably be interviewed by one or several people representing the following interest groups. Learn from this list what that person or group wants so that you can shape your answers to be effective for that particular audience.

Higher administrators: associate deans, dean, provost, president
Head or chairperson
Associate head or associate chair (in a large department)
Directors of program committees (the undergraduate program, graduate studies, the service courses, plus various subdivisions representing different departmental missions)
The search committee that chose you out of hundreds of applicants
The personnel or promotion and tenure committee
People in your general area (e.g., American literature, Francophone literature, language acquisition, creative writing)
People in your specific area (pedagogy, classical philosophy, Old French, military history)
People in adjacent historical periods (or people whose interests someone thinks overlap yours)
Junior faculty (untenured recent hires)
Some member of staff (who will tell you how/when you will be reimbursed for your flight tickets)
Graduate students
Undergraduates

Higher administrators operate above the departmental level. The dean wants research productivity (in a research school), and all deans want competent teaching. Avoid professional jargon (which would probably be interpreted as your being unable to pitch your material properly to undergraduates). Be lively and stress the importance of your research, its implications and applications. Work in a reference to your teaching evaluations, using your best student evaluation scores. Make it clear that you have future research projects in mind and talk a bit about the next one. If this is primarily a teaching school, then stress teaching and collegiality; you may also want to make a point of mentioning community contacts, outreach, lectures to alumni, and service. Make much of any extra practical skills you might have, such as experience teaching ESL or Business Spanish.

In a research institution, the associate dean for research and graduate study will be able to tell you about grants, support for travel, and support for putting on conferences or lecture series. If the dean is out of town, the associate dean will be the person to meet with you. One or the other will also be able to tell you about possible support for faculty development.

In a small school, you may actually be interviewed by the provost or the president. Stories abound of such interviews being rather weird, for these dignitaries rarely know anything about your field. If you interview at a sectarian school, however, this administrator may be the person to examine you on your faith and its appropriateness for this job. The push for orthodoxy and conservatism in such schools tends to come from the upper administration (appointed by trustees) rather than faculty. If you are an international student, the higher administrators will probably be assessing your fluency in English; since you have to function in an English-speaking university, they will take a dim view of poor proficiency, even if the job you are applying for is in a language department.

When asking an administrator questions, you may wish to inquire about the future of the department and of the university. Does the dean think your department is improving? What changes does the dean hope to see take place in the department over the next five years? If you talk to a higher administrator of a state university, you might ask how well the legislature supports education in general and at this school in particular. Have raises been possible on a regular basis? Is the legislature threatening another major cut, and if so, might this interfere with future tenurings? A university in bad financial shape might not be your best bet, even if the job looks good in other respects. A dean is unlikely to admit that the school is in straits, but you may pick up hints.

The *head* or *chairperson* will tell you about salary, benefits, work conditions, and terms. If you have spousal-hire problems or desire same-sex partner benefits, this is the person who will tell you what might be possible, though save such questions until after you receive an offer. If you are an international student needing a green card, the head and associate head will be the people with whom you need to discuss the necessary steps. Do your homework and give the head or chairperson a sheet of paper with the name, e-mail, telephone number, and office of the administrator on that campus who handles green card matters.

A word of clarification on terminology: In many schools, a head is appointed by the dean and answerable to the dean in a top-down flow of power; a chairperson is elected by the department and answerable to the department in a bottom-up flow of power. The distinction, however, has never been absolute, and head is becoming the more common title, since it avoids the extra syllables of chairperson or chairwoman and avoids confusion with named-chair holders. Whatever the label locally used, you should be aware that departments tend to be autocratic or democratic, and the pattern will almost certainly be college-wide, maybe university-wide. Both systems have advantages and disadvantages, but you want to figure out which you are dealing with.

An *associate head* is usually found only in large departments. In such a hierarchy, the head deals with higher administrators and the rest of the university, while the associate head handles the daily running of the department and such chores as scheduling. An associate head will be concerned with how useful you might be. The head or associate head may actually decide which of the three candidates best fits overall departmental needs (as opposed to the search committee's infatuation with a particular candidate's style, or some powerful professor's desire to acquire a flunky).

The *search committee* will be measuring you against the other two candidates they chose out of the conference interviewees. They have the most invested in the unstated aims of the search, since they have argued for weeks over what it should accomplish. You can ask them what they hope this hire will gain for the department, and show your willingness to work up the necessary courses or skills. If you got them to articulate such an aim in the conference interview, you can indicate what preliminary steps you have taken to prepare yourself to meet that need. You do not know what credentials the other candidates bring, so you can only try to be impressive and friendly.

The *personnel committee*, sometimes called the promotion and tenure committee, is looking ahead six years to the tenure decision. Since their successors will have to decide whether to support your bid for tenure, their first concern is your research, at least in a school with any emphasis on research, and you will be asked to tell them about your future projects. They will look for signs of professionalism, and will count naïveté or ignorance of professional matters against you. They will also look for signs of competent and imaginative teaching. After that, they will tell you (or you can ask them) about the local promotion and tenure procedures and expectations. Ask what their department's expectations for tenure might be and ask what the records of the last few to get tenure look like—what books published at what presses, and how many articles in what kinds of journals. You might ask if their publication standards are rising, especially if you are interviewing at a regional campus or regional state university—and if so, from where is the pressure to do so coming? If this is a teaching institution, you will want to learn about other professional activities that are adjudged equivalent to publication in their scheme of rewards.

Directors of programs want to know what you can teach in their program and how useful and flexible you are about teaching. If a specialist in literature, will you fit into the department's elementary language acquisition programs? If a classical philosopher, do you have much to contribute to the more contemporary mission of the department? If you are a medievalist, can you teach history of the language? If a Victorianist, can you do Romantics as well? The smaller the department, the more you must be able to function as a generalist. Essentially, anyone with a PhD should be able to teach the survey courses associated with the field.

As you meet *people in your historical period or specialty area*, give some thought to how your presence would affect their power structures. What, for instance, will your relationship be to the senior person(s) in your area? Is he or she about to retire? Is the department hiring you deliberately to push aside a nonpublishing or bad-teaching nonentity? Is he or she traditional and are you cutting-edge and theoretical? How do your research interests mesh and overlap or complement each other? You might also seek answers to the following: Does this historical period or interest area work as a unified group? Is there a reading group, and if so, is it for faculty only, or for faculty and graduate students?

When socializing with *junior faculty*, you can ask how they feel they are treated (if no senior faculty are present who might tattle on them). You can ask *graduate students* how they find the faculty in your area. Are they helpful and supportive, or are they too wrapped up in their own work to help students? Learn about the dissertations the graduate students are writing. A job candidate at Penn State failed to click by showing no interest in the work of the local graduate students. Be very interested in their work, and make as many helpful suggestions as you can. After all, you may well be put on some of their committees if you are hired. If you are given a lunch or discussion-time with *undergraduates*, ask them about themselves, the program, what they would like to see from you as a new department member, and what about the major they wish were different. The latter might give you some interesting conversational fodder for chatting with faculty.

Questions to Which You Would Like Answers

Basic Conditions

- Course load? nature of courses?
- How big are the classes? (A 4–4 load with ten students per class is very different from one with larger classes. 4–4 is also easier if you do not have four separate preparations.)
- Above what size enrollment are graders supplied, if they are?
- Salary?
- Will the school help pay for your move?
- Could the school pay to extend your medical benefits to cover that yawning gap between graduate-school employment and your assistant professorial job?
- What do the records of people who have gotten tenure recently look like?
- Are the standards for tenure being raised?
- Do new people get office computers? How fancy and high-powered a computer can you hope for?
- Do office computers have some kind of high-speed connection to the net or does it run through phone lines?
- Do the servers have large enough capacity to permit personal web-pages? (For many small schools, the answer is no.)
- What is the library like in your areas? Does it have any particular holdings or special collections that might be useful to you? Do they have or will they get databases you need?
- What is the emphasis of their graduate program? In what schools have their best graduate students landed jobs? You can ask about any aspect of graduate placement that interests you, and you can make plain that you would enjoy helping train job hunters. You know a lot about the hunting process now, so you can show informed interest. If the school is a college or community college, you can ask what kinds of jobs their students move on to after graduating.

Resources

Stress things from which more people than you alone would benefit, and, obviously, only ask about those that truly interest you.

- Are there funds to underwrite the development of an innovative teaching idea you have?

- Are there facilities that permit computer use in classrooms?
- Are there opportunities for interdisciplinary teaching?
- If you wanted to sponsor a conference, would it be possible to do so? What sources for funding a conference are there?
- Is your department or university part of some institutional affiliation—with the Folger Shakespeare Library, with a university abroad? (Better yet, if you have heard of such a connection, ask how it works.)
- Is there money for adding books to the library? Databases? Films?
- What are the facilities for film screening for classes? DVD/VHS projector or only a TV screen?
- Most schools will pay something toward sending a faculty member to a conference, but would it be willing to do the same to send a Film Studies specialist to a major film festival? While you wouldn't give a paper, attendance and the exposure could be very important for professional development.
- Can you create and teach some new courses?
- How complex is the process for bringing new courses into being?
- If you got money from an outside source, would it be possible to take time off to work on a book?
- What funds are available to subsidize summer research? for course release time? for a research assistant? (Be careful on the last few questions; they can make you sound selfish and not committed to the school or being there.)
- Does the school offer a paid semester's research time to junior faculty?
- Does the school offer sabbaticals, and how are people using them to develop their teaching and research?

Department and University Community

- Is there a research colloquium?
- Are there brown-bag lunch discussions?
- Is there much interaction with other departments?
- Where do junior faculty live?
- Is there a faculty club or campus eatery where you can join other members of the department at a table without having to set up a date in advance?
- Are there good local book stores? If so, where?
- What do houses rent/sell for in the area?

- Which areas of town should you look at? Which should you steer clear of? (the fraternity area, for instance, or a dangerous area to the north of campus).
- Can you rent a house for the year from a faculty member going on sabbatical? Ask the dean who might be out of town. Some schools have housing offices that deal with this sort of arrangement. Some schools offer subsidized housing to faculty.
- Which rental agents are the best to deal with? (Graduate students might be better informed than faculty.)
- Which townhouse complexes do junior faculty members favor for their first year or two?
- What lecture series does the department run? (You have an idea for one, or for speakers, or for a speaker.)
- Are there reading groups? Publication workshops?
- Does the school have a good film series? Jazz series? Concert series?

As with interviews, look on these interchanges as conversations with people about things that matter to you. The multiday interview is stressful because you are always on stage, but keep trying to learn about the place, and do your best to seem like someone who would be helpful to department endeavors, someone with good ideas but not someone who rides roughshod over faculty or staff members with other ideas. Indeed, many campus interviews are largely social, and your aim is to be fun to talk to, a good listener, a smart suggester of solutions to problems, and someone who would fit in. Neither fawn nor play hard to get. Be eager and genuinely interested in these potential colleagues, their work, and the school.

Remember, some schools do not know how to arrange such visits, and you may find yourself with awkward blocks of time on your hands. Furthermore, many people do not really know how to conduct interviews, and will ask you pointless questions or not ask you anything at all. You may be stuck with an awkward group at lunch who will talk of nothing but local town issues about which you know nothing. Try to work your way into the conversation by making it more relevant, but do not panic if this does not work. Shrug it off; these things happen. Interviewing takes practice and thought on both sides.

During campus visits, schools are looking to see if you will be useful (administrative view), collegial (faculty view), and productive, probably in that order, since research productivity will have been established as much as possible during the conference interview. Whenever possible, present ideas that are conducive to collaboration, collegial good feeling, and working in your area with a group, not as an individual.

Awkward or Illegal Questions

The campus interview is where you are most likely to run into really awkward questions; the questioner may be fully aware of the breach of decorum or may just be clumsy and ignorant. Here are some sample situations.

- Why was our student who went to your graduate school so dissatisfied with the Renaissance program? What's wrong with those jerks? That student was brilliant. (This questioner kept probing for feedback on the professors. You will have to try to turn aside such inappropriate questions.)
- If we offered you the job, would you take it?
- What sort of job does your spouse need?
- Is your taking this job contingent upon your spouse being hired?
- Here's our offer. Do you accept it?
- Which schools have invited you to campus interviews?
  Have answers prepared. You should not say which schools. This is very important: If you are being pursued by schools no one has heard of, the person asking may decide you are unworthy and pass that judgment on; or the head might decide that the department need not offer you a good salary to compete against these rivals. If you have interviewed with an extremely prestigious school, the one you are visiting may figure it has no chance and not make an offer. Never name other schools interested in you. You can just say, if asked about other interviews, "Yes, I'm interviewing and finding this a very busy but stimulating time, what with teaching and travel." If pressed, refuse outright to name other schools. Say your supervisor told you not to name other schools, and if someone tries to jolly you along and ask why anyone would enjoin that, explain the logic of obscure/good schools. Say that you are looking at each school as a separate entity and wish to be viewed by that school in the same fashion, without reference to other job possibilities. Then turn the conversation by describing why you are interested in this particular school and wish to be taken seriously by it.

Remember, your supervisor or placement officer says that you will be skinned alive if you give an immediate oral acceptance. You need to bargain first. If you really like the school, you can say that this school is your first choice and you would certainly expect to accept it if the written offer were the same as your understanding of the oral, but you prefer not to make a final commitment until you discuss the offer with your supervisor and see it in writing. Once you have been given the basic terms orally is the time to start bargaining, before anything has gone on paper. You want the written version to include whatever you have bargained for.

One advantage to demanding the offer in writing before giving final acceptance is that it may give you extra time to hear from another school. Some schools take three or more weeks to churn out a letter; more efficient ones fax it to you the next day. Those that take lots of time will strongly resist sending the letter unless you promise to accept. Do not give in to that pressure, and be sure to bargain for salary or moving expenses before you are sent the written offer or contract. If you commit yourself to the terms negotiated orally, the only thing that could justify turning the written offer down would be a serious discrepancy between what was promised orally and what is offered in writing.

Discrepancies do occur. Heads are sometimes overly optimistic about what the dean will provide by way of salary or moving costs. Some schools do this version of bait-and-switch routinely, and you only realize that you have been had when you get the written version. Watch out for situations in which, after you accept, the offer and your acceptance must be okayed by dean and provost. If either of them in theory could veto your appointment, then you do NOT have a firm agreement, and you can consider yourself free to talk to other schools that approach you. The school would argue that you are committed to them, but if they are not committed to you, then you should not tell other schools to remove your name from consideration because you have accepted a job.

Presentation

When making arrangements for the visit, ask whether you will be giving a presentation, and if so, what sort of presentation. Ask if the department would like to hear about any particular part of your work. The person arranging the visit may specify one of these formats or some new combination:

- A forty-five-minute talk, with fifteen minutes for questions
- A thirty-minute talk, with thirty minutes for questions and discussion
- A twenty-minute after-lunch talk, with indefinite time for questions

- Two twenty-minute presentations, one on research, one on teaching
- A roundtable discussion of teaching
- A talk about your research in general
- You may be asked to give some article or chapter as a talk. (Check first before using your writing sample as the basis for the talk.)
- You may be asked to send an article/chapter in advance, which the department will read. They would then discuss it with you for thirty minutes, asking you to summarize it briefly and informally at the outset.
- You may be given a class, whether on some standard topic in grammar or rhetoric in a required elementary course, or some canonical text in a survey course. One well-run department managed to have its three candidates teach *Gulliver's Travels*, book I on Monday, book II on Wednesday, and book IV on Friday, and thus could compare them on a similar text.
- You may be asked to provide a suitable short story or poem for a class in your specialty; the class will read it and you will teach it.
- You may be asked to take a standard text and "teach" it to a group of faculty members. (If you are supposed to "teach" a text to a mixture of students and faculty, urge the students to come up front so they will not feel intimidated into silence by faculty sitting on either side of them. You should be able to phrase this invitation so that you get a laugh.)

Prepare the talk to last five minutes less than is called for, since you will want to give a few thank yous in your opening remarks, and you will probably make a few impromptu asides. Besides, the head may waffle and wander in introducing you. Before your visit, read the talk aloud many times so it is semimemorized. This way you can look up frequently and make eye contact, which is very important. Try to make eye contact at least once with everyone in the audience.

Work hard in preparing your talk. Unless the school says it wants a conference-style presentation of your work (all the jargon included), do not just read an article or chapter part. Written discourse does not perform and communicate well orally. You will still have it in front of you and be able to refer to it, but oral material needs more drums and trumpets, more repetitions, more hand waving and emphasis on main points. It should be lively. Remember, your audience will judge your potential for the classroom from what you do here. A low-key, dry presentation will damage you. Jargon from your field will probably count against you; many members of the department will not be up on your specialty. You may wish at one or two points to say "If I were teaching this, I would now develop the historical dimension of this idea a bit further" or "Since

I know you need to know how I would handle an idea like this in a class, let me give you the definition of this specialist term as I would in a class and illustrate it."

If they stress that they do not just want a chunk of a chapter or article, you might consider the following. Draw up a talk on your whole thesis project, one that emphasizes what is most original and powerful about it, what it permits you to do with the texts, documents, or artifacts you discuss, and why it matters. You can make this lively and easy to follow— and then when the search is over, you can go rewrite your preface incorporating all this lovely material. You can genuinely improve your book project by having done the thinking necessary to deliver such a talk.

Give some thought to the logistics of your talk. Do not go straight from lunch to the talk, if you can avoid it. If you cannot, eat very lightly and stay away from dairy products because they gum up the vocal cords and make you need to clear your throat often. Coffee and tea tend to dry the throat, so skip these, if you can. If the talk comes after dinner, do not have more than one alcoholic drink. Many people consider meals the most difficult part of the interview process. Forget looking at the menu with an eye to gourmet delectation. You will taste nothing. Pick things that you can eat easily without having to worry about mess or etiquette.

Prepare for antagonistic as well as friendly questions. Most departments have a curmudgeon or a pompous loon, and if your work is at all controversial, it is bound to rub someone the wrong way. Indeed, what you do may be a denial of everything that their old-fashioned specialist in your field believes in. You must always be polite, no matter how hostile the question. Some job hunters, probably out of nervous defensiveness, interpret badly phrased questions as hostile when in fact they are offered by strong supporters of the appointment. A snappish response loses you that support and embarrasses your supporters.

Be sure you know the published work of people in your area. You might be able in discussion to make some point of connection between what you do and what the questioner does. Even if the questioner hates your guts, your referring to something she or he published ten years ago will prove that you have done your homework, and dispose others well to you.

You can handle a hostile question like this: "Your assumptions seem to be A and B. I am working from assumption C. Given that basic divergence, we'll probably have to agree to disagree." Always try to identify the assumption behind someone's query or challenge. If you are not sure, ask: "I can answer that better if I understand where you're coming from. Are you assuming X or Y in asking that, or have I missed your point?"

If you're given one of those long, rambling questions that has no articulable focus, listen for something you can connect to and then start your answer like this: "That's a complicated question. Let me answer this part that jumped out at me, and then we can explore other implications."

Remember that anyone's query about representation or hybridity or exit exams will be coming from a definition of whatever that term is, and his or her definition may not be the same as yours. You can always start an answer by saying, "I define performativity as thus-and-such, so I would argue the following."

Try not to look at this as an exam, but as a chance to talk about your ideas with people who are interested in them. They may indeed be able to make useful suggestions. If someone does start a useful train of thought, you cannot really afford to take notes while dealing with everyone, but ask them to talk to you a moment after the presentation and let you jot down their suggestions.

In this stressful period, you may well come down with a cold and have to manage these visits in less-than-wonderful shape. If you are smart, you will already have had a flu shot, and even in January, it would still be a good idea. Be sure you have on hand the requisite cold remedies. A swig of cough syrup might make it possible to continue through your talk, but be sure to get one with uppers (decongestants), not downers (antihistamines).

Miscellaneous Problems

You may find gaps in your day's schedule of interviews. Carry a paperback with you. If your stay includes a holiday, see if you can arrange for one or more faculty members to show you around the town or city. Find out from the web what natural beauty spots, museums, or other points of interest might be in the vicinity. Then you can ask to see these rather than sit in your hotel room. If you are a cross-country skier or hiker and the weather is appropriate, you might manage an outing.

Unions and Step Systems

If you were trained at a university where the graduate student teaching assistants are unionized, you will know the kinds of questions you will want to ask if the school interviewing you has a faculty union. If you have no exposure to unions and step systems, then you need to learn enough to ask useful questions.

The University of California has a step system (non-union); the City University of New York (some branches) and the Keystone system in Pennsylvania, for just a couple of examples, have union versions of such a step system. In either situation you enter at a specified level, and can only rise through levels at a set pace, even if you are a whiz publisher and become famous fast. While beginners do not have much maneuvering room, you should polish up your arguments for starting at better than bottom—namely, your publication, teaching experience, experience in organizing conferences, and the like.

Some schools have local teachers' unions, organized by The American Federation of Teachers or the American Association of University Professors; others were organized by teamsters or another national union outside of education. In most union schools, you have to pay union dues whether you join the union or not, because you get the benefits and conditions that the union has negotiated. If the union is any good, the advantages will be superior medical benefits, a good retirement plan, and better-than-average wages, as well as security and clear guidelines on tenure and promotion. The drawbacks may be a lack of reward for outstanding performance and productivity, lack of punishment for the egregiously bad performance of others, unwieldy bureaucracy and paper-work, lack of flexibility in terms of what you teach and when, and the threat of union action. You may be grateful for what such action does for your paycheck, but the threat of a strike can generate a terrible atmos-phere on campus, anger among the students, and distrust all around. These drawbacks were listed by a Penn State job hunter who landed in a union school. A more recent hunter, who read this book in manuscript, protested that his school union had no such unwieldy bureaucracy, provided excellent merit raises, and granted complete freedom in terms of teaching. The union was entirely beneficial, from his standpoint. No general statements, therefore, are possible. You simply need to find out how a particular union operates locally. Another job hunter who got a job at a unionized school furnished some questions to ask on campus or after the offer has been made.

- How often is your contract negotiated?
- Is your salary negotiated separately from the basic labor contract?
- If the contract is under negotiation at the time you are being hired, do you come in under the old or new terms?

- Is membership mandatory? If not, what percentage of your department belongs?
- Do department administrators count as management or members of the union?

Unionization is a hotly contested topic at some schools, and you may be questioned about your views on unionizing. Members of the department who are militantly anti-unionization will probably respond badly to enthusiasm for unionization from you. Unless you have researched unions and have seen their workings personally, your safest answer may be to plead relative ignorance, since what you know or have heard rumored may not apply at all to the particular union system at issue. Where possible, seek information about the local circumstances rather than offer opinions.

The Offer

You may receive the offer orally while you are still on campus, but usually the department wants to discuss all the candidates, so you first learn that you are their choice by phone. The MLA says you must be given two weeks to make up your mind. Few schools can afford to give you any more than that because if you turn them down, they want to get on to their number two choice before she or he has accepted elsewhere.

Do not accept on the spot. You need to talk it over with your supervisor and friends, and you want to be sure that you understand what the offer actually means. You will want to know how it compares to other offers being received that year. Bargain for the improvements you most desire and then ask for the offer in writing. Despite requests, the MLA has not issued a clarification of an ambiguity: Does the two-week clock start with the oral offer or the written? Schools, obviously, wish to consider the oral the starting point, but job hunters would benefit in major ways if the two weeks began with receipt of the written offer.

For some schools, the only piece of paper involved will be the letter of offer. Others have a contract filled with legal jargon as well. If the letter of offer does not cover all the points you discussed with the head, your answer should list these and state that you accept contingent upon these points you discussed and agreed on being included. Get any understanding you have on paper.

Many first-time hunters are surprised that the contracted time offered is only one or two or three years, renewable. Very few schools give you a contract for the full six years' probationary period. They need the right to get rid of someone totally unsatisfactory in less than the full period. Of course, this also means they can get rid of you if the university falls on particularly hard financial times; being thrown out of the troika to the wolves is one of the functions of untenured faculty. You cannot do anything about this, so put it out of mind. Normally, you will be carried through until the tenure review, when final decisions are made, unless your teaching is unsatisfactory or unless you are publishing too slowly and are in a research school, in which case, you may be cut off some time before the sixth-year review.

If you get only the letter, do not feel antsy because you have no contract graced with "whereinas" and "the party of the second part." A contract is, truth be told, not much good in a face-off between you and the university, particularly before you have actually started teaching. If a provost unilaterally abrogates a contract, as one did with a job hunter of mine who did not have a green card (although she had been completely open about this), you can do nothing unless you have thousands of dollars to sue, and even then, the court would almost certainly find for the university, since the university is under no obligation to hire you.

Whether you have a letter or a contract, save this document. You never know when it might become useful. Years after accepting our jobs, my husband and I were very grateful to have these letters on file because the local IRS office decided to challenge expenses on research trips to London as frivolous, saying that research was our private hobby. Having the letter, which made explicit the expectation of publication, saved us.

The points you will be most likely to bargain over are as follows.

Salary

If you have lots of teaching experience and some publication, you can try for a bit above the beginning level. If you have taught eighteen courses and their load is 3–3, that amounts to three years' worth of experience by their scale. I know of no one who bargained the salary up more than a few thousand, but every bit helps. You cannot count on getting that increment, though. A school may have a policy about all first appointments starting at base level. Perhaps the department head has strong-armed the dean into improving beginners' salaries and has hired six people your year at that new level. Going back to the dean and asking for more just for you may be beyond practical politics. The head and dean also have to worry about the morale of people hired three years before you who will not have made it to the new beginners' level yet. The head may also figure that your experience was the reason you were interviewed, not something for which you now deserve extra credit.

Policies on salaries differ wildly. Some schools offer the lowest they think they can get by with. A few may startle you by asking what you think your salary should be, and hint that you should aim high, or ask you to suggest a salary but give you no sense of the local scale. The latter can be very disconcerting. You may have no idea at all about what a beginning salary should be for this school and in this part of the country, but you can do a bit of research. The tables in the Almanac issue of the *Chronicle of Higher Education* can help you out a bit; before your campus visit, you can have researched the school and compared its average salaries with averages elsewhere. Cost of living varies widely and can explain some salary differentials. A four-bedroom house may go for $125,000 in the Texas panhandle, but for a million or more in Los Angeles. Auto insurance may vary from less than $500 a year to more than $3,000, depending on location. Issues like salary are something to discuss with your supervisor and placement officer prior to the campus visit. They will know the range of salaries earned by last year's hunters, and can find out roughly what their own institution is offering. Type "cost of living comparison" into your search engine and try the different sites. Some are more helpful than others, listing small towns as well as large cities, for instance. If you know the beginning assistant professorial salary at your graduate institution, you can compare that with what you are being offered at another school and see how the buying power differs.

Course Reduction

Some people get their load lowered from 3–3 to 3–2 for the first year. Sometimes you can get the teaching rearranged: Instead of 3–2, you get 4–1, which would give you substantial amounts of time in the one semester for research.

Computer and Other Equipment

Think big here. A school unable to do much on salary or moving might spend freely for your computer. Computers are often paid for from year-end money, so be sure to get your order in promptly if you do not wish to wait long into the autumn for the new budget to be in place. You need to know enough about computers to order intelligently, so get advice if you need it. The same goes for film equipment if your field demands that.

Moving Expenses

The university may have a policy against spending money in this fashion, in which case the department will probably have no independent say. If the department can choose to distribute its money for that purpose, though, it might do anything from paying you $1,000 to paying the moving company for you.

Summer Money

You would be making a serious mistake to teach in the summers. You need that time for research, writing, and other professional development. However, it does not hurt if the school makes easy research money available during your first few summers so that you do not "have" to do summer teaching. The school cannot promise such money, since it is given in competition and availability may vary with the state of the budget, but the head can promise to support your application strongly.

Money for Getting to Archives or Conferences

Schools vary enormously in what they will offer. Some will pay all expenses for one conference or trip to an archive, which can easily run $1,000 or more. Some will just pay airfare, permitting you to apply that amount to other costs if you get yourself to the conference in some other fashion. Some only pay if you are giving a paper, while others will pay whether you perform or not. Some will pay for an international conference, while others must go through quantities of red tape to get funds for international activities. Some will give you airfare to one conference and a smaller set amount toward another conference. A few schools just offer a flat sum to any department member for conference going or research expenses. Annual budget fluctuations can affect all of these forms of largesse. If you plan on attending a number of conferences, you will have to pay many of the costs yourself, but what a school initially offers you for conferences may make that aspect of professional activity less destructive to an assistant professorial salary.

Subsidy for Your First Book (Should that Prove Necessary)

I will discuss this topic in chapter 4, but you might wish to look ahead and bargain for this now. One school's generous and foresighted solution is to offer assistant professors in the humanistic disciplines a lump sum of $10,000 as start-up package. This they can use to get to extra conferences or archives, buy materials needed for research, or anything else, but one big-tag item they are warned to save it for is subsidy. The school would write the check, but this fund would be the source. A less wealthy school might be willing to promise subsidy should it prove necessary. The promise costs nothing now and the money might never be called for if the book were to land without a demand for subvention.

Databases for the Library

If your research depends heavily on having access to a particular database, such as *Past Masters* for a philosopher or the *English Short Title Catalogue*, you might start bargaining for that now so it will be in place when you arrive. If you need films, these also are something you can dicker over: a budget of so many thousand dollars to start a relevant film collection?

Credit for Past Publication

A school may or may not count your past publication toward tenure. Many do not because their judgment is to be based on what you produce during the six-year probationary period. However, if the school has a system whereby an article gives you points for two or three years in faculty activities and this scoring system affects your merit raises, you might ask that the two articles that have just appeared should give you points during the next two years toward merit raises.

Medical Benefits

Find out if there will be a gap between your current policy and the starting date of your new one. If there will be such a break, see if the new school will subsidize a continuation for your current plan. This is expensive, but if you let your insurance lapse, you may find that your new policy will not cover pre-existing conditions, and in any event you would be highly vulnerable during the time without coverage. This particular cost will hit you just when you are most likely to be without salary, paying for a move, and coming up with a damage deposit, so help in this realm will be worth a great deal to you.

Beyond identifying the points you wish to bargain for, you need to collect information on the retirement plan options and the possible medical plans. Really bad plans might make your first-choice job less attractive than second- or third-choice schools with good benefits and retirement. Some medical plans, for instance, may be better if you have children, or better if you have a pre-existing condition, or if you expect to be out of town or out of the country frequently. You may have to choose between an HMO and a non-HMO plan, between your paying a percentage on all drugs or paying a much smaller percentage on chronic medication but more on occasional medications: These and other options will bedevil you. The school may contribute a lot or very little, in which case you will have to contribute more. Many schools let you change the medical package once a year, so a bad choice is not likely to dog you for too long, but you do need to be ready to deal with such choices.

Similarly, you need to check out retirement plans. Some schools offer just one option, while others make two or three available. Usually the choices will consist of a state system, an independent insurance-company-based system, and TIAA-CREF (Teachers Insurance and Annuity Association-College Retirement Equities Fund). My preference is for TIAA-CREF, but you will have to evaluate the terms offered at that school. If you have two offers to choose from, you will wish to compare the percentages contributed by the school toward retirement, any lag time before the school starts contributing, and the period before the money vests and belongs to you. For more on retirement and reasons for taking an independent rather than a state system, see chapter 4. When you get a huge, confusing packet of material on retirement, work through it immediately and send the requisite forms back promptly. At a state school, you probably will not be paid if this paperwork has not been done and returned on time. Your best bet is to talk to faculty at your new school and learn what they chose and why, and get the best advice you can.

Campus Interviews in Retrospect

Campus interviews are strenuous. If you have many, you will be worn ragged by the end. You will also feel about ten years older and you will, in fact, be ten years more mature in your understanding of the academic world. If you get six campus invitations, pursue all six, even after you have gotten an immediate offer from number four and plan on accepting it. You may be mortally tired, but going to see the last two campuses will continue your education in just how different schools can be. Numbers five or six might prove worth considering on totally different grounds, or might make you more deeply grateful for the virtues of number four. You will also pick up good curricular ideas that you can apply elsewhere; cross-pollination is a useful by-product of the interview circuit.

You will come out of this with increased self-esteem. You managed even when the plane was rerouted and you had to bus the rest of the way. You managed when no one met you at the airport and you had to stay the weekend in an empty guesthouse that had no private phone and no lock on the door and unshoveled sidewalks piled high with snow. You taught the class, even though it was not on the material you had prepared. You survived a badly run visit during which you were only offered machine sandwiches by the head, apparently because the school was too poor to have an entertainment budget. You survived a head who was too green at the job to know she should tell you the terms of the job and waffled on about her field (not yours). You will in future dine out on the story of the small college president who insisted that you were a candidate for journalism because (he claimed) he had never authorized one for English. You kept a straight face with the writing director who proved to be a control freak determined to make you teach creative writing lockstep with her, although your publications were far more impressive than hers. You kept a cheerful mien at the depressed campus where everyone hated everyone, had had no raises for five years, and only stayed because they wanted to live in that part of the country. You learned a few things when dealing with a head who was a particularly offensive male chauvinist boor. You survived the school at which Protestant evangelicals were persecuting Catholics (you being Catholic). You are still trying to think of the right retort to a southern department head who said baldly that he didn't care what your field was, he was interested in your candidacy because you were African American. You were non-plussed when you sensed that the chic little overnight guest quarters were probably once the slave huts behind the mansion that became the college. You learned a lot about a school when you were asked how one of your graduate school professors (an alumnus of that school) was carrying out his Christian mission. These are all real experiences of recent job hunters.

At the end of all this, you are a somewhat different person, with a lot of unexamined assumptions rethought, and your image of yourself shaken into a new configuration. You are ready to take up a job as a faculty member. Figures vary, but something like thirty to forty percent of PhDs in the humanities are getting tenure-track academic jobs in their field their first year of hunting, and the percentage goes up if they keep trying, though nothing guarantees success. If you have found a job, particularly if you have found one you like pretty well—no place is perfect— you have done something to feel proud of, something that should provide you with a sense of satisfaction for some time to come. Now you have some new homework.

Having found out where you will be next year, do a bit of research on the history and politics and ecology of that region of the country. Learn about Appalachia if that is where you are bound; bone up on the Civil War if you will be living in a part of the country still attuned to its issues; learn the basics of California history if you're heading for the West Coast. Read a novel or two set in the region of your new university, and if your department has creative writers, read one or two of their novels. Such proof of interest in the school and area can always be made to work for you. One successful job hunter recommends getting an article or two sent out in that summer before the new job starts, because their landing in journals will take a great deal of pressure off you in your first year or two.

If you did not get a job in this cycle of hunting, you are now much more polished and experienced, and have four or five months in which to add to your credentials and work on your book manuscript before you start looking again. Because of the market, fresh PhDs are trying to compete with people a couple of years finished who have landed their books. While this is discouraging, it also shows you what to work toward while preparing for the next round: Get that manuscript polished and propagandize presses until one will look at it. Plan on going to your field's big conference so you can push your prospectus to publishers' representatives. This is one of the best and most efficient ways of getting a press to look at a prospectus and respond promptly. Spending a year or even two in limbo while getting a book out might work in your favor in the long run. If a press accepts your manuscript during your first year on the job, you will seem a *Wunderkind* to your colleagues; your status will be higher than if the book had taken in your third or fourth year, irrational though that may be. Surprisingly often, the people who were deeply depressed at not getting even bad jobs in one cycle got good ones the next because their credentials were better or because they simply had better luck, so a bad year may be a disguised blessing and lead to a happier future with a better job.

Your greatest problem when tackling the cycle for the second or third time is to put your discouragement and despair behind you and practice as earnestly as if this were your first time out. If you cannot bring yourself to practice as you know you should, then offer to advise and share your experience with those going out the first time; to do that properly, you will find yourself having to brush up on the information and skills that you need, but more pleasantly than if you were just feeling sorry for yourself in your study. You have ultimately to recapture that eagerness and optimism. If you do not think you can succeed, you probably will not.

Four

The Economics of Being an Assistant Professor

This chapter may at first seem something of a grab-bag, since its concerns range from the problems of publishing a first book to planning retirement. While publishing the book may seem irrelevant to financial matters, you might not have such problems getting your book taken in time for a tenure decision were it not for the economics of humanities publishing. Furthermore, the probable future demand for subsidy makes the topic more money-oriented than it would have been a decade ago. Granting the somewhat miscellaneous nature of the topics here, I do not propose to force them to fit a procrustean framework. Book publishing involves more than economics and will be given its due. Following that will come retirement, the kinds of financial records you need to keep for tax time, and the long-term economic prospects for a humanities academic. As you compare two jobs, if you are lucky enough to have more than one offer, you will be looking hard at the economic implications of your choice: salary versus cost of living in those areas, percentage the school contributes toward retirement, the generosity of the benefits, the kinds of support available for faculty activities, research, and development. If you can foresee some of your needs in advance, you may be able to bargain for the school to meet them.

Publishing Your First Book

Publication has become the currency of the humanities community. Articles and books can be counted easily and they can be judged, albeit with somewhat more difficulty. Your department and your college unit (usually Liberal Arts or Arts and Sciences) are always in the midst of benchmarking exercises. How does your department measure up against the "top ten" in your field, as established by the *U.S. News and World Report* ratings, or against the National Research Council ratings or against the Big Ten or against the other members of your football consortium? Your department's placement in a *U.S. News* list is a given, but your administration may wish to show how you rate against other universities in your conference or locality, or find numbers to argue that you have been improving in praiseworthy fashion since the last such report. Your head may, for instance, produce a list of the department's top twenty journals and then see how many articles your department has published in those journals over a set span of time and compare that figure to those from equivalent departments. Your dean may release statistics on how many more books one of the unit's departments has published in the last five years than the previous five. Or someone may come up with figures of how many books per capita a department can boast. Candidates for senior positions may be checked in the citation index to see how often other scholars refer to their works.

Most of these measurements correlate very badly with quality, but they are reducible to numbers, which good thesis supervision—alas—is not. You will be making a mistake if you disdain these clumsy comparisons and try to hold aloof from them, for they have real-life economic consequences. If your department has a higher per-capita number of books than other humanities departments in the unit, that may prove a good talking point with the dean for more money and the chance to hire more faculty. If your college can create the right sort of statistical comparisons, it strengthens its hand for bargaining with the central administration. Raises, hires, travel funds: All these depend in large part on publication statistics and, increasingly on your ability to get grants. Similarly, your personal standing within the department—economic, political, and psychological—depends on your publication in most if not all schools. Indeed, in a research-oriented school, you may not have any standing at all if your first book is not accepted for publication in time for the tenure decision, for you may not get tenure.

Book publishing has become so difficult that its central role in tenure decisions is now being challenged, and teaching institutions sometimes accept articles instead of books. Nonetheless, you would be unwise to figure that the demand for a book in a research school will be replaced by something else very soon. Ideally, your supervisor will have encouraged you to write your dissertation in as press-ready a form as possible.

Dissertation versus Book: What's the difference between them?

Dissertations written in the old-fashioned way—as dissertations—will suffer problems that must be corrected before they are shown to a press.

If you and your supervisor plan ahead, you can avoid that extra stage of revising by writing a book from the very beginning. Here are the differences for you to keep in mind. Dissertations tend to reflect your process of educating yourself in the topic; books simply offer the conclusions. A dissertation spends a lot of time differentiating you from all your predecessors in the field. After all, one of its functions is to prove that you know the field. Your knowledge should and must be assumed in a book. Dissertations are also larded with jargon; you had to prove that you understood the tools of the advanced work in your realm. A book, though, will sell even fewer copies than otherwise if it communicates with only the half-dozen most advanced people in the field. Jargon now turns presses off, whereas once upon a time a jargon-filled book was trendy.

Dissertations reflect your insecurities regarding your status in the field, often offering far more support for an argument than is necessary, or defining your position by attacking those of others. A book projects the confident voice of an expert telling other experts new ideas that will be of interest to them. You may differentiate your position from another scholar's, but no hostility is called for. Someone whom you scornfully belabor is undoubtedly the first person you will set eyes on at the next conference or will be the reader chosen by a press or the person who will review the book for a major journal. Try to disagree fruitfully, in ways that your opponents would find interesting and that would encourage amiable intellectual debate.

Tone is one of the most obvious characteristics that a publisher will look at. If your manuscript sounds like a dissertation, a press wants nothing to do with it because far too much effort will be required to edit your work into proper professional shape. One experienced editor tells me that he can open a manuscript at random and read a single page and decide whether the piece is worth publishing or not. If the tone is right, the rest probably is.

Look at recent books. Look at the length of their chapters (none twelve pages, none eighty). You, too, must think and argue in the accepted normal units. Look at the nature of the preface or introduction; make sure that yours covers the same kinds of material. If you do all of this before you write your dissertation, you can save yourself a lot of rewriting at later stages. If you produced an old-fashioned dissertation rather than a book manuscript, however, you will have to devote serious labor to revising before you can send it out with any hope of success.

Prospectus

A prospectus package consists of a short cover letter, a document describing the project, a table of contents, a preface or introduction, a sample chapter, and your CV. The cover letter must stress what makes your study exciting and important (the descriptive document and the preface will also have that material, but some overlap is inevitable). Be sensational and be specific, but also keep it short, preferably no more than a page. The acquisitions editor is almost certainly not a specialist in your field, and may not even be a specialist in your branch of the humanities. You cannot assume knowledge and must do what you can to explain without dumbing down. The cover letter or document is what makes the editor bother to look at the rest or not, so it must be persuasive. The descriptive document, the prospectus itself, may have some of the following subheads: context, rival studies, audience, research methods, chapter contents, new discoveries, and conclusions with their narrow and broad applications, pedagogical value, the author's credentials, articles the author has written relevant to this project, and the status of the manuscript. The chapter you send must be self-contained and flashy. It must excite readers. You ruin your chances if the chapter involves much description of your predecessors or if it simply covers ground. It must have an exciting argument.

You should send the prospectus packet out when your manuscript is very close to being finished. You can send it to one press at a time (the best policy, but only in an ideal world), to two or three at a time, or to thirty. Be warned: If you send an ineffective prospectus and thirty presses say no, you have made it impossible to approach those presses later with a good prospectus. Sending to more than three at a time is ill-advised. Even this can hurt you, because if two say they want to see it, you can only send the manuscript to one at a time, and the other will know that it was not your first choice.

In commercial publishing and even in some social sciences, multiple submission is acceptable with permission of all the presses involved. In humanities, you almost never get that permission. Authors need not be granted any concessions because what they hope to land at a press will not make the press any money. After all, a press spends a minimum of $200 for two readings. Academic presses do not want to pay that money for something that might be withdrawn because another press accepted first. You will merely look foolish if your cover letter airily says that you will give them right of exclusive reading if they agree to make up their mind quickly; they won't accept it unless they alone have it, and making presses behave decently about turn-around time is, alas, something we all daydream about, and the fantasies tend to involve boiling oil. As one scholar put it to me, "Publishers aren't civilized. They're not even housebroken." The central problem, though, is not as often the press as it is the shocking irresponsibility of some readers—your fellow professors.

Even though presses seem to misbehave, you cannot afford to. Multiple submission without permission is in many eyes one of the deadly sins of the profession, almost as bad as plagiarism and falsification of sources. No one objects to multiple submission of prospectuses; publishers accept that as standard procedure. Multiple submission of books or articles, however, can deservedly damage your career. The system of handling publication is rickety and fragile enough. With articles, all the reading is done gratis, as a service to the field. The economics of scholarly book publishing are extremely marginal. If everyone multiple-submitted, the system would come crashing down about our ears.

Figure it will take you a minimum of two years to land a manuscript, even supposing that manuscript to be top quality and well revised. The process will probably take three years, and maybe four—and that would not necessarily mean that the manuscript was not good, just a bit unlucky. Hence the urgency to your getting your manuscript sent out by the end of your second year in a job if you are at a research-oriented school, since you will probably not get tenure if it has not been accepted by the sixth year review. Hence, too, the need for you to turn immediately to your next book project after you send the first one out. Not only do schools want you to get your thesis printed, they want proof that you will not just collapse and cease to be productive. Many people can write a thesis with a supervisor standing over them cracking the whip. Indeed, some schools are reluctant to count thesis books toward tenure for fear that the underlying ideas are really the supervisor's, but most schools recognize this fear to be unwarranted in the humanities. However, statistics show clearly that few academics are self-starting and motivated to do their own project from scratch with no outside help, and research schools do not wish to tenure those who do not belong to that small group. Tenure at a research-oriented school is given for a rate of productivity and for proof of continuance, not just for a book and six articles. If you get up to the tenure point and your book has not taken but you have most of a second manuscript complete, the school will be more likely to consider you anyway than if you have no new, substantial project underway.

Why is Publishing Books so Difficult Now?

In 1970 the standing library order from prestigious American academic presses for humanities books was over eight hundred copies. A press would price the book to pay for itself at eight hundred sales, and make a small profit on purchase by individuals. Around the year 2000, the standing order had sunk to about one hundred and seventy copies. The figures I have heard from publishers for producing literary monographs are $8,000–$10,000 in direct costs, and $16,000–$20,000 in indirect costs. A press may use nine or more people to handle editing, production, marketing, sales, and the like. Add building overhead and you see why indirect costs run so high. To get that $30,000 back with sales of three hundred at best, a press would have to net upwards of $100 per book. Hence, most academic presses are losing money even when they charge more than $50 for a book, and they must be bailed out by their universities—reluctantly and less fully every year.

Many academic presses are now essentially unwilling to consider standard scholarly books unless some form of subsidy is available. One I know, for instance, will not take literary criticism without subvention; it loves books on German subjects, though, because the German Embassy is generous with publication grants. Since humanities units are fiercely resisting having to undertake this extra expense for their faculty, you need to know the arguments on why it may well be necessary if your book is to be published. You also need to think of ways of making such an outlay palatable. For instance, you might suggest a swap—teach summer for free, say, if the dean or department will cough up several thousand dollars as subsidy.

Subsidy to get a book published is increasingly going to be a fact of life. One group of presses is considering demanding subsidy from any author's school if that school does not itself support an academic press; demanding a book for tenure but not supporting a press whose mission is to publish such books makes that school a parasite on the system. If your job is with such a school, you may well be forced to persuade them to produce a subsidy, so prepare yourself. Those of you who have done rhetoric or Cultural Studies theses that touch on a nonliterary field (sports, League of Women Voters, labor unions) or those whose work involves foreign literature whose embassy believes in supporting its own culture might be able to find sources for subsidy-sized handouts from these outside sectors.

Subvention in the humanities usually takes one of two forms: subsidy or the subsidy-equivalent of Camera Ready Copy (CRC). Subsidy from your school may come from the departmental or college level, or from a publication fund (e.g., Cornell's Hull Fund if you are a faculty member at Cornell). Your being able to produce CRC means you become your own typesetter, and thus save the press several thousand dollars. For this procedure, desktop publishing programs like PageMaker or Quark are unnecessary; you need only Microsoft Word or WordPerfect. You will need to learn much about the program that users normally never hear about, but technology-conscious state universities have staff members who can help you. Their computer centers may well have some very high-powered experts in printing. Most American presses do not need very elaborate templates for setting type to their specifications. Learning about templates, running heads, crop marks, and other niceties will take time, but the knowledge will be useful. If you start learning it while you are still at a major university with a large computer staff, it could become an element on your CV and something you could teach other members of your new department.

Here are some further arguments you need to be able to deploy. By the time a research school has supported you and paid your benefits for six years, paid for travel to conferences, and given you a semester off with pay, it may have spent close to half a million dollars (those benefits are expensive). For it to balk at $5,000–10,000 more is foolish economy; this is a tiny amount in the overall scheme of things. Another argument involves the reason that subsidy might be needed. The diminution of library sales from eight hundred to one hundred and seventy is caused by the rising costs of science books and journals; libraries cannot afford to buy the less-crucial humanities books. Science journals not only charge libraries hundreds or even thousands of dollars per year per journal, they also get page costs from the authors of articles. However, in the sciences, such money comes out of the author's grant or department, and even if it came from the author, that payment would not make the product a vanity publication. Science journal publishers coin money. Humanities publication is being destroyed by that greed, but that's the way things are now. Because most humanities books cannot make their costs, presses raise their prices, and so fewer individuals and libraries buy copies. They sell fewer copies and have to raise their prices still higher, so fewer individuals and libraries buy copies, so. . . . You get the picture.

Alternatives will eventually spring up, including online publication and print-and-bind on demand, but all have drawbacks and at present, non-standard publication may not count for tenure. The likelihood of any particular online publication still being available online twenty years from now is practically zilch. Websites come and go. The publisher maintaining your book on its site might be taken over and the backlist cut; your book would then cease to exist. In theory, online publication should be easy, but the practice is likely to prove otherwise.

Academic presses now take as much time to scan a prospectus and decide whether to read a manuscript as they used to take to decide whether or not to publish. Six months' wait to hear if your book will be read is not uncommon. If you have talked to an acquisitions editor at your professional conference or if a senior professor pulls strings with the press, you may be given permission to send the manuscript without bothering with the prospectus stage, but mostly, you have to scrabble to get someone to look. Being able to state in the cover letter to the prospectus that you are able to produce Camera Ready Copy or that your school has sometimes produced subsidies in the past might help them take your prospectus more seriously. Subsidy for publication must come—at least officially—from some institution, not yourself, and in theory it should be asked for after acceptance, not before. If you, yourself, offer subsidy before acceptance, then technically you are producing a vanity publication (even if the same rules are not applied in the sciences), and it would not count toward tenure.

You must understand the difference between genuine academic outlets (university presses), academic-style commercial outlets (Routledge, Palgrave Macmillan, which are fine), highly respected commercial outlets (more likely for biographies than scholarly books—Norton, Knopf, Random House, again very prestigious), and fringe presses that are sometimes okay as minor outlets but are sometimes outright vanity presses. The reputation of fringe presses varies over time, and from field to field. In a school serious about the prestige of its research, publication with some of these would not count, since it would be seen as nonrefereed publication. According to a *Lingua Franca* exposé (September–October 1993), one such fringe press actually sold PhDs. The prospective buyer had to collect that diploma in person from an offshore location so the company could not be prosecuted for mail fraud. I am advised that naming presses that might hurt your tenure prospects could prove legally actionable, so I do not include their names. You will have to talk with your mentors and collect that information on your own.

You must take responsibility for knowing how any particular press reaches its decision. Many years ago when I called one of these fringe presses, I was told that it made its decisions in-house within two weeks, which means that books were not sent out to two experts in the field, as is the custom for academic presses. Many universities make a fetish out of the refereeing process. Sometimes a good editor of a series who makes his or her own decisions will give you much more careful readings and advice on how to improve. Nonetheless, given the values that operate now, such an editor's modus operandi might not count as refereed publication and many schools will not accept unrefereed publication for tenure, so you have to know how the press works. You also have to know your own department's customs. People in history, English, and philosophy departments have numerous possible outlets; scholars in language departments have fewer, so those departments consider some of the marginal presses acceptable.

When you arrive at a new job, ask the head whether the department has a list of favored journals, and start enquiring about how the department would view some of the possible presses you are hoping will consider your book. If the school is not strongly research-oriented, you might ask whether your turning your thesis into articles would be acceptable, or whether a book is the *sine qua non* for tenure. You want to be sure you understand the local rules, since the consequences of not doing so will be unfortunate, to say the least. Once you know the rules, you will find it much easier to work efficiently toward an unproblematic promotion and tenuring.

Retirement

Retirement may be the last thing you are thinking about when you first get a job, but among your earliest chores will be to fill out wads of paperwork, some of which will involve the details of your retirement plan. The wrong choice at this point could cost you a lot down the road, so you need to understand the basic possibilities. You do not have any choice about signing up for retirement; at most, you will have a choice of TIAA-CREF (Teachers Insurance and Annuity Association-College Retirement Equity Fund), another independent plan (probably run by an insurance company or a mutual fund company), or a plan local to that school or state. Consult with your new colleagues about what they chose and why. Consult your thesis supervisor about the issues and principles involved, and if you know anyone who is financially competent in investment, consult that person too.

State plans often offer defined benefit pensions. This means that your retirement income will not go up and down with the market, but is instead calculated by means of a formula like the following. You get two percent for every year you work for that state applied to the average of your last three years of salary before retirement or leaving. If your final salary averages $80,000 over those three years and you worked for forty years, you could retire with eighty percent (40 × 2%) of $80,000 or $64,000 per year. Some state plans offer a more generous percentage that makes retiring at 100 percent possible. Other state plans are not formula-based, but invest money paid by you and the school. If the school pays a large percentage and you a small one, this can look very attractive. Such local plans tend to be most advantageous, however, if you never move from that state or from that retirement plan; if you do either, you may find getting full value from them difficult and withdrawal of your funds to put them elsewhere may be impossible. Furthermore, defined benefit plans may leave you badly protected against inflation. Cost-of-living increases are currently part of some such plans, but that clause is being cut out in the business world, and states will almost certainly follow suit, so figure that additional personal investments will be needed to protect you from inflation. All this may seem Greek to you, and your retirement hardly seems a burning issue. Being lazy or careless now, though, might prove expensive: The small amounts of money you put toward retirement at age thirty can grow a lot more than the bigger sums you invest at fifty. Take some time and trouble to do this right!

I know little about insurance company–run funds, but given the fiduciary misbehaviors in all sorts of major financial institutions during the last twenty years, I feel less confidence than I would like in an independent, for-profit institution. Among other things, the company could be taken over disadvantageously, and pension schemes have been damaged in company take-overs. One item to check is the annual charge for their services; many mutual funds charge high fees. Only local faculty can give you much information about such a plan.

My own choice, based on what has been available where I have taught, is TIAA-CREF, but I admit that it is losing market share. Many educational institutions in the country offer it, though salary percentage contributed by school and teacher vary widely from institution to institution, and the contract struck by each school with TIAA-CREF differs, so some schools may offer less advantageous conditions than those I have experienced. If you choose this option, start by putting about eighty percent into the stock-related funds (CREF) and twenty percent into the non-stock instrument, TIAA. When you are fifty or fifty-five, you will probably want to change your annual contribution proportion to something closer to fifty-fifty. You can move money from CREF to TIAA immediately at any time, but not vice versa. TIAA-CREF runs what has been until now one of the most successful large-scale retirement plans in the country, and it has followed very sound principles. The TIAA half will ultimately provide you an annuity, a fixed sum per annum. The CREF part will also provide an annuity, but one that will rise and fall with the market, which is unsettling when it goes down, but the upswings help protect you against inflation. The TIAA protects you when the market is down; the CREF keeps you from starving on an inadequate annuity when the market is up. If you are an aggressive risk-taker in investing, you may find TIAA-CREF stodgy, and the nonliquid nature of TIAA investments means that you cannot transfer money out of that plan quickly. Those are the chief objections one hears to this retirement plan. Its handling fees are low. Financial institutions do change (for better and for worse) and TIAA-CREF is changing rapidly as of 2004 (on which, see discussion in *Forbes* magazine, 16 February 2004, 117ff.). For the present, TIAA-CREF's track record plus its nonprofit status make it seem safer to me than a commercial pension manager, but this is a personal opinion and it rests on local circumstances. You need to consult the faculty in your new school about what is available locally.

If your school has a good contract with TIAA-CREF (that is, beneficial for its faculty rather than the school), all the money in the account vests immediately and you can transfer the account from one school and state to another. Less advantageous contracts delay vesting of the school's contribution, and some accounts cannot be transferred, in which case you will have to start another account at your new school. Another advantage is that TIAA-CREF gives you several ways of investing your money (e.g., stock, growth, index, global, social choice, and bonds funds) and it permits you to change the emphasis from growth to income as you get older. It also offer Supplemental Retirement Annuities (SRAs) and other ways of putting aside tax-sheltered money beyond the basic retirement contribution.

A final argument for taking TIAA-CREF is that neither the state nor your school has any control over your retirement money once it has vested. If at some point your school feels you have behaved criminally, your school can very probably seize its own contribution (and maybe yours as well) in a state plan, leaving you with no retirement funds whatever—a grim prospect given that social security may not last your lifetime. I have heard of a professor who pilfered from some special funds, and to avoid prosecution, he lost his job and all the retirement funds in his state pension. One need not be "soft on crime" to find this a disturbing story. Of course, you have no intention of doing anything criminal, but rules of the universe change. Sexual relations between faculty and graduate students have long been ignored, but some schools are now trying to make it grounds for dismissal from tenure and declaring it a crime. Given current practice that the "victim" must be believed, you might falsely be accused of sexually harassing an undergraduate who was mad over a grade and be deprived of your job and your retirement money. Homosexuality in some schools might qualify, given laws on the books or laws that might be passed in some states. Some political activities might draw the wrath of the trustees; any ties to groups accused of terrorist sympathies could get you fired and worse, even though those groups were considered harmless two years earlier. Protecting your money from changes in social values is highly desirable.

As early in your career as you can scrape up the money, invest in an SRA. If you don't want all your eggs in the TIAA-CREF basket, try a Vanguard fund. They charge less for their services than almost any other fund family, and their investment record is very good. An SRA's value compounds, so the sooner you start, the better the end results. If you don't have children, start investing on your own as soon as you can; if you do have children, you may be able to invest only trivial sums until they have finished college, but even if you only start serious investing then, you can make a major difference to the comfort of your retirement.

Here's a good plan to try to follow: Every time you get a raise, cut it in half. Put half of the raise into your independent investments, and use the rest to improve your salary. You will feel the pinch, but better while you're young than when you're old.

Keeping Financial Records

The tax system in this country—ever shifting and often irrational—leaves much to be desired. If you are to get all legitimate deductions, you need to keep the right kinds of records and you will need a good Certified Public Accountant (CPA). As a graduate student, you probably filed the simple form and settled for standard deductions, and figure you can do so for some years to come: Wrong! You need to make appropriate deductions right from the first year of employment, even though the sums involved are trivial. According to my experience, based on the tax laws in effect during my professional life, your very first tax return as a faculty member should have those professional deductions. If you wait until the amounts involved are worth the hassle of setting up the deductions, the IRS will ask you why you had no such expenses previous years, and will say that if it did not matter then, it does not matter now. You cannot afford to let this slide by.

You will need to keep two kinds of financial records to help you with taxes. One will keep track of your professional expenses during your ordinary life involving teaching and living at home. The other applies to professional trips to conferences or archives and to sabbaticals.

Start either a notebook or a computer file and enter your professional expenses in a set of logical categories. These categories will include books, office supplies, computers and their expenses, professional long-distance calls, and expenses attached to conferences, visiting archives, and sabbaticals. Your very first year, you may be able to deduct something for your moving expenses and for the set-up costs at your new job, although that will depend upon the tax laws at that time. Check stubs and credit card bills will help you make out your records every month, but you will do better if you remember to enter items in a notebook or computer file the day you purchase them.

Get a Certified Public Accountant as soon as you can afford one. I cannot give specific advice on many points—to deduct or not for your home office, for instance—since practices vary widely from one IRS office to another, and tax law changes every year. You should be conservative in your claims; if you lose an audit, the result is very expensive. Ask colleagues what CPAs they use and trust. Such a person must understand the academic life. A nonspecialized tax-preparation service does not provide sufficient expertise, and will do you little good, while a good accountant can often get you substantial refunds—some years a couple of hundred, some years a couple of thousand, and even many thousands for a sabbatical year if you go abroad.

Not only do you want to protect money in this fashion, you want to spend it effectively. Invest in yourself and your future. Money spent on professional development or to make your publication better is always well spent. If you cannot get grants, pay your own way to conferences, to the School of Criticism and Theory and NEH summer seminars, to Folger Library seminars and Cultural Studies think tanks, to other countries to study the language or participate in advanced seminars. For many years at the assistant and associate levels, my husband and I figured that by driving one cheap car, we saved enough money (percentage of purchase price per year, insurance, gas, repairs) to pay for his spending a month in London every year for his archival research. You are not owed grants; your career is yours to build and invest in.

When you are away from home while engaging in professional pursuits, very different kinds of records need to be kept. The assumption behind these records is that you are involved in extra expenses that would be routinely covered at home, so those extra expenses are part of the total cost of your time away. The easiest system I've found for these records involves a notebook and an envelope or set of large envelopes. For a conference, use a small pocket notebook, in which you enter every penny you spend and the item purchased. Save all the receipts, stubs, tickets, and cash register tapes in an envelope labeled for that conference or trip. For a sabbatical, keep a steno notebook, one dated page per day, and enter every single expense, no matter how minor the item. When away from home, your coffee, railway reading, and cough drops all count. Save all receipts: ticket stubs, credit card copies, and cash register tapes. During a sabbatical just put each month's worth of receipts in nine-by-twelve-inch envelopes labeled January, February, etc. Your notebook keeps a written record of all those expenses; the receipts provide supporting testimony should the IRS challenge your claim. You need not sort them other than by month. With luck, you will never look at them again. Only if the IRS is feeling dubious about you would you have to match receipts to the expense record, but they are unlikely to bother. This amount of corroborative evidence is highly persuasive by its sheer bulk.

The Long-Term Economics of Being an Academic in the Humanities

What kind of future can you expect, economically speaking? You could make much more money in law, medicine, or business. Real computer expertise can be peddled in any part of the world in which you fancy living. While some academic fields are flourishing, the humanities do not enjoy much respect at present, and salary differentials are likely to increase somewhat between humanities fields and fields in which grants and sponsored research are the rule. If you do not get a tenure-track job, you may face long hours and low pay, and such lecturers are teaching more of the courses at universities than ever before. That's the bad news.

The good news is more diffuse, and depends upon your enjoying a certain kind of lifestyle. One can enjoy the academic life at many levels of school. Even if you came out of graduate school wishing to land a research-oriented job, you may find yourself quite happy in a teaching-oriented school, where pressure to publish is not nearly as fierce. If you get any tenure-track job, you can probably create for yourself more or less the kind of life you wanted, always assuming that you do enjoy teaching undergraduates.

Academics have to be patient. The rewards of being an academic take time. You will need about a dozen years, if you are in a historical field, to be recognized as a potentially major scholar or critic. Some cutting-edge fields are different, particularly if you put things out on the web, but the time from writing something to acceptance, to being in a backlog, to publication, to appearing in bibliographies, to being picked up and read and used by others takes at least five years.

Contented academics also enjoy some kinds of security more than they crave large amounts of money. The MBA starts at twice the salary of an assistant professor, and gets raises that may run ten percent or more, whereas academics in recent years have rarely seen more than a three to four percent raise, at best. Those same MBAs, however, may find themselves jobless with no warning, and must face the little problem of paying a mortgage and eating without any income, often for many months at a time. A doctor may not lose a job that quickly, but faces malpractice suits and skyrocketing malpractice insurance. Lawyers are in such an oversupply that many are barely eking out a living. While some states are clearly hoping to break the tenure system, they are unlikely to be able to do so retroactively; the courts would prevent that. If you get tenure, you have something that should protect you for the rest of your professional life. The security may not be glamorous, but it appeals to those who prefer practicality to thrills.

While your early years will not produce nearly as much money as you might wish, the latter half of your career can be quite comfortable if you play by the rules and publish steadily, or are generous and energetic in the collegial ways demanded by a teaching institution. You will need twenty to twenty-five years to hit good enough earnings to have enough money to put a substantial amount aside. However, once you have been in the field for twenty-five years and if you have been steadily productive, your salary will start increasing steeply. The three or four percent that did little to improve your assistant professor's salary will be real money if given on the basis of a good full professor's salary. If you get the university's average raise throughout your career, you can expect to end up modestly comfortable, and anyone who publishes steadily can hope to get noticeably more than that average. You can also improve your circumstances by moving a couple of times to other schools; sought-after outside hires are given rather special salaries (though they usually then receive smaller raises so that others in the department gradually catch up). An employed spouse will also make a great deal of difference to your economic well being. If your spouse makes approximately the amount you do, you can be very comfortable indeed without children, and able to cope with college expenses if you have kids. While you could definitely make more in some other lines of endeavor, you need not live a church-mouse existence if you plan well, publish steadily, partner with another professional, and start investing early.

Five

The Politics of Being an Assistant Professor

Talking about the politics you need to understand after you get a job may seem premature. Why put that into a book on hunting for the job? My reason is as follows. When you go into an interview, your interlocutors are looking for a colleague, and all too frequently, they see a nervous, immature, and ignorant graduate student. Naïveté will not endear you then or during your early years. If they see you as someone whose hand will have to be held, who will say silly things in department meetings, and generally be a pain in the ass for not understanding how an institution works, you may not come out at the top of their list. Interviewees who make the best impression are those who already seem grown up. Such students can imagine themselves as faculty; they understand life in this particular institutional structure, have accepted its demands and adapted to it, and know that they are satisfied with their life-choice. This chapter is intended to help you make this mental change. Some of the things you need to understand include networks, the protocols of department meetings, the mysterious ways in which department decisions favor some voices over others (and rarely address the true subject in dispute), the need for compromise, the timescale of institutional change, what to do during department turmoil, and how to protect yourself.

Networks

Despite your having been a member of an academic institution for years, you have probably not thought effectively about the nature of institutions and the rules that govern their behavior. Many of these rules are found in any institution—government, business, the church, or the military; others are specific to academia. Most people don't get very good at understanding an institution until they've been in a job at least ten years and many never do understand, and doom themselves to a great deal of frustration. A creative writer once remarked to my husband, "I understand the firehouse politics of small towns. I'm comfortable with that. And I can tell that something of that sort is going on in the department. I can't understand it, though. I don't understand the rewards. I don't know why people fight for some things and ignore others. I sense the currents, but it's as if the politics were all being carried on in a foreign language." You need to learn this foreign language.

The essence of institutions is networks, spiderwebs of interconnections. The first step to institutional wisdom is realizing that you are no longer a private individual. Your professional actions all have network-touching implications. Naturally, you are aware of your chosen network of friends, people your own age and maybe a few professors who were friendly and helpful. Smart people keep that network alive and extend it. You keep such people informed of your advances, and make sure they know of your successes. You ask advice. Maybe you get some members to read work in progress.

By joining a college or university and a department, you become part of a nexus of networks, and you are a member whether you recognize it or not. These unchosen networks are what most graduate students and assistant professors do not understand. They think when they say something, they are speaking as an individual, and individual ideas and stances are all that matter. That will never be the case again for you if you get a job. You are always part of such networks, and the smart person learns to cultivate them as assiduously as she or he does the chosen ones. You still may sometimes choose to speak out against something in the institution and set the spiderwebs vibrating angrily, but you want to understand what the consequences can be; you want to choose your stands carefully. Here are a few examples of political errors that stem from ignorance of such noncultivated networks.

The first regards a grad student, but an assistant professor could just as easily make such an error. This student wrote a letter to the college newspaper, following up some article, and said some highly critical things about the MFA program. The criticisms may have been completely justified, but here are some of the nonvisible responses. One professor saw the letter and asked me who this cretin was who had written it. He shook his head and said that in departments in many schools, that person would never get a PhD. The head at that time did not operate in such a vindictive fashion, but seeing that someone does not get a degree need not involve any serious unfairness; it could be more a matter of doing no favors. No reminders about this or that deadline. No summer teaching. No fellowships.

You may wonder why a head would be so horrified by a critical letter. Aren't academics supposed to enjoy free speech? The head is always involved in a complicated process of getting money from the dean for new hires, for improving graduate student stipends, for new TAships. The head had been involved in negotiations for more faculty slots for the MFA, and overall for more hires for the department. If a dean, who has been told that the MFA is wonderful, reads an eloquent letter calling it lousy, that dean is going to resent having been conned, and might take it out on the department. Another invisible result: Politically savvy faculty would be extremely careful with what they said to that letter writer, and might wish not to supervise him or her. If you can't trust someone to refrain from shooting off a big mouth, you are better off not saying anything of any political import to that person. His or her naïveté can be as damaging as malice.

So, this degree candidate thought to speak as an individual, but the nonvisible networks touched upon involved English department negotiations with dean, the dean's view of department, willingness to mentor, and potentially the person's own future in the program. Given that the person had an MFA, one has to wonder if it might not reduce the necessary glow in any future letters of recommendation from the MFA professors. This does not mean that you must always overlook shortcomings in a program— far from it. Working to improve the school that employs you is a major component in a satisfying career. Sounding off in the newspaper, however, is not the way to tackle internal problems. Every criticism may be justified, but this is not the institutionally intelligent way of approaching the issue.

Here is another example of someone acting as an individual and ignoring the institutional networks. This story comes from a West Coast university some years ago. The placement officer did not have a very good opinion of the students, and at MLA, she sounded off to friends, saying that her university's products were good for nothing. When one operates as an individual, one may (unfortunately, but very typically) gain lots of feel-good sensations from persuading oneself that one is better than the institution that employs one. The woman in question may indeed have once been at a school with a better graduate student pool. However, the bush telegraph was soon reporting this attitude back to faculty at her current university. The networks mean that nothing remains secret very long. You have got to be very careful about slamming your school or department in public. You can work very hard to improve it, and gain great satisfaction from doing so, but don't make a practice of grousing about its weaknesses to those outside the school, even to close friends.

Here is another example, along with one of the secrets for doing well in this world: Share your successes by understanding who benefits from them and how. Corollary: Realize that nontenured rivals and tenured deadwood do not benefit from your successes, and be modestly quiet about them with either of those audiences.

You see all the work you did on your thesis as your own titanic struggle, your own creation. If you had a competent supervisor, though, one who put time into advising and criticizing, the result genuinely remains yours, but someone else has a vested interest in it. To a minor degree, that person and your department will deserve brownie points if your thesis lands well as a book and if you get a good job. You may not wish to share the glory of getting a good job, but a competent department puts considerable effort into preparing you to do that. If you land well, some credit goes to the job-preparation team, the faculty who made time to do mock interviews, those who wrote letters of recommendation, and your supervisor. If you are smart, you will keep those people well informed at all stages for some time to come, particularly of your successes. People who have helped you succeed (however marginally) feel well disposed to you by virtue of your success, in part because they gain brownie points from your success. Your succeeding does them good within the system. Why throw away a network of people who feel well disposed when they might be helpful in some future way? You may not like this sense that your successes must be shared and involve a feeling of indebtedness, but if you realize that your success spreads around credits for others in that local system, you can benefit from their well-wishing. Learning how to spread those credits effectively is a sign of a good politician. Future letters of recommendation will come much more willingly and glowingly from someone with whom you have kept in touch. Requesting a letter out of the blue after six years' silence does not rouse much enthusiasm to do you any favors.

Here is a positive example of how networks function. A former job hunter came back to her graduate institution to see friends, and she invited me, as placement officer, for coffee. We talked about revising her book manuscript, for which she had received a preliminary contract from a very prestigious press. Her initial impulse called for doing lots more research and expanding the manuscript in several directions. I pointed out that she might well lose the contract if the manuscript were expanded beyond the thirty or so pages called for by the readers' reports. She was thus saved some possible grief by keeping in touch with her network.

She also noted with some sense of gratitude that her graduate department had sent her as a graduate student to a European conference, paying all her expenses; her current employer was trying to find funds for that same conference, but she now realized just how unusual it was for a school to have done that for a graduate student. She was strongly urged to write the dean who had supplied those funds, copying in the department head, commenting gratefully on what her school had done for her as a graduate student, and pointing out that one result of such support was an acceptance for her book manuscript with a very major press. Now, by keeping the network informed, she has saved herself a mistake in revising her book; and by writing a letter or two that spreads news of the book and offers thanks, she gives both the dean and the department points and builds up capital for the future. If her former department wishes someday to drum up money to send another graduate student to a very distant conference, the precedent can be invoked for strengthening the head's letter to the research committee for funds. Future graduate students may benefit.

She was also advised to write a nice note (much the same content) to the donors of the thesis fellowship she had enjoyed. Knowing that the thesis is becoming a book should make them feel very positive about what their generosity is achieving, and may well produce more fellowships at some point for that university. Indeed, news of success in publishing can help the dean secure more such fellowship money from donors. Keep your network informed of your successes, and write thank you notes freely. In a couple of years' time, if you want to spend a month using your graduate school's library resources, that dean or head might be able to find a bit of spare cash to pay you to give a lecture that would help you finance that visit. Gratitude need not be registered by subsequent deans or heads, but for a little while, your doing the right thing may give you a string you can pull.

Thank-you notes are one of the major currencies of networking. A short e-mail will suffice in most instances. If someone on the staff from your department (or library or computer center) does you some service particularly well, thank not only that person but also write a note of commendation to that person's supervisor. If you take a computer seminar, e-mail the instructor your thanks. By individuating yourself in that fashion and letting that person know your name, you create a kind of bond that lets you send him or her a computer question six months later. If you have not sent a thank you, any further demand you make on that person's time is selfish and inconsiderate. Why should a note matter? If that person is planning on job hunting or building a case for a raise, your little note can go in the file of supporting evidence. By sending written thanks, you are literally putting credit into the system; this allows you to draw on it later. If you hear from a good undergraduate that a nontenure-track lecturer is doing an especially helpful job of teaching, let that lecturer know what good things you've heard, and let the head know too. Positive feedback is remarkably rarely given, but can be extremely helpful. By passing on good news, you contribute to the network. If you remind yourself to see such acts as putting credit into the system, and if you understand how it operates as credit, then you will make it possible for you to draw on that network when you need help.

When facing a political, institutional, or publishing problem, use your network. Collect advice from your thesis supervisor or from senior people in your new department. You may want to be "all grown up" and cut any ties of dependence and subordination with your supervisor. Why, though, lose contact with someone who gains credit for your doing well and should be willing to help and advise you? If people differ in their advice, go back and ask for the logic behind their stand if they didn't give it to you in the first place. Each increment in the conversation strengthens your ties to the network.

If you have an article draft, try it out on some new colleagues to build network connections. The main thing to be wary of is someone trying to corral it for a collection or third-rate journal that he or she edits. You need to avoid this. You can argue that such an acceptance will not look good when you come up for tenure; such a personal or institutional connection might even keep the acceptance from counting as refereed publication. You can claim that your thesis supervisor warned you to beware of any such local connection for your early publications. Most people are happy to give advice, and many will be inclined to think well of your work and of you if you have taken their advice and made some of their suggested revisions. Remember this, with regard to tenure votes.

If the problem you face regards teaching, you might prefer not to take it to local people if you are untenured. Use people at your graduate institution as sounding board. You do not wish to expose weaknesses that will be remembered against you at tenure time. If the problem stems from local student culture, however, you will need local suggestions.

Advice is a network function, and you need to recognize advice when you see it. If your chair calls you in and asks whether she can help in some fashion because it seems to her that your personal life is interfering with your professional life, do not walk out of the office burbling how wonderful and motherly she is and how glad you are she's so helpful. Your boss has just told you that you are messing up your professional life, which means your contract may not be renewed. You'd better clean your act up immediately, and make a few contingency plans in case you are on the market again soon. If someone keeps popping into your office and asking how your freshman composition course is going, this may be a slightly inept way of indicating that the person would be happy to give you advice or fill you in on local solutions to local problems—in other words, offering connection to a helpful network. If the person coordinating the course is notoriously difficult to deal with, you may need all the local know-how you can acquire, no matter how good a teacher you think yourself.

A significant part of good network politics is treating the staff well. Go in and introduce yourself to the administrative assistant and secretaries as soon as you get to your new department. Take them out to lunch. In a small department, there may be only one secretary, and that person can make it easy or difficult for you to get what you want—everything from prompt appointments with the head to an office that doesn't hear every flush of the toilets in rooms beside and above it. The secretaries know what forms you have to fill out—to register your publications, obtain reimbursement for travel on professional business, get permission to leave town during the teaching semester—and can walk you through those. Some secretary or administrative assistant may have an invisible institutional power because she has experienced four or five heads and their administrations, and knows far better than the current head (who may be new to the university) how things are done. She can tell the newest head why two members of the faculty do not get on well and have been on opposite sides of departmental issues for fifteen years. Some administrative assistants have PhDs and are brighter than you are; do not condescend to them.

Whether you think well of staff members or not, go out of your way to say thank you when they do something for you, even though it is routine and you think it deserves no special recognition. You will find that even the less competent or less helpful members of staff will try harder for you if you are personally friendly. One former job hunter found that the secretary of his department had been given a new computer in a box with no information and no support. She had not the faintest idea how to set it up and install programs. She was practically in tears. He took the better part of a day to do it for her during his first week on campus. Now, if he wants someone to rob a bank, he knows whom he can ask and get a cheerful affirmative answer.

When you first go to a school, the administration will offer orientation functions for new faculty. Do not skip these because they promise to be boring. Enjoyment is not the point. Believe me, attendance will be being taken, formally or informally, and in a small school that values collegiality, your name will go out on the networks as not committed to the school and not doing your part if you skip the function. So, have tea with the dean, go to that department retreat, attend that seminar, take that historical walk around town. Such functions may last beyond the first year. If your chair gives a party for all of last year's new hires, you had better be ready to cancel prior engagements and attend. Here is another possibility: The school may have an orientation program for incoming students, involving a book or two that they are supposed to read. If you read the texts in advance, you will have some common ground with your first year students, and you might gain a point or two in network chatter by showing up for the discussion of one of the texts.

Gossip networks also exist—faculty, staff, and student—with just enough crossover that nothing stays secret for long. Remember this before you talk about private matters. A former student of my husband's, coming back to visit after two years away, stopped fifteen miles out of town to see his favorite car repairman, and was surprised with an elaborate analysis from this rural mechanic of who was sleeping with whom in his former department. You never know where information will go or how it will get passed on. Sensitive information can cause a lot of trouble once it is let loose.

Department Meetings: Hidden Realities and Unmentionable Subjects

One thing that new faculty rarely understand is that department meetings often talk around a subject rather than address it directly.[1] In most schools, local culture will prohibit direct expression of at least two things: Arguments based on self interest is one; criticism of a colleague for lack of productivity, bad teaching, or bad behavior is the other. Nonetheless, these unmentionables underlie many department issues. Hiring is one such issue. Say that the twentieth-century specialists are pushing loudly to hire someone in the first half of the twentieth century. They cannot say, "Yes, we have three people in that field already, but none of them is productive and two won't speak to each other." What they will say is that they need someone in that area to build national recognition in that field and strengthen an already strong area. You may feel that wasting a position on a field with three turkeys is throwing good money after bad, and you may wonder whether a really stellar scholar would wish to join this unsavory flock unless fleeing a sexual harassment charge at home.

You cannot say that, however, and must find other terms in which to oppose that allotment of a line.

Curriculum is another issue that provokes doublespeak. Your medievalist cannot say, "If you remove the Chaucer requirement, I will have no graduate seminar and will be shunted off into teaching freshman composition." Instead, this scholar will argue that no one who has not studied the Wife of Bath can be considered educated, and the department would be disgraced if it lowered its standards by getting rid of the requirement. The Renaissance people may add their support because they see their field as next most likely to suffer if requirements for historical fields are dropped or changed. The desires of your theory students or rhetoricians (who have no need for Chaucer) will be totally ignored in the high-flown arguments about standards and the meaning of "well-educated."

When a topic falls afoul of both self-interest and collegial shortcomings, the two cognitive holes merge into a black hole. It swallows all discourse that approaches too close, so departmental discussion stays well back beyond the event horizon. This happens, for instance, when the dean demands that the department raise its publication standards for tenure. Many who now have tenure would not qualify by the new standard, but are naturally unwilling to admit this in public. Even those who have been prolific publishers usually hesitate to say in a meeting that certain colleagues should be disqualified from voting on tenure because their records are inadequate. The department will raise an ornate and complicated cloud of objections to the changes, but none of those will reflect the true problem.

An emblematic experience for the new assistant professor is for her to say something in a department meeting, and after a hiccup of silence, the discussion resumes as if nothing had been said. Most universities operate in a manner reminiscent of both the military and the Catholic Church. Few members of those establishments would suggest that a general or the pope should be voted into office by the draftees or parishioners, let alone expect this idea to win immediate welcome. The academic equivalent is an assistant professor proposing a concentration in Media and Cultural Studies to be built out of thin air in a traditional literature department, or wanting the department to give far more weight to teaching in its tenure procedure. Very often, the assistant professor argues for something that is too clearly self-interested and that damages the self-interest of others. More seminars in Cultural Studies mean fewer for historical areas. Reduce the publication requirement to accommodate more dedicated teaching (with computerized bells and whistles), and the department and college would both lose in the benchmarking studies of publication that determine everybody's raise and the unit's standing in the university. The neophyte has no idea what the network effects of such a change might be or indeed that such network effects exist.

Or consider the techno-literate assistant professor who sincerely believes that all historical courses would be more effective if augmented by professor-created websites loaded with art, readings, and music of the period. The older professors are unlikely to know how to produce such a thing, and probably feel no need for it, having never experienced it. Those who do not greet the idea with cries of joy are thinking about the time it would take them to learn to create what they consider a dubious good at best.

But why the silence? The assistant professor is sincere, idealistic, and devoted to student interests. However, proposing something that only he or she knows how to do is self-interested. That person would lose no time in learning the skill and might gain prestige from leading the department in new directions. Others would lose months of working time that could be spent writing a couple of major articles, for which they anticipate real rewards. The department's inability to "hear" such suggestions relates to the lack of language with which to reply without referring to self-interest or the issue of collegial competence. As that assistant professor, you should create your own website and demonstrate it to all who express interest. Encourage and help friends to create similar sites. Finally, in return for a course reduction, offer to teach those now convinced of its worth how to build such sites, and you will gain that prestige in the long run. Just don't try to make websites into policy at a department meeting.

Because issues of self-interest, collegial criticism, and department history may be invisible to you as a newcomer, you may not know what the real issue is in a department discussion. When the head promulgates some stance as department policy, do not stand up in the meeting and argue against it, no matter how silly or badly thought out it may seem. In a department in a southern school, a disgruntled faculty member (originally from the North) routinely badmouthed the school to job candidates, and had actually prevented desirable hires. The head publicly promulgated the policy that criticizing the school and the local culture to candidates was not professionally appropriate. A junior member, knowing nothing of this history, objected to this curtailment of free speech and honest discussion with a potential colleague. That assistant professor merely labeled himself politically naïve. Instead of speaking up, wait until after the meeting and ask some senior department politician or the head privately what was going on under the surface that you couldn't quite grasp, and maybe he or she will explain. If you gain a reputation for being dangerously naïve, people won't confide in you because they can't trust you to know when to keep information to yourself.

Here is a different kind of example of how surface and reality differ, this time from an umbrella communications department in a big western state university. After lengthy department meetings, the head would ask a judicious senior member, "What's the wisdom, George?" George would scrupulously and thoroughly sum up all the issues and all stances taken on them, giving everyone from every division due acknowledgment. Then he would suggest that the arguments pointed to one particular solution. The department, feeling that all the issues and feelings had indeed been fairly weighed up and recognized by a judicious, impartial senior statesman, would happily vote for that solution. A junior person there saw the head coming out of George's office prior to eight A.M. a few times on the days of department meetings, and eventually realized that they were deciding then and there what the wisdom would turn out to be. This is not something to get furious about, nor is it necessarily corruption, though obviously it can be called that. Rather, this is how most institutions work, and indeed is how well run institutions work.

Only a politically inept administrator raises an issue and invites free-ranging open debate. This just blows up in the administrator's face. Open debate in meetings can go in any direction, and decisions arrived at this way will make long-term planning impossible. Mutually incompatible decisions will be made in different department meetings. Votes will be swayed by temporary alliances and hard feelings over an issue voted on ten minutes earlier. A good head never just throws an issue on the table and invites the department to come up with a solution. Much better to state the problem and, in the agenda for the meeting, offer two or three possible solutions, point to their strengths and weaknesses, and ask for departmental thoughts on them. A good head knows how to sound out a department (possibly with the help of program directors), and does not push for a result unless the votes for it are there, because the head does want the department's acquiescence. The head, remember, is trying to obtain results that will keep a constituency happy, that are consistent with other departmental policies and plans, and that will avoid setting bad precedents. Some of what the head wants (raising department standards for tenure) may go against the majority will, though such a development may be necessary and demanded by the dean. Throwing it open to the department to debate would most certainly not get the desired results. The smart person doesn't fight this manipulation of issues, but learns how it works and learns to make the system work for her or him. This is institutional politics, and it deserves study.

Here is another form of currents beneath the surface. At one school, a head wished to preserve his stance as a reasonable, kindly, positive, and unpartisan figure by having someone else make the unpleasant criticisms of the department in a department meeting meant to push for reforms or for raising standards. Therefore, another member of the department produced the deserved but very unpopular criticism. The associate head came to him after the meeting and said mournfully, "How could you say such terrible things about the department?" He was blandly answered, "I didn't say anything that the boss didn't okay beforehand." The associate head, who was not a savvy politician, thought for a long time and then said, shaking his head, "I should have realized that, shouldn't I?" Well, yes. In that instance and given the person involved, he should. Such wheels-within-wheels will not be evident to you for some years, but be aware that they may exist.

Not all departments work in this fashion. Here are a couple of alternatives. More common forty years ago than now was the perpetual dictator-head. Some people were dictators for twenty years, and what they decided became law. They could grant your tenure by snapping their fingers (no paperwork back then). If you are not in opposition, this has virtues and will at least save you the time spent in committees. At the other end of the spectrum are those departments that are to a very high degree truly democratic. They do have open covenants openly arrived at. Even in this kind of department, though, the chairperson is likely to have an inner circle of people who are trusted above others. In most departments, untenured faculty are not likely to belong to the inner circle, and their ideas will probably not win support against the department's preferred patterns and the self-interest of those already tenured.

Compromise

What do you need to gain the power to make changes and be listened to seriously? You need longevity. You need proven productivity, primarily as a scholar, but also recognition as a good teacher. You also need a track record of giving sensible advice. In addition to these things, you will need patience and the ability to accept compromise graciously.

No one without tenure carries much weight, for the obvious reason that such a person lacks longevity, productivity, and track record. Until you have tenure, you are ephemeral. Making departmental changes that will affect everyone along the lines suggested by an untenured person raises the possibility that the department will be stuck with a new development, though the person who pushed for it has disappeared and is not available to help implement it.

"Sensible" advice is obviously a loaded term. Those at intellectual or political extremes (the young radicals and the most conservative elders) tend to be ignored, as are those perceived as unstable troublemakers and loose cannons. You are far more likely to be taken seriously if your advice lies toward the political center of the department. If your stance lies somewhat on the radical/younger side, but does not come across as extreme, you have some chance of leading the department a few steps in the direction you wish to see taken. Over time, such steps may translate into genuine change, but you will need patience and must tolerate compromise.

Young faculty members tend to want change and want it now. They do not reckon with the weight of institutional tradition and the self-interest of others, and they are impatient with compromise and incremental change. You do not accomplish major change—such as increasing the technology component in traditional historical courses—by arguing for it in open meeting. You have to work indirectly and accept a step-by-step set of changes.

Always, you need to allow time. Most departments that have tried to make research more important found that it took a dozen years to get serious standards in place and applied. I watched a department take a decade to change the graduate comprehensive exams step by reluctant step from a weird set of spotty coverage exams to specialized exams designed to be helpful for the thesis work. The incremental shifts happened every two or three years, and eventuated in a useful set of exams. No large department would vote for radical change all at once: After all, many faculty members benefited from students taking their courses to gain coverage for the original exams. To bring about departmental change, you need creative arguments, patience, long-term vision, and willingness to implement change in steps.

If networks are the essence of institutional life, compromise is the essence of departmental decisions. Recognize the self-interest in your own suggestions. Then, work as much as possible with, not against, the self-interest of others. Department members at the political extremes of the department tend to make demands that violate the boundaries of self-interest and collegial criticism; for that reason, they rarely achieve their ends. You will never get all you want, or anything like it. If you keep up pressure in a certain direction over time, however, and if the swing of the pendulum is in your favor (say, you are young, and more young people with similar views are hired), then step by compromised step you can come closer to what you want. Assistant professors who understand the cognitive blank spots in departmental discourse and learn how to maneuver around those holes will quickly become audible in departmental meetings. Those who do not doom themselves to frustration and alienation. Cast your mind ahead to your distant future and note this corollary: Votes tend to go slowly in the directions favored by the young, so as you approach sixty, more and more votes will go in directions you dislike. Focus on your own work, and cultivate other interests in order to avoid becoming bitter.

Protecting Yourself

As an untenured faculty member, you have to protect yourself from many kinds of demands and dangers. Hard-fought departmental issues might damage you if you side with the wrong faction. Unreasonable demands on your time for service can prevent you from publishing enough. You can fall into unproductive and harmful social patterns. Here are some of the situations you need to recognize and deal with.

If you are totally in disagreement with departmental policy, you gain nothing by nursing your sense of outrage at the department. Forget about trying to lead a revolution, particularly if you are untenured. Above all, do not try to make a public fuss—letters to the student paper or to the *Chronicle of Higher Education*. Making a fuss will haunt the department and you. Fifteen years after a head resigned in an explosive public meeting in the 1960s, that battle resounded in academic memory because that head went elsewhere and complained violently about this "decapitation." Whenever that department did an outside search for heads, it got echoes of that ruckus ("You're the place that treated Marmaduke Slumgullion so badly; no thanks, I'm not interested in being considered!"). Your creating or associating with an explosion does you no good, and can have an impact on the department's ability to hire desirable candidates.

Usually a department just outwaits an unsatisfactory head and chooses someone else when his or her term is up. If, however, a coup really is needed to get rid of a very unsatisfactory administrator, let senior people do it. If they are politically competent and the head is sane, it will take place behind the scenes and be invisible to the department and the larger world. In an Ivied instance, a head received a letter from the dean accepting his resignation and offering sympathies for his poor health. The head protested that he was fine and was not resigning. "Oh yes you are" was the answer—and he did. Sensible administrators know that if the dean says "enough," the thing to do is declare victory and withdraw gracefully.

As a junior member of a department in the midst of such turmoil, withdraw as much of your emotional commitment as you can from the department and put your effort into your own work. You control your work; you do not and never will control a department or all its policies, even if you someday become a head. Remember when you are in the opposition that heads come and go; you may be in favor with one, out with the next. If you produce publication steadily and teach enthusiastically and if you do not embrace a gadfly role, you will not suffer much when out of favor, and will make up when in. Your work is what you control. If you land it in prestigious journals and get books taken, you will be able to move elsewhere or rise in general power where you are through productivity and longevity. You will also be relatively invulnerable to shifts in policy. This is true even at a school that considers teaching its primary mission. Most such institutions want some publication, and they use it for benchmarking, so even if you do not produce articles at the rate demanded by a flagship state university, you still protect yourself and make your record marketable to other schools if you publish steadily.

As minority faculty members, you may hit special obstacles to focusing on your own work so you can be productive. Your university will want you to be involved in mentoring and offering role-models, in advising, in recruitment and retention, in writing grants, in providing a presence on various policy committees, and in outreach. You may specialize in some field that has little or nothing to do with the literature or history or other cultural artifacts produced by your minority group, but you will be pushed to involve yourself in all activities regarding that minority group, whether they are intellectually relevant to your work or not. You may also find white colleagues asking you to talk to their minority students about late papers or problematic classroom behavior because, these colleagues say, the students will listen to you. Such colleagues are, of course, trying to evade such confrontations because criticism from them can be interpreted as racist, but they thereby contribute to minority student perceptions that their white professors don't want to give them the time of day. You should do your best to make your colleagues take responsibility for their own students, or you will be adding considerably to your advising burden. In addition to such minority-specific service, the department will want the usual committee service, and such young faculty members may find themselves dangerously and quite unfairly overextended.

Any new faculty members, minority or not, can also find excessive demands being made on their time. Involvement in setting up a new program, for instance, will devour attention and effort as you write grants, work out curriculum, administer a lecture series or conference, or work up publicity for a film series. Because technology-oriented jobs are new, you may be the first member of a department to cover that area, and students will flood to you, wanting you to supervise their MA and PhD theses. All junior faculty members should protect themselves by keeping time sheets on all things related to service during the untenured years. That includes time spent at presentations and supper parties for visiting job candidates and receptions for donors as well as committee meetings, trips to high schools, and the number of theses supervised. If after the first year or two, you realize you are being asked to do a grossly unfair amount of service, you will have the hard facts in terms of hours and dates to argue for an adjustment.

Where, though, in the system can accommodation be made? You must present your credentials for tenure in that famous triad of activities: publication, teaching, and service. Your school will be uninterested in letting you publish less; that damages the school in its various benchmarking processes. You cannot spend less time and effort on teaching; worse class evaluations will not help you or serve your students well. You can, of course, demand a reduction in service, but if the school values what you are doing for its public relations, it may be reluctant to see reason. The feasible point of attack is teaching load. If the university is demanding excessive amounts of your time and you can prove that (with time-sheet comparisons between your service time and that of a normal service load), then you are in a position to ask for a reduction in your course load. If your head refuses that, then regretfully inform him or her that you will have to withdraw from many service functions that you now provide, and write the dean a letter explaining why. You will want the dean to know what the problem is, since the dean is always monitoring your progress toward tenure and needs to know why you are not publishing much. If the dean values your services for minority recruitment or founding a new program, then the head may be made to rethink your teaching load.

You must protect your time for work if you are in a research school. Automatically assuming that you must fly back home for cousins' weddings or uncles' funerals or the winter holidays may be familial, but it deprives you of invaluable time. Think when choosing your friends. Nonpublishing people have wonderful ways of filling time with enjoyable activities that have kept them from publishing and will do the same for you. Remember that the senior people who vote on your tenure will judge you by your associates. If you are always doing things with the department's nonpublishers, this fact will be noted as a bad prognostication. An assistant professor took her boyfriend from town to a university party, and the boyfriend got into a screaming quarrel with a member of department. The assistant professor wondered naïvely to her former supervisor if this might be held against her. Of course it would be. Who you run with and what they do will be noted. That is cultural and social politics, not just institutional. That one incident is hardly fatal, but you do not want to make trouble for yourself.

Departments are often ideologically split. English departments have passed through the following sequence, but other departments have their equivalents. In the 1950s, philology, historical work, and editing faced off against new criticism. Then new criticism confronted early theory. Then early theories were attacked by more recent theory. Now you also get splits between those oriented to the printed page and the web-surfers, those who rely heavily on films in literature courses and those who consider that dumbing down Shakespeare. Most students going on the market now have had considerable training in pedagogy; virtually anyone older will not have, and that split can ruffle feathers. Any such ideological departmental division may put you in a prickly situation and you need to think of strategies to protect yourself. You are given a bibliography and research methods course your first year, say, and the person overseeing it is web-phobic, though you wish to include a good bit of web research. Or you come to a new job with lots of good ideas about how to teach technical writing, only to learn that one elderly incompetent teaches it and has sworn to destroy anyone who tries to do it differently. Wait until you have tenure before taking that one on, or make sure that several people are involved in taking over the course so you cannot be shafted individually. In the methods course example, be tactful; do a reasonable amount with conventional bibliographic sources, but do web work as well, and get advice from the head or some mentor where you teach or at your graduate institution as to how to lessen tension between you and the person overseeing the course.

Here is a very common trap that junior people fall into. You and others in your untenured state and of your up-to-date theoretical bent gather every Friday afternoon and bitch over beer about the frightfulness of the contemptibly old-fashioned department. You feel so grown up and sophisticated as you savor knowingly all the many faults of your institution, every one of which is probably real. Looking down on the department makes you feel so superior to the school, so deserving, and so misunderstood and undervalued by a stupid institution. Your cynicism is unearned though, because you do not know enough other institutions to know what your institution's virtues are. You make yourself feel good temporarily by encouraging yourself to feel bad and misused. Assistant professors pool ignorance and paranoia and feed each other's hang-ups. Developing paranoia when you are untenured is all too easy, although usually unjustified; most people and institutions really do have more important things to do than persecute you, and most schools offer a pretty clear statement of what is expected for tenure. Most people dislike the first few years of their initial job. I certainly did, and talked endlessly with my husband about the flaws of the institution. When we moved, we swore never to fall into that trap again, and have been much the happier for the decision. All that time spent deprecating the institution was a terrible waste of energy better spent on positive endeavors. Try to avoid negative outlooks. The negatives do not help you develop anything useful, and furthermore, they do not really make you happy, just smug or self-pitying. Protect yourself from that temptation.

Do not let feuds start. A search committee for a new head practically came to blows when one member of the committee wanted to ensure that the candidates would be respectable scholars, and another did not care if the publishing records were contemptible as long as the candidates had administrative experience. They ended the meeting screaming at each other, with other members of the search committee wishing they could hide under the table. The older of the two of them came around the next day and said, "Let's go to lunch." They talked about noncontroversial things, and by that simple act made it possible to go on dealing with each other amiably, even though they disagreed violently on this one issue. You are far better off learning to be mature and handle disagreements in a nonpersonal manner. A feud helps absolutely no one, and damages the department for years. Be the first one to offer the olive branch, and hope the other party has the sense to respond appropriately.

Note the ease with which you can make yourself needlessly miserable if you have low standards at a higher-standard institution. Some associate professors have filled their lives with bitterness over the demands for promotion to full. The standard in some departments calls for an article per year and a second book "of own words" (meaning not an edition and not an edited collection); furthermore, this second book must be in print before promotion can be considered. Those whose friends were promoted at other institutions as soon as their second books were accepted felt miserable that they had to wait for their book to come into print, perhaps as much as three more years if they were dealing with a slow press. They could have cut that time by being more technologically sophisticated and offering Camera Ready Copy, but had not bestirred themselves to acquire the know-how. I was taught in graduate school that only books in print counted for that second promotion, so although it took me more than three years to land my second book, I was mad at various presses but did not feel abused by my university. I was a lot happier at this stage than they were because I held myself to the higher standard.

Another common source of needless anger regards people from outside being brought in with lesser credentials—brought in as full professor, for instance, with the second book only in press while everyone inside must wait until the second book is in print. Hiring often operates on a double standard: In order to get someone, a school naturally tries to catch him or her just before the next big project appears because if the book comes out when that person has joined the new school, it will bear the new school's name as place of author's residence, and so will bring credit to that institution. That book goes in the department's list of publications for the year, and in the college's equivalent, gaining them all sorts of points in the various ways of measuring departmental and collegial virtue. This is just the logic of hiring. Instead of getting angry, remember its applications to yourself and your getting outside offers. As soon as your book is accepted, be sure to give some related talks at conferences, and let friends in other schools know that you have a book accepted. This is a prime time to go on the job market if you are dissatisfied where you are. Remember, too, that a well-run department will manage to get equity raises for prior members whose publications are more substantial than those of the newcomer. One dean said to a department chair, "Your job is to create inequities and then demand that I give raises to the deserving so that things are fair again." A head who gets you that equity raise will see to it that you do not suffer in the long run from bringing in the new person on less-demanding terms.

Consider the standards at research-oriented institutions: You should think of producing what's expected for tenure every six or seven years, on the average. For many humanities departments, that means a book every seven years and annual articles that are not just chapters in the book. For a larger, more complicated book, allow ten years, but keep up the article per year. This is the blueprint for a very satisfying and potentially lucrative career, and anyone in the humanities who meets this set of demands can expect to end up as a distinguished or chair professor some day. A few elite private institutions tenure virtually nobody, so even producing at a higher rate will not gain you tenure there, but at most flagship state universities and other research-oriented schools, this formula almost invariably suffices. What amazes tenured observers is the number of assistant professors who know this but do not apply it to themselves; they do not send their manuscripts out at the end of their second year, or they produce only three or four articles, and then feel embittered when they fail to win tenure. At institutions that do not judge themselves primarily by research, you may find the expectation something more like an article per year *or* a book during a seven-to-ten year period. Almost no "pure" teaching schools exist anymore except community colleges, where publication is only one of several acceptable forms of professional activity; some publication is expected at most former state teachers' colleges and regional campuses, and if it is not when you get there, it will be when the institution next hires a new president or provost or dean.

For better or worse, publication has become the primary benchmark by which institutions measure their worth, partly because the humanities are mindlessly aping the sciences, but also because publication does lend itself to being measured. What you will find at schools that are less research-oriented is that an article a year or every other year is desired, but they will not be fussy about where the article appears. Indeed, they may fail to be impressed by your landing in major journals because they have too little feel for the relative prestige of outlets. Such schools are also likely to be in a turmoil of changing standards, and what you are told about expectations when you accept the job may be disastrously inaccurate two years later, yet changes in policy may not be announced publicly. Main campuses pressure regional campuses to raise standards, and this puts nonpublishing seniors at those campuses in the position of firing publishing juniors for not having published enough even though the juniors have published more than the tenured members. You have got to bring your own standards with you. If you ever wish to publish your way out of such a school, you must maintain standards for yourself that are higher than those of the school. Do not indulge in feeling superior to the school that hires you, but do demand more of yourself.

The nature of institutions is such that longevity can be important. Church, university, and state bureaucracies: Administrative problems are much the same in any institution. Businesses may fire you at the drop of a hat, but those people who do survive have all the more weight through longevity. Longevity, among other things, provides a sense of institutional history, of what will be acceptable in the local subculture, and it provides knowledge of the inner workings—whom to contact. Committee work at college and university level helps you learn about your institution. You learn who gives good advice and who seems flaky, who works well toward committee consensus, who understands how to make things happen, and who is dangerously sloppy about procedures. You learn about the ways that leadership differs at different levels. Only after seeing examples will you realize, for instance, that skill as a dean or provost may not translate to skill as a head. A dean or provost works with staff subordinates who will dutifully present various approaches, but who then fall in and accept the decision and make it work, even if they do not like the decision. A department head or chairperson faces a rambunctious and irresponsible department, where those outvoted often work to undermine and destroy the majority policy. Similarly, someone who has been chairperson of a ten-member department may prove helplessly inept with a sixty-member department.

You have to learn to read between the lines. Letters of recommendation for job candidates, for head candidates, for promotion and tenure reviews, often tell you things by indirection, since our litigious age may make a candid letter of assessment actionable. Enthusiasm for the potential of a thesis with no comment on how soon it will be done is a danger signal regarding a job hunter. Saying that a head candidate is blunt and direct may be praise, or may mean that this person has no tact and antagonizes people right and left. This need to interpret can also go for spoken words. As a graduate student, you learned that your thesis supervisor's saying, "You might want to look at that book" meant that you had better go read it right away. That same polite locution—"You might want to do that"—remains a fairly strong imperative when it comes from someone senior to you or administratively overseeing you in some fashion. A head who had once been a provost carried back to the department level an upper administrator's desire never to speak too directly. He would say in a dreamy tone, "I wonder if that's the right thing to do?" The feckless department members who did not know how to interpret this got in trouble because they did not realize that in admin-speak that means "Don't you dare do that or I'll break your kneecaps."

If you get drawn into any sort of administrative duties, particularly when untenured, an important rule you must memorize is to adhere to the stated protocols and keep a complete paper record. Always print e-mail related to such an administrative job. This protects you. While you may make the wrong decision, you will not be "in the wrong." This makes a world of difference if it comes to any kind of hearing before a higher administrator, ombudsman, or court of law.

Institutional politics for you as an assistant professor will be rather different from any level that you have seen up to now. This is not to say that you should flatter your tenured colleagues and be obsequious. You need to stand up for some programs or ideas you wish to see fostered. You will not want to hide your true outlook, but you also need to learn how not to push it in others' faces. You need to learn to disagree fruitfully, and in ways that provoke interested discussion rather than anger. You need to see that you can support your ideas effectively or ineffectively, and that the ineffective way may be damaging to you. You need to learn to take the long view, and to accept the inevitability of compromise, while realizing that you can push toward your goal in steps. You should vote as your own judgment dictates, even if the stand is unpopular in the committee and you know your position will not win. You do not owe anyone a unanimous vote, although some schools will pressure you because unanimity is prized in the local culture. Just learn when to stop arguing aloud and trying to twist arms. The next time the issue arises, your stance may be more familiar. You may have worked up a bit more departmental sentiment in its favor, and you may get a more positive hearing.

You have to accept that the eternal verities you absorbed in the course of your thesis writing will be viewed with derision by someone coming along five years later, and furthermore, may seem pointless and peculiar to older faculty when you arrive. Fields change constantly, and you will have to change, accept others with very different attitudes and values, and learn to get on with them even when you disagree quite fundamentally. Nothing is stable. Remind yourself that the department you enter will be considerably different when you come up for tenure in six years. The head and dean will almost certainly be different. You cannot plan around any one person or policy. Plan what you want to be, apply your own standards, and do the work that will make you your ideal kind of scholar and professional. Shape your career according to an abstract pattern you have decided upon rather than looking for local loopholes. This will help protect you if you don't get local tenure.

You need to learn the limits of arguing in department meetings. An assistant professor attended a meeting in her department her first year. A problem was raised and she described the obvious answer from her perspective, but the little hiccup of silence followed, and she was ignored. She sensibly said to herself, "I'm not going to win this, and there's no point in fighting on grounds not of my own choosing." She now has tenure.

Unless you go to an elite institution that rarely tenures anybody, you will probably find yourself one day in a school that expects and hopes to tenure you. Financial exigencies may cause problems; so may heavy overtenuring in the department. In the great majority of cases, though, people who follow the rules get tenure. You must, however, hold yourself to a high standard, and not plan on just scraping by. You have to push yourself hard: Get that book out by the end of the second year and start another book promptly, if that is the school expectation. Remember that if you wish really to flourish, you need to continue at this assistant professor pace and not slack off. You must husband your time and not fritter it away on inconsequential activities. You must learn the rudiments of politics and try not to draw opprobrium or anger. Above all, you must learn to seek out what is good about your school. By all means, work to move if you wish something different, but never make the mistake of thinking yourself too good for the institution that hired you. Work instead to improve it, and try to feel proper gratitude for its virtues. So variable are schools that your next may have none of those virtues, though it may have others, and it will possess a whole new range of vices. Concentrate on the advantages, concentrate on your own work, and make yourself the kind of scholar you look up to and would like to be. If you manage this, you will do just fine in your chosen profession.

Note

1. Portions of this discussion first appeared in somewhat different form in the *Chronicle of Higher Education* in the *Chronicle Review* section, vol. 49, issue 21, p. B5 (31 January 2003), in a piece called "Department Politics as a Foreign Language."

Six

Epilogue for Placement Officers

I have found the following to be useful for training job hunters: three or four group sessions, two mock interviews, mock campus presentations, personal conferences, and e-mail availability.

Start a notebook of successful CVs and other documents related to applications, or put them on a website. If people are willing to share copies of their contracts, put those in the notebook too, as they let job hunters see what such a document looks like. Start a database of who has interviewed at which campus. Invite back to campus former PhDs who have landed in a variety of jobs, academic and not, to talk about their experiences. Invite next year's job hunters to sit in on the general meetings and guest lectures with this year's job candidates; they can work to get some of the tasks accomplished early, and can help out as audiences for mock campus presentations. If graduate students are permitted to serve on search committees, the year before going on the market is a good year to serve. Future hunters can see it from the other side and see what works well. If they attend the conference, they might participate in their search's interviews and so observe how interviews are played out. This helps demystify the process.

Depending on your school's calendar, you will want to set up your schedule something like the following.

- August or September—*first meeting*: The placement officer gives a general description of the job hunting process and discusses the documents needed. Send the hunters off to work on their CVs, letters of application, teaching portfolios, and writing samples, if they have not already worked these up the previous year, as advised. Have all job hunters present you with an information sheet on their interests, qualifications, and the kind of job they hope for. A CV and a brief statement on the nature of the job would do as well. Remind them in September to get their references to write letters. Have them send to you a copy of the dossier so letters can be checked for glaring problems. Because job hunters are busy, they tend to skim material like this book once, casually, and then forget most of it. Tell them to read it once a week for the next six weeks; much more will sink in.

- Early October—*second meeting*: This meeting should focus on conference interviews. Tell job hunters to start practicing the questions, the ninety-second version of their thesis description, and their three or four points about themselves. The placement officer and some other faculty member can conduct a short mock interview on the spot with one person, preferably someone who has interviewed before, and then ask every person on the market that year four random questions from the list. The point is to let the job hunters experience the paralysis (or the motor-mouth response) that hits the unprepared, and make very real to them the need for memorized answers. Let everyone present give feedback on each interviewee's performance.
- November—*first mock interview*, preferably with video camera.
- December—*second mock interview*.
- Early January—*third meeting*: Discuss campus interviews and negotiations.
- January and February—Set up mock campus presentations when and as needed.
- April—*fourth meeting* as pot-luck party

  Debriefing—let job hunters tell anecdotes of what they went through. This proves highly instructive for all concerned (including those who will be on the market the next year), and a useful catharsis for some.

  Discuss nonacademic employment, both for the unsuccessful hunters present and for those with jobs. The successful hunters may be training job hunters the next year at their new institution, and will have to produce information on nonacademic possibilities. Those I talk about are data-mining (for stock brokers, computer companies), technical writing/editing, university centers for improving pedagogy, teaching in private schools, and working in publishing.

  Discuss what they need to do to turn their dissertations into book manuscripts, plus the economics and politics of being an assistant professor. If you have recent PhDs willing to make a trip back, get their input on how free they feel about speaking out in department meetings, and what they have learned about department dynamics and politics.

Getting faculty to volunteer their time to do mock interviews takes persuasion. Mass e-mail to your faculty is ineffective, in my experience.

The placement officer really needs to send personalized notes to individual department members. Post a sign-up sheet outside the graduate office door and try to get a minimum of two, and preferably three, faculty members to sign up by each job candidate's name and time slot.

Start a database on who does campus interviews where. The next year, when someone gets invited to the same school, put that person in contact with the previous hunter to go there. Valuable insight can be gained from sharing such information. The information is probably only good for three or four years at most, so keep the year of the interview and remove the oldest as you go along.

One-on-one conferences with the students are part of a placement officer's job. The job hunter who is interviewing at a small liberal arts college may need special coaching if all the higher education she has received has come from large universities. Once someone secures a job, he may wish to rehearse some possible political problems he foresees and get advice. Those who have searched in vain in previous years will need heartening and encouragement, as well as the occasional kick in the pants to stop any wallowing in self pity. Keep in touch with the unsuccessful ones. Even if they have only negative results to report, they tend to be glad that someone asks and cares. Their supervisors may already have withdrawn their emotional commitment.

For those seeking nonacademic employment, a listserve called WRK4US (http://www.woodrow.org/phd/WRK4US, run by the Woodrow Wilson foundation) can be helpful. For seeking government employment, try http://www.federaljobsearch.com.

If, in the course of using this book, you become aware of omissions, if some practice in your field differs from those described here, if you disagree strongly with one of my stances, or if your job hunters undergo strange experiences, I would like to know. A second edition could incorporate such modifications.

Kathryn Hume (iqn@psu.edu)
The Pennsylvania State University

Appendix I

Examples of Job-Hunting Documents

For legal reasons, these documents have been slightly fictionalized. Names of hunter, supervisor, referees, named fellowships specific to a school, schools, and some personal details have been altered. The journals in which these hunters landed articles are the actual journals, but the issue, volume, and page numbers have been scrambled. Formats and fonts have been preserved so you can get ideas and see what seems effective to you. I have altered phrasing very slightly in a few letters. In all meaningful respects, though, these are real CVs of job hunters.

Contents

CVs

Letters of Application

Thesis Descriptions

Teaching Philosophies

Brief Teaching Portfolio

Jorge Colón

910 Oakridge Lane
University Town, State, Zip
(555) 236-1847   jxc149@univ.edu

EDUCATION

Ph.D., English, Graduate University, May 2001.
>   Specialties: 16th- & 17th-Century Literature with emphasis in
>   Drama, Shakespeare, Shakespeare and Film, Milton, and
>   Cultural History.

M.A., English, Graduate University, May 1997.
B.A., English, Undergraduate University. *Summa cum Laude*, 1995.

Dissertation   *Sport, Literature, and Politics
in the English Renaissance*

Defended with "Highest Distinction" on 12/4/00. The dissertation argues that sport mediated the poles of excess and control in the Early Modern imagination. The subject is a popular conception of sport as a functional phenomenon and, more specifically, the gradual transformation and reinvention of it between the early Tudor and Restoration periods in England. By revising the traditional argument that sport was merely synonymous with holiday revelry, gambling, and other disorderly activities, the study establishes sport's integral place—both literal and metaphorical—in contemporary politics, polemics, and the formation of the emergent national identity.

Committee   Dr. Susan Ridgeway (Director)   Dr. Arlin Foster (Engl.)
                 Dr. David Soames (Engl.)   Dr. Giovanni Ricci (History)
                 Dr. John Willis (Another University) Dr. Nicholas May (Engl.)

ACADEMIC EMPLOYMENT

Teaching Assistant, Graduate University, 1995-present.
>   English 497: Shakespeare and Film (1 section-Spring 01)
>   English 444: Shakespeare (1 section-Spring 01)
>   English 129: Introduction to Shakespeare (1 section)
>   English 221: British Literature to 1798 (2 sections)
>   English 202B: Writing for the Humanities (5 sections)
>   English 202D: Business Writing (4 sections)
>   English 15: Composition & Rhetoric (6 sections)

Research Assistant, Graduate University, 1996-7.
>   Aided in researching, editing, and indexing of Prof. David Soames's
>   *Intelligence Work in Renaissance England* (Major University Press, 1998).

Tutorial Writing Instructor, Undergraduate University, 1993-5.
>   Instructed undergraduate students in researching, writing, and
>   revising composition papers.

ARTICLES

"Recasting Shakespeare on Film." In *Collection of Essays on
>   Shakespeare and Film*, ed. Nancy Mitchell. Forthcoming
>   (2003) ms. 16 pp.

"John Milton and the Poetics of Restoration Sport." *SEL:
>   1500-1900*: 40.2 (2002).

"The 'Two Guises of Game': Anti-Play Polemics in Renaissance
>   Prose." *Prose Studies: History, Theory, Criticism*: 18.2 (2001).

"Sport and Contest in Shakespeare's Roman Histories." *Renaissance
>   Quarterly*: 45:3 (2001).

Notes   "Teaching Shakespeare on Film." *Shakespeare and the
>   Classroom*: 18 (2001).

HONORS AND AWARDS

Graduate Assistant Award for Outstanding Teaching, 2000.
>   One of 5 recipients of annual university-wide award.

Andrew W. Mellon Institute Grant, 2000. Awarded on a competitive
>   basis for participation in seminar, "Tradition and Change in
>   the Renaissance."

Ben Jones Research Grant, 1999. Awarded on a competitive basis by
>   Graduate University English Department.

University Research Grant, 1998. Awarded on a competitive basis
>   by the Graduate University Research Office.

Phi Kappa Phi National Honor Society, 1998.

English Department Travel Grant, 2000 and 1998.

Folger Institute Grant, 1997. Awarded on a competitive basis to
>   attend seminar, "Shakespeare and Film."

Charles H. Michaels Merit Scholarship, Undergraduate University, 1995.

Golden Key National Honor Society, 1993.

Alpha Chi National Honor Society, 1992.

CONFERENCES

Will Present Paper, "The Danger of 'Innocent, Harmless Mirth':
   Walton's *Compleat Angler* in the Interregnum." "Drink and
   Conviviality in Early Modern England" Conference at
   University of Reading, England. July, 2001.
Presented Paper, "Shakespeare's *Animated Tales* and the
   Construction of Today's Children." Southwest/Texas
   Popular Culture Association/American Culture Association
   Conference, Albuquerque, NM. March 2001.
Chair, "Teaching Shakespeare and Film." Central New York
   Conference on Language and Literature, SUNY College at Cortland,
   NY. October 29-30, 2000.
Presented Paper, "Scar Wars: Richard III and Darth Vader:
   Teaching Meta-theatricality through Film." Workshop at
   Shakespeare Association of America Annual Conference, Montréal,
   Canada. April 2000.
Presented Paper, "'When to their Sports they Turned': *Samson
   Agonistes* and the Politics of Restoration Sport." Central
   New York Conference on Language and Literature, SUNY College at
   Cortland, NY. October 1999.
Presented Paper, "The Hydras of Discourse: Ben Jonson's *Poetaster*
   and Comedic Language Planning." "Making Contact: Natives,
   Barbarians, Strangers" Interdisciplinary Conference at University of
   Alberta, Canada. October 1998.

PROFESSIONAL SERVICE

Chair, Graduate and Fixed Term Employees Organization, 2000-2001.
President, English Graduate Organization, May 1999-May 2000.
Departmental Delegate, "Re-envisioning the Ph.D." seminar, 2001.
Judge, African American Read-In Writing Contest, 2000.
Departmental Delegate, Graduate Student Association, 1999-2000.
Founder, Health Care Writing Preparation Series, 1997-2000.
   Established, organized, and taught writing workshops for
   Graduate University students entering the health care professions.

PROFESSIONAL AFFILIATIONS

Modern Language Association
American Association of University Professors
Renaissance Society of America

Folger Shakespeare Institute
Shakespeare Association of America
Phi Kappa Phi

REFERENCES

Professor Susan Ridgeway
Department of English
Graduate University
University Town, State, Zip
Home: 555/231-8785
sxr28@univ.edu

Professor David Soames
Department of English
Graduate University
University Town, State, Zip
Home: 555/237-6521
dxs18@univ.edu

Professor Nicholas May
Department of English
Graduate University
University Town, State, Zip
Home: 555/235-9514
nxm21@univ.edu

Professor Arlin Foster
Department of English
Graduate University
University Town, State, Zip
Home: 555/237-4647
axf7@univ.edu

Professor Giovanni Ricci
Department of History
Graduate University
University Town, State, Zip
Home: 555/863-9475
gxr25@univ.edu

Professor Jaelle High
Department of English
Graduate University
University Town, State, Zip
Home: 555/ 238-7334
jxh15@univ.edu

CREDENTIALS

My confidential dossier, containing letters of recommendation and my transcript, is available from Graduate University's Career Development and Placement Office. To receive a copy, please contact me, and I will have the Placement Office mail it to you.

Ann Molina
http://www.personal.univ.edu/axm120

479 Topley Ave. #24   University Town, State, Zip
e-mail: axm120@univ.edu   home (555) 234-9793   cell (555) 792-4438

EDUCATION

Ph.D.   English (Native American Studies, 20th-Century U.S. Literature)
Graduate University, University Town, State, Zip (Expected May 2002)

M.A.   English, Western State University (1996)

B.A.   English, Political Science Minor, *summa cum laude*, Undergraduate College (1994)

Dissertation (all chapters drafted): "Pueblo Cultural Narratives and American Indian Law"
Thesis Committee: Janine May (chair); James R. Mulday, Jr.; Crystal Wynn; Amos Pond

I combine readings in American Indian storytelling and pottery traditions, or what I call "cultural narratives," and American Indian law to show how Pueblo cultural narratives are more than the histories of an oppressed people. Rather, I highlight how the Pueblos have used their traditions to counter federal attempts to forcibly transform them into "Americans." Pueblo stories, as survival narratives, have helped the Pueblos preserve their cultural identities and maintain a unique sense of self. Even in the midst of catastrophic change, Pueblo peoples have turned to their stories for lessons that teach the value of renewed traditions and revitalized ways of looking at life.

PUBLICATIONS

Miscellaneous
"Of Fire and Memory," in *Research/Graduate University*, Graduate University, January 2001

Jaune Quick-to-See-Smith, *Indian Country Today*. Gallery Brochure for The Museum of Art, Graduate University, Fall, 2000

"Anglo Perceptions and the Authentic American Indian," in *The Image of the American West in Literature, the Media, and Society*, eds. Steven Kaplan and Will Wright, Pueblo, CO: Society for the Interdisciplinary Study of Social Imagery, 1996.

Book Reviews
Maurice Kenny, ed., *Stories for a Winter's Night: Fiction by Native American Writers*, in *World Literature Today* (forthcoming)

James Welch, *The Heartsong of Charging Elk,* in *World Literature Today* (Spring, 2000), pp. 174

Diane Glancy and Mark Nowak, eds., *Visit Teepee Town: Native Writings After the Detours*, in *World Literature Today* (Spring, 1999), pp. 800-02

Joane Nagel, *American Indian Ethnic Renewal: Red Power and the Resurgence of Identity and Culture*, in *Rocky Mountain Review* (Winter, 1998), pp. 82-84

Reference Book Entries

American National Biography. Gen. Ed. John A. Garraty, New York: Oxford University Press, 1999. "William Riley Burnett," 4: 7-8. "Walter Stanley Campbell," 4: 302-303. "Edwin Corle," 5: 516-517. "Thomas B. Costain," 5: 557-558. "Harold Lenoir (H. L.) Davis," 6: 196-197. "Jean Kenyon Mackenzie," 15: 253-254. "Merrill Moore," 15: 775-776. Co-authored with Dr. Susannah Grinder

FELLOWSHIPS AND AWARDS

Ford Foundation Minority Dissertation Fellowship, 2001-2002

Sixteenth Annual Graduate Exhibition in Arts and Humanities. Third place award for poster presentation of dissertation project and ability to explain and defend research to faculty, students, and the general public. Spring, 2001

Sigma Lambda Gamma National Sorority Leadership Award in "Cultural Awareness." This minority student organization advocates standards of excellence through five principles: Academics, Community Service, Morals and Ethics, Cultural Awareness, and Social Interaction. Spring, 2001

Fifteenth Annual Graduate Exhibition in Arts and Humanities. First place award for poster presentation of dissertation project and ability to explain and defend research to faculty, students, and the general public. Spring, 2000

Research Office Dissertation Support Grant, 1999-2000

Graduate University's Humanistic Studies' Interdisciplinary Dissertation and Creative Projects Award, 1999-2000

Graduate University Graduate Fellowship, 1997-1998

CIC Predoctoral Fellowship (four-year award), 1994-1998

Numerous travel grants

TEACHING

Courses

English 15—Composition and Rhetoric (3 sections)

English 15—Learning Edge Academic Program [L.E.A.P.] (1 section)
A collaborative teaching and learning program that combined Composition and Rhetoric, Political Science, and Library Studies

English 135—Alternative Voices in American Literature (1 section)

English 200—Introduction to Critical Reading (1 section)

English 435—The American Short Story (1 section)

Invited Lectures

"Museum Studies," Art History 497B, Graduate University, Spring, 2000 (Associate Curator: Roberta Jelsem). Team-taught course on Native peoples' representation in American museums. Taught in conjunction with an exhibit of Andy Warhol's 1986 "Cowboys and Indians" series and Jaune Quick-to-See-Smith's "Indian Country Today"

"Mythology," Comparative Literature 108, Graduate University, Spring, 1998 (Instructor: Rose Streams). Lectured on N. Scott Momaday's *The Way to Rainy Mountain*

"Ethnicity and the American Experience," American Studies 405, Graduate University, Spring, 1997 (Professor Amos Pond). Lectured on N. Scott Momaday's *The Way to Rainy Mountain*

"Contemporary American Literature," Liberal Arts College, Spring, 1994 (Professor Laura Grass). Lectured on Sandra Cisneros's *The House on Mango Street*

SCHOLARLY PAPERS DELIVERED

"New Age Thought: Blazing New Frontiers or Traversing Colonialist Trails?" Society for the Interdisciplinary Study of Social Imagery, University of Southern Colorado, March, 1997

"Anglo Perceptions and the Authentic American Indian," Society for the Interdisciplinary Study of Social Imagery, University of Southern Colorado, March, 1996

"Reading Double-Consciousness in Sandra Cisneros's *House on Mango Street*," National Undergraduate Literature Conference, Weber State University, April, 1993

"Ghosts in the Attic: Henry James's *The Turn of the Screw*," National Undergraduate Literature Conference, Weber State University, April, 1992

PROFESSIONAL PRESENTATIONS

"Cultural Difference in the Classroom," Invited speaker: Composition Department's Brown Bag Lunch Series, Graduate University, Fall, 1999

"Graduate Opportunities for Black and Hispanic Students," Invited speaker representing Graduate University: Thirteenth Annual Fattah Conference on Higher Education. Provides information for minority students interested in attending graduate school, February, 1999

"'Multiculturalism' and Composition: Teaching Writing with a Difference," Invited speaker: Composition Department's Brown Bag Lunch Series, Graduate University, Spring, 1998

"The Conference Interview Process," Invited speaker: ABD Support Group, Center for Minority Graduate Opportunities, Graduate University, February, 1998

"Negotiating Your Way Through Graduate School," Invited speaker: First and Second Annual Retention Conference, Center for Minority Graduate Opportunities, Graduate University, August, 1997; August, 1998

"On the Eve of the Millennium: Expectations, Hopes, and Goals," Invited speaker: Welcome Address—1995 CIC Predoctoral Fellowship Conference, Graduate University, October, 1995

PROFESSIONAL SERVICE

American Indian Studies Consultant: Planning and implementation of *Andy Warhol: Cowboys and Indians* exhibit in conjunction with Jaune Quick-to-See-Smith, Museum of Art, Graduate University, Spring, 2000

"Negotiating Your Way Through Graduate School," Planning Committees: Second and Third Annual Retention Conferences, Graduate University, Spring, 1998-1999

Minority ABD Support Group Coordinator: Facilitated and coordinated group meetings for new and returning minority ABD students, Graduate University, 1998, 1999

U.S. Latino/a Studies Search Committee: English department, Graduate University, June, 1997-July, 1998

Ph.D. representative: English Graduate Organization (EGO), Graduate University, 1997-1998

McNair Scholar's Program: Conducted GRE workshops for program that assists first-generation college students, Graduate University, July, 1996; April, 1997

Graduate University's Educational Partnership Program (PEPP): In connection with graduate summer course entitled "Hybridity and the Poetics of Mestizaje," conducted reading and writing workshops for Latino/a youth and senior citizens at Casa de Amistad (Latino Senior Center), Graduate University, 1996

Founding member/elected secretary: Movimiento Estudiantil Chicano de Aztlan (M.E.Ch.A.), Mexican-American student organization at Graduate University, 1996-1997

REFERENCES

Professor Janine May
Department of English
116 Barrow Building
Graduate University
University Town, State, Zip
555/865-2082   jxm15@univ.edu

Professor Crystal Wynn
Department of English
227 Barrow Building
Graduate University
University Town, State, Zip
555/863-2348   cxw4@univ.edu

Professor Lindsay Rofort
Assistant to Dean of Minority Affairs
College of Agriculture
120 Agricultural Administration Building
Graduate University
University Town, State, Zip
555/865-7531   lxr25@univ.edu

Professor James R. Mulday, Jr.
College of Education / 300 Renlan Building
Director, American Indian Leadership Program
Graduate University
University Town, State, Zip
555/237-4540   jrm2@univ.edu

Professor Emeritus Amos Pond
Department of English
113 Barrow Building
Graduate University
University Town, State, Zip
555/865-7416   axp9@univ.edu

Janet Evans
Department of English
120 Barrow Building
Graduate University
University Town, State, Zip
555/863-9543   jxe6@univ.edu

Thomas Hearns
106 N. Corliss Road
University Town, State ZIP
555 233 3948   thearns@univ.edu

EDUCATION

PhD, English,   Graduate University   May 2003

Research and teaching interests: African American Rhetoric, Technology Theory, Technical Communication

> Dissertation: *Rhetoric In the Divide*
>
> > This project uses the concept of the "Digital Divide," or systematically differentiated access to computers and Internet technologies as a lens for re-examining relationships between technologies and rhetorical production throughout the history of African American struggles for freedom and equal participation in the American nation. By analyzing several sites where technologies and rhetoric converge, I attempt to develop an approach to African American rhetoric that focuses on the sites and goals of African American struggle rather than individual strategies employed by individual rhetors. This emphasis on the goals and sites of rhetorical production reveals a tradition of African American orators, writers, performers, and designers that has sought complete access to the larger nation and its technologies not merely for the sake of access, but in order to transform both the nation and those technologies that design, construct, and sustain it.

Committee: **Dr. Marvin Hagler, Director**   Dr. Steven Thomas (English)
                  Dr. Carmen McRae (English)   Dr. Raymond Robinson (AAAS)
                  Dr. James Johnson (MWU)

MA, English, Graduate University   **2001**
BA, English, Undergraduate University   **1992**

PUBLICATIONS AND WORKS IN PROGRESS

"Rhetorical Pugilism: The Black Jeremiad in Critical Race Theory." Under Review: *JAC*. ms. 27pp.

"Chattin that Chat: African American Electronic Discourse." Under Review: *Computers and Composition*. ms. 25pp.

Thomas Hearns 2

"Canon Jackin': Rhetorical Resistance through Master Narratives." Under Review: *Black Renaissance/Renaissance Noire*. ms. 32pp.

"Rhetoric in the Divide: Technological Responses to African American Struggle." Forthcoming in *African American Rhetorics: English Perspectives*. Richardson, Elaine and Ronald L. Jackson, eds. Carbondale: Southern Illinois UP, 2003. ms. 22pp.

"Just Another Angry Black Man? An Open Letter on David Anson's Firing." With Steven Lindsell, Morris Monkton, et al. *Black Issues in Higher Education*. June 3, 2001. p. 34.

Review of *Race in Cyberspace*. Kolko, Beth, Lisa Nakamura, and Gilbert Rodman, eds. *TCQ* 9:3, Summer 2001, 70-74.

PRESENTATIONS

"Composition in the Underground: Recreational Spaces as Sites of Rhetorical Education." *Thomas R. Watson Conference on Rhetoric and Composition*. October 10, 2002. Louisville, Kentucky.

"Composition's Three Card Monte Goes Digital: Race, Technology Access, and Silence in the Field." *Conference on College Composition and Communication*. March 21, 2002. Chicago, Illinois.

"Talking B(l)ack to the Divide: Language, Literacies, and Technology Access. *D3: Digital Divide Doctoral Conference*. August 12, 2001. Ann Arbor, Michigan.

"Crossing Composition's Discursive Divide: Technology Access and Writing Instruction." Invited Presenter, *Computers in Writing Intensive Classrooms*. June 18, 2001. Houghton, Michigan.

"Just the Fountain Will Never Do: Imagining Pedagogical Possibilities in and Beyond the Service Course." *Association for Teachers of Technical Writing*. March 16, 2001. Denver, Colorado.

Thomas Hearns 3

TEACHING EXPERIENCE   29 total sections

Composition and Technical Communication Courses

Teaching Assistant, Graduate University, 2000-present

> Technical Writing (ENG 202c) 2 sections
> First Year Composition (ENG 15) 1 section

Teaching Assistant, Another University, August 1998-May 2000

> First Year Composition (ENGL 150) 1 section
> Technical Communication (ENGL 398) 3 sections, including 1 hybrid
>   distance education/computer classroom section

Instructor, Nearby Community College, March 1997-May 1999
> Basic Writing (ENG 097, 099) 6 sections
> First Year Composition (ENG 101, 102, 103) 6 sections

Teaching Assistant, Undergraduate University, September 1992-June 1994
> First Year Composition (ENG 101, 102) 3 sections
> African American Masterpieces (ENG 207) 1 section, co-taught with Ed
>   Ringler

Summer Bridge and Student Success Programs

Instructor, Pre-Engineering Freshman Program (PREF), Graduate
   University, Summer 2000, 2002
Instructor, LINK Program, Undergraduate University, Summer 1992, 1993
Instructor, Health Careers Opportunities Program, Undergraduate University,
   Summer 1992, 1993

PROFESSIONAL WRITING EXPERIENCE

Communications Consultant, National Consortium for Graduate Education for
Minorities in Science and Engineering (GEM), South Bend, Indiana, 2001-present.
Assisted Executive Director in planning strategies for recruiting graduate fellows and
alumni and corporate support. Prepared annual reports, wrote and reviewed documents
including student handbooks.

Thomas Hearns 4

Public Information Officer, Office of the Mayor, Major City, Midwestern State, 1993-1994. Wrote, edited, and collaborated on speeches and opinion editorials. Managed Mayor's written correspondence.

Writing Consultant, Office of Minority Affairs, Undergraduate University, 1993. Wrote text for booklet marketing the university to students of color nationwide: "Students of Color and Undergraduate University: Changing Odds, Changing Circumstances, Changing Lives."

PROFESSIONAL AFFILIATIONS

Conference on College Composition and Communication
Modern Language Association
Association for Teachers of Technical Writing

REFERENCES

Unless otherwise indicated, all addresses are Department of English, 297 Barrow Building, Graduate University, University Town, State ZIP

Marvin R. Hagler (Chair)
Professor of English
555 865-2902
mrh34@univ.edu

Steven Thomas
Assistant Professor of English
555 865-4342
sxt323@univ.edu

Carmen McRae
Assistant Professor of English
555 865-9789
cxm98@univ.edu

Raymond Robinson
Professor of African Studies
133 Williams Building
555 867-3567
rxr76@univ.edu

James Johnson
Professor of American Thought and Language
296 Belton Hall
Midwestern University
Midwest Town, State ZIP
555 869-4859
jjohnson@mwu.edu

CREDENTIALS

My confidential dossier, containing letters of recommendation and my transcript, is available from Graduate University's Career Development and Placement Office. To receive a copy, contact me, and I will have the Placement Office mail the dossier to you.

JULIE C. PETERSON

123 Main Street, University Town, State ZIP (555) 235-4487
Department of English, Graduate University, University Town, State ZIP
petersonj@univ.edu

EDUCATION

Ph.D. in English (Concentration in Rhetoric), Graduate University, University Town, State, May 2001.

> *Dissertation*: *Women Teach the Soldiers: Volunteer Writing Instructors in the World War One Era*. Using several archival sources, this project investigates the pedagogical methods of a large cadre of American women who volunteered to teach writing to illiterate American soldiers during the late 1910's.

> *Committee:* Jane Deacon (Director), Frank Corrigan, Amy Gregg, Jose Manez

M.A. in English, Midwestern State University, University Place, State, 1996.
Specialization in Composition and Rhetoric

B.A. in English, Small College, Small Town, State, 1992.
Summa Cum Laude, Phi Beta Kappa

RELEVANT COURSEWORK

Theory and Teaching of Rhetoric and Composition
African American Women's Rhetoric
Writing Across the Curriculum
Bakhtin and Composition
18th- and 19th-Century Rhetoric
Feminism and Rhetoric

Composition History
Composition Theory
Research Materials and Methods
John Dewey & the Educational Tradition
Gender in American History
Critical Theory
Psychoanalytic Feminisms

HONORS AND AWARDS

Spencer Foundation Dissertation Fellowship for Research Related to Education. My dissertation project was one of thirty selected from over 600 applications nation-wide to receive this $20,000 award.

AAUW Dissertation Fellowship. My dissertation project was selected from over 700 applications to receive this $15,000 award. (Due to my award from the Spencer Foundation, I was unable to accept the fellowship).

Research and Graduate Studies Dissertation Award, Graduate University. This $1,200 award enabled my March 2000 dissertation research at the Library of Congress.

Interdisciplinary Dissertation Research Award, Graduate University. This $1,200 research award provided support for my research at the National Archives.

Award in Rhetoric, Department of English, Graduate University. As the first recipient of this award, I received supplemental funds to cover course-related expenses such as books and supplies.

PUBLICATIONS

"Teachers' Organizations and Pedagogical Missions." *Composition Pedagogy Review,* 10.1 (Fall 2001): 30-52.

"Using Archives, Saving the Past," in *Research in Teaching: Primary Materials and Archival Methods.* Eds. Sarah Jones and Mark Johns. New York: University Press, 1998: 25-42.

"Bakhtin and Composition Instruction among Volunteer Literacy Teachers, 1910," in *Theories and Pedagogical Rhetorics.* Ed. Kyle Pine. CD-ROM Princeton, NJ: Academic Disks, 1999.

"The Heroine as Teacher in Early 19th-Century American Literature." *Women in American Literature,* 1.7 (1997): 11-23.

Book Manuscript Under Consideration
Co-editor (with Jane Deacon) *Teaching Composition in the Academy.* This collection has received one positive review at a university press, and we await a second reviewer's response.

In Circulation
"Naomi Phelson, A Teacher for the Troops" (12 pp)

PAPERS PRESENTED

"Teaching Writing, Teaching Literacy: What Makes the Difference?" Academic Society, Washington, DC, May 2000.

"The Rhetoric of Teaching," Teaching and Learning Conference, Austin, TX, October 1999.

"Composition in Historical Contexts," Conference on College Composition and Communication (CCCC), Atlanta, GA, March 1999.

"Bakhtin and Composition Instruction among Volunteer Literacy Teachers, 1910" North American Composition Studies Conference, Seattle, WA, June 1999.

"The Pedagogy of Literacy in Nineteenth-Century Novels," CCCC, Chicago, IL, April 1998.

"Using Archives, Saving the Past," Rhetoric Society of America, Chicago, IL 1997.

"Dealing with Student Resistance as a TA," CCCC, Phoenix, AZ, March 1997.

"WAC in the First-Year Composition Course," The Future of Composition and Rhetoric Graduate Conference, Midwestern State University, State, 1996.

"Group Conference Strategies from the Writing Classroom," Illinois Writing Centers Consortium, Anytown, IL, November 1995.

"Interpreting Writing Assignments," National Conference on Peer Tutoring, University of Vermont, Burlington, VT, November 1991.

TEACHING HONORS

Teaching Mentorship, Midwestern State University Writing Program, 1994. This program matches nominated teaching assistants with faculty members in an effort to provide extensive training in writing curriculum and instructional resources development.

TEACHING EXPERIENCE

Graduate University:

Business Writing. Upper-division course in which students learn business writing genres and conventions and develop strategies for analyzing and composing written, oral, and online texts. My syllabus included a service-learning component through which small groups of students composed brochures and pamphlets to meet the needs of local non-profit agencies.

Social Science Writing. Upper-division course familiarizing social science majors with conventions of research and trade writing in various social science disciplines. My course familiarized students with the conventions of writing in social scientific fields through units in which they produced proposals, progress reports, job application packages, literature reviews, formal reports, and rhetorical analyses of published sources.

Introduction to Rhetoric and Composition Summer Program. Special summer session offering linked a typical Introduction to Rhetoric and Composition course (see below) to an intro-level Speech Communication course in order to provide an integrated curriculum for incoming first-year students. I collaboratively designed the syllabus for the course with the Speech Communication instructor.

Introduction to Rhetoric and Composition. First-year course in which I emphasize argumentative writing and rhetorical and cultural analysis, with a special focus on collaborative invention and revision in the writing process. I also require students to meet with me individually at least two times per semester in an effort to familiarize them with their audience and to familiarize myself with the struggles they are encountering most frequently.

Midwestern State University:

Writing Consultant, 1995-96. Weekly tutorials at the University Writing Center designed to help students recognize and address the strengths and weaknesses of their invention, composing, and revision strategies.

The Rhetoric of Community. Junior-level writing course stressing cultural analysis and rhetorical analysis of discourse communities. Students analyzed and composed texts addressing community formation both within their disciplines and within the world beyond the university.

Literacy & Learning Across the Disciplines. First-year required writing course discussed argument and analysis by examining disciplinary conventions. My semester project assignment asked students to keep a reflective journal and perform a rhetorical analysis of one course they had taken.

American Rhetoric of Opportunity. This class asked students to critically assess historically and culturally specific descriptions of "the American Dream." Analyzing both fiction and non-fiction sources, students worked toward their own redefinitions of "opportunity" in America.

Exploring Identity in the University. This course emphasized the writing skills of argument and analysis through an exploration of what it means to be a university student. Students composed texts evaluating identity in the university for various audiences both in and outside of the academy.

Other Teaching Experience:

Senior Peer Writing Tutor, Small College, 1991-92. Trained new peer tutors; prepared center publications on various writing skills for tutor and student use; studied and reported on patterns of center use.

Peer Writing Tutor, Small College, Small Town, State, Fall 1989-Spring 1992.

Introduction to College Writing Teaching Assistant, Gifted Youth Program, Anytown, State, Summer 1991. This three-week course for academically talented youth between 12 and 16 years of age introduced students to argument, arrangement, style, and collaborative revision.

PROFESSIONAL EXPERIENCE

Web Coordinator, Graduate University Writing Lab, 2000-present. Use HTML and web writing software to expand the web site for center that provides writing support to undergraduate and graduate students and faculty.

Composition Assistant, Graduate University, 1999-2000. Worked with Director of Composition to train and mentor program teaching assistants and lecturers. Coordinated "Brown Bag Lunch" series of informal talks on pedagogical issues and "Rhetoric Reading Group" discussions of recent scholarship. Oversaw undergraduate grade appeal process for students who believed they had been evaluated unfairly by their instructor.

Assistant Director, Conference on Composition and Pedagogy, Graduate University. Assisted in development of conference theme, schedule, and speakers. Corresponded with featured speakers and other university units involved in planning. Developed conference web site to make participants' papers available on-line prior to the conference so that more time might be spent discussing them in sessions.

Research Assistant for Dr. Jane Deacon, Department of English, Graduate University, 1997-99. Helped plan and coordinate Professor Deacon's graduate seminars. Assisted Professor Deacon in locating and exploring library and archival sources for various research projects.

Coordinator of Graduate Organization's Speaker Series, Graduate University, 1997-98. Planned monthly talks by university faculty on topics related to rhetoric, critical theory, and literature.

Writer, English Update, Alumni Newsletter of the Department of English, Graduate University, 1997-98.

Graduate Mentor for Peer Writing Consultants in training, Midwest State University, 1995-96. Met weekly with two new undergraduate writing tutors in order to develop their skills in the Writing Center. Observed tutoring session and provided written feedback noting strengths and difficulties.

SERVICE

Composition and Rhetoric Search Committee, Department of English, Graduate University, 2000-present.

Writing Across the Curriculum Committee, Graduate University, 1999-present. Work with representatives from several different disciplines to advise Director of WAC.

Composition Committee, Graduate University, 1997-98. Worked with Director of Composition, Assistant Director of Composition, and several composition faculty members to evaluate developmental and upper-level writing courses.

Graduate University Essay Contest Review Committee, 1998-99. Read and evaluated over 200 essays written by local high school juniors for this yearly contest.

Graduate Organization Representative, Graduate University, 1997-98.

Grievance Board, Small College, 1991-92. Heard and mediated several harassment complaints involving students and faculty.

REFERENCES

Jane Deacon, Professor of English, Graduate University, University Town, State ZIP (555) 862-5435, deaconj@univ.edu

Frank Corrigan, Professor of English and Director of Graduate Studies, Graduate University, University Town, State ZIP (555) 862-2152, corriganf@univ.edu

Amy Gregg, Professor of English and Department Head, Graduate University, University Town, State ZIP
(555) 862-2253, gregga@univ.edu

Michael Yarano, Associate Professor of English, Graduate University, University Town, State ZIP
(555) 862-0708, yaranom@univ.edu

Phyllis Aravande, Assistant Director of Composition, Graduate University, University Town, State ZIP
(555) 862-3994, aravandep@univ.edu

CREDENTIALS

My dossier, containing letters of recommendation and my transcripts, is on file at Graduate University's Career Center. To receive my dossier, please contact me at (555) 235-4487 or petersonj@univ.edu, and I will have the Career Center mail it to you.

Melanie Wilkes

107 NORTH THOMPSON STREET #2 • BAXTER, STATE ZIP
PHONE (555) 246-5632 • E-MAIL MEW202@UNIV.EDU

OVERVIEW

Teaching: I am an experienced teacher with particular interests in medieval literature, religion and literature, and rhetoric and composition. I can teach composition, British Literature from Beowulf through Aphra Behn, Old English, Chaucer, Milton, medieval "theme" courses (Saints' lives, medieval women, etc.), and religion and literature, using both contemporary and medieval texts. Allowing for preparation time, I can teach rhetoric theory; fantasy literature; history of rhetoric; Arthurian lore; mythology; and Renaissance, seventeenth, and eighteenth century survey courses. I have taught more than twenty college-level courses in literature and rhetoric/composition.

Research: I am interested in the rhetoric of religion as it is played out in literary, institutional, and alternative settings. I have several articles in hand, all in medieval studies. These include a paper on the Old English Mary of Egypt, an article on teaching medieval literature based on my Medieval Congress presentation from 2003, and dissertation chapters on Old English eschatology and preaching. I have two proposals for longer projects in progress. One is a monograph on the influence of seventeenth and eighteenth century philosophy on John Wesley. Another is an informational guide to scholarship for non-academic pagan "reconstructionists."

EDUCATION

Ph.D.—English

Graduate University

Defense Planned Summer 2003

Dissertation: "Christian Subjectivity and Time: The Rhetoric of Early Medieval Eschatology." Working from the homilies of Ælfric and Wulfstan, as well as anonymous vernacular homilists of the Anglo-Saxon period, I argue that the various rhetorical and poetic formulations of "judgment day" sermons conditioned readers/auditors to see themselves as inhabitants of "Christian" time and history, thus forming an important early step in the creation of "modern" subjectivity. *Committee: Dr. Henry M. Jones, Director; Dr. Nancy Sorrel (English); Dr. Frank Corrigan (English); Dr. Jean-Pierre Alençon (French)*

Comprehensive Examinations Passed Fall 2000. Areas: Medieval Studies, Rhetoric, Renaissance Studies, Chaucer

M. A.—English

Southern University, Fortville, 1998

B.A.—English

Undergraduate College, 1993

Graduate Coursework in Literature: Plautus, Tacitus, Old French Literature, Old English, Beowulf, Studies in O.E. Prose, Chaucer, Middle English non-Chaucer, Boccaccio, Medieval Historiography, Paleography, Medieval Latin, Milton, Eighteenth Century Novel, Victorian Novel, Modernism, Religion and Literature

Graduate Coursework in Rhetoric: History of Rhetoric, Rhetoric Theory, Issues in Invention, Composition Teaching and Theory, Kenneth Burke

TEACHING EXPERIENCE (NINETEEN SECTIONS TOTAL)

Graduate University

English 221: Survey of English literature through 1798
My emphasis is on placing literary texts in a historical and rhetorical perspective; we examined ways in which texts define the subject in terms of religion, gender, and nationality. Worked with traditional literary texts as well as "popular" texts such as saints' lives and slave narratives. *Three sections*

English 202A: Writing for the Social Sciences
Explored the concept of "discourse community" in terms of the varied disciplines and interests represented in the class. Emphasis on workshop, peer response, and individual consultation. *Nine sections*

English 015: Rhetoric and Composition
Emphasis on classical, stasis-based argumentation. Students applied argumentative techniques to current issues of their own selection. *Five sections*

Southern University, Fortville

English 102: Writing Literary Arguments
Emphasis on reading literature rhetorically and writing arguments about literary texts; instruction in grammar and composition. *Two sections*

English 101: Rhetoric and Composition
Based on the Toulmin method; introduced students to reading and writing arguments; basic grammar and compositional instruction. *Three sections*

Writing Center
Worked with non-traditional and other undergraduate students; worked with ESL students. *Two semesters*

ACADEMIC AND PROFESSIONAL ACTIVITIES

"Doubt, Belief, and the Alien: Reading Medieval Texts with Undergraduates"
Accepted for the 2003 International Congress on Medieval Studies, Western Michigan University, Kalamazoo, MI

"Ælfric's Homilies and the Process of Interpretation" Presented at the 2001 International Congress on Medieval Studies, Western Michigan University, Kalamazoo, MI

"Sayers's Pauline Commentary on the Modern: The Law of the Flesh and the Law of Love in *Whose Body?*" Presented at the 1999 Dorothy L. Sayers Conference, Grove City College, Grove City, PA

Phi Beta Kappa Membership 1993

LANGUAGES

French, Latin, Old English, Old French, ASL (alphabet only), learning Italian

REFERENCES AND CREDENTIALS

Dr. Henry M. Jones, Distinguished Professor of English, Graduate University

Dr. Frank Corrigan, Professor of English, Graduate University

Dr. Laura Benison, Professor of English, Western University

My confidential dossier, containing letters of recommendation and my transcript, is available from Graduate University's Career Development and Placement Office. To receive a copy, contact me, and I will have the Placement office mail the dossier to you.

Peter Emmett

Communication Arts
Graduate University
123 Dustie Building
University Town, State ZIP

p.emmett@univ.edu
(555) 862-5435 (office)
(555) 243-5223 (home)
(555) 397-5557 (cell)

EDUCATION

Ph.D., Communication Arts, Graduate University. Defense scheduled for February 2003. Dissertation: "Communication Politics and Communication Ethics." Committee: Redmond Innis (Chair), Kenneth Malcom, Benjamin Rounweil, Abel Tull (Philosophy).

M.A., Communication Studies, Small State University, 1997. Thesis: "A Quantitative Study of Debate Anxiety." Committee: Cher Fausta (Chair), Colin Insel, Warren Kellogg, June Yrmin.

B.A., Communication Studies, Undergraduate University, 1995.

RESEARCH INTERESTS

My research focuses on two fields: contemporary rhetorical studies and communication ethics. These two fields are not separate or even merely complementary areas of study. Rather, from the very beginning of rhetorical studies scholars have developed and deployed both implicit and explicit political and ethical theories in the study of rhetoric. Postmodern and poststructural accounts of communication open new ways of thinking about the functions of rhetoric, ethics, and politics. In the search for poststructural accounts of rhetoric, ethics, and politics, I find assistance not only in philosophical and rhetorical texts, but also in the concrete practices of popular media, social sciences, legal argumentation, and policy making. Through contemporary rhetorical studies and philosophy, I strive to articulate accounts of rhetoric, ethics, and politics that provide alternatives to the humanist grounds of universal essence and immutable reason.

JOURNAL ARTICLES

"**Deconstructive Rhetorical Arts in the works of Jean-Luc Nancy.**" Accepted pending revisions at Philosophy and Rhetoric.

"**Communication Ethics from the View of Kant.**" Philosophy and Rhetoric 23 (2001): 251-278.

"**Continental Philosophy and Violent Films: Congruent Critiques of how Criminologists Construct Subjectivity.**" Critical Studies in Media Communication 28 (2000): 123-147. To be reprinted in Studies in Film Violence, Edward Cline and Ryan Tyrrell (Eds.). Madison, WI: University of Wisconsin Press, Forthcoming.

"**Some 20th-Century Philosophical Perspective on Argument Pedagogy.**" Argumentation and Advocacy 15 (1999): 153-168.

"**Applying Political Science Theories to Modes of Argument about Public Policy.**" Contemporary Argumentation and Debate 19 (1998): 99-111. Reprinted in Essays on Contemporary Argumentation and Debate, Stuart Dodsley (Ed.). New York: International Debate Education Association, 2002. 165-191.

"**Pedagogical Concerns about New Technologies in Intercollegiate Debate.**" Speaker and Gavel 20 (1997): 42-53.

CHAPTERS IN EDITED VOLUMES

"**Arguments from Definition: A Reconsideration.**" Forthcoming in the selected proceedings of the 5th International Conference on Argumentation, Frans H. van Eemeren (Ed.). Publication expected in early 2003.

"**Interrogating Humanism in Stanley Kubrick's Later Films.**" Co-authored with Anne Giulini. Studies in Kubrick, Derek Lynn and Owen Hensing (Eds.). Madison, WI: University of Wisconsin Press, Forthcoming.

"**Researching your Arguments in Cyberspace.**" Intercollegiate Forensics 2nd ed. Brandon Young (Ed.). Dubuque, Iowa: Kendall/Hunt, 1997. 99-127.

BOOK REVIEWS

"<u>A Reference Book on Rhetorical Theory</u>, Editors: Sue Doyle and Mark Baily."
<u>American Communication Journal</u> 4.3 (2001): acjournal.org.

CONFERENCE PAPERS AND INVITED LECTURES

"Ethics in Early Speech Communication." (to be presented at the 2002 National
Communication Association Convention in New Orleans, LA.)

"Troubling Definitions: Challenging Argument from Definition." (2002 International
Society for the Study of Argumentation, Amsterdam, Netherlands.)

"Limit, Alterity, and Ethics: Between Foucault and Levinas." (2001 National
Communication Association Conference in Atlanta, GA.)

"Toward a Deconstructive *Tekne* of Rhetoric: Jean-Luc Nancy's Politics of
Communication and Community." (2001 International Communication
Association Conference in Washington, DC.)

"Being *for* the Other: Ethics, Justice, and Communication." (2000 National
Communication Association Convention in Seattle, WA.)

"The Potential Excesses of the Advocacy of Outward Activism: Critiquing the
Outward Turn from the Inside/Outside." (2000 National Communication
Association Convention in Seattle, WA.)

"Polemics and Dialogue in Argumentation Theory and Pedagogy: Toward a
Democratic *Techne* of Argument." (2000 International Debate Education
Association Conference on Debate and Democratization in Budapest, Hungary.)

"Turning Kant Against the Priority of Autonomy: Communication Ethics and the *A
Priori* Community." (2000 National Communication Ethics Conference in Gull
Lake, MI.)

"Stoic Ethics and Rhetoric: The Risk of Rationalism's Excess." (2000 Eastern
Communication Association Conference in Pittsburgh, PA.)

"Michel Foucault's Critique of Humanism: Radical Subjectivity and Possibilities of
Freedom." (2000 Eastern Communication Association Conference in Pittsburgh,
PA.)

"The Owl of Minerva: The Perils and Possibilities of Writing the Future." Co-authored with Anne Inspiration. (2000 Southern States Communication Association Conference in New Orleans, LA.)

"Gender/Power/Kubrick." (Invited lecture for the interdisciplinary symposium, "The Eyes Have It: Stanley Kubrick, Film, and the Uses of History," Center for the Study of History and Culture, Albion College, Albion, MI, 2000.)

"Foucault's Historical Methodology: Uses and Implications for Rhetoric." (1999 Southern States Communication Association/Central States Communication Association Joint Conference in St. Louis, MO.)

"Discourse Ethics: Communication Ethics in Nietzsche and Foucault." *Selected as one of the top four papers in communication ethics.* (1998 National Communication Association Conference in New York, NY.)

"Deviant Subjects in Foucault and *A Clockwork Orange*: Critiques of Social Scientific Constructions of the Self." (1998 National Communication Association Conference in New York, NY.)

"Ships in the Night: Debating Postmodernism." (1998 National Communication Association Conference in New York, NY.)

"Teaching Argumentation Existentially: Argumentation Pedagogy and Theories of Rhetoric as Epistemic." (1998 Nascent Methodologies Conference at University of Maryland.)

OTHER CONFERENCE PARTICIPATION

"Calling/Reading/Writing: Doing Justice to Levinas." (Short position paper for pre-conference workshop on Levinas at the 2000 National Communication Association Conference in Seattle, WA.)

"Taking Ethics as First Philosophy Seriously: The To/For Distinction in the Writings of Emmanuel Levinas." (Short position paper for pre-seminar workshop on Levinas at the 1999 National Communication Association Conference in Chicago, IL.)

Respondent. "Kritiking: The State of the Art." (1999 National Communication Association Conference in Chicago, IL.)

Panel Debate on Issues in Health Care Reform. (1999 Southern States Communication Association/Central States Communication Association Joint Conference in St. Louis, MO.)

GRANTS AND FELLOWSHIPS

Research Office Dissertation Support Grant. Received one semester of course release. Graduate University, Fall 2000.

Open National Communication Graduate Student Fellowship. Received room, board, and fees for the National Communication Conference, 2000.

Undergraduate Technology Enrichment Grant. Received $5,000 for new computers for the Graduate University Communication Student Program and Lab, 1999.

AWARDS AND RECOGNITION

Cheryl Ambler Award for Academic Excellence in Graduate Scholarship, Graduate University, 1999.

Graduate Scholar Award. Graduate University, 1998-99.

Graduate Scholar Award. Graduate University, 1997-98.

Master's Degree conferred with Distinction. Small State University, 1997.

Outstanding Communication Graduate Student. Small State University, 1997.

ACADEMIC EMPLOYMENT

Graduate University: Fall 1997 – present.
- Taught courses in rhetorical theory, public speaking, informative and technical communication, and small group communication, Fall 1997 – present.
- Developed and coordinated the new civic engagement project, including recruiting students, creating public events, and connecting students to campus and local political organizations, Fall 2002 – present.
- Worked in conjunction with the Graduate University Marketing Department to teach marketing students how to present market analysis and to communicate effectively in project teams during their capstone course, Fall 2001 – present.
- Developed and directed the new Center for Public Speaking, including hiring, training, and supervising student tutors, Fall 2001 – Summer 2002.
- Directed the debate program, including maintaining budgets, training students, and supervising assistants, Fall 1998 – Spring 2000, Fall 2002-present.

Small State University: Spring 1996 – Fall 1997.
- Taught courses in argumentation and small group communication.
- Served as the senior coach for the intercollegiate debate program.

Additional Summer Teaching
- Residential High School Honors Program at Ivy University, 1997–2000. Taught courses in legal argumentation. Co-authored research guides for students.
- Faculty, Debate Institute at Landmark State University, 1995-1999. Taught mass lectures in debate theory and directed research teams. Co-authored research guides for students.

COURSES TAUGHT (25 total course sections)

Introduction to Rhetorical Theory: This survey course covers the major movements in rhetorical theory from ancient Greek texts through late 20th-century theorists. (1 course section, 24 students)

Argumentation and Debate: An upper-division course covering the theory and practice of argumentation in interpersonal, organizational, and political contexts. (2 course sections, 24 students each)

Informative, Technical, and Presentational Speaking: An upper-division course focusing on communication skills related to business and technical environments. (2 course sections, 24 students each)

Effective Speech: A basic course covering the theory and practice of oratory, with additional material covering small group communication and rhetorical criticism. (12 course sections, 24-30 students each, also some mass lectures)

Public Speaking and the Law: A college-level summer course for extremely advanced high school students covering the practice and criticism of legal communication, ranging from successful trial advocacy to the analysis of appellate decisions as rhetorical texts. (4 course sections, 24-32 students each)

Small Group Communication: A basic course in the theory and practice of group discussion and decision-making, covering core perspectives on group dynamics. (2 course sections, 28 students)

Using Debate in the Classroom: A two-weekend short class on the integration of debate as a teaching tool in elementary, secondary, and post-secondary educational settings. (1 continuing education section, 8 students)

Mastering Library Research: A two-weekend short class on the effective and efficient use of library and research facilities, covering paperbound indexes, computer databases, and Internet research. (1 continuing education section, 6 students)

SIGNIFICANT GUEST TEACHING

"**Poststructural Views of Social Science**" for a graduate seminar on epistemology of the social sciences; "**Using Theory in Criticism**" for an undergraduate course on rhetorical theory & criticism; "**Ideology Critiques of Popular Film**" for an undergraduate course on film theory and criticism; "**Michel Foucault and Theories of Rhetoric,**" two mass lectures for an undergraduate course on rhetorical theory; "**Foucault and Derrida as Rhetorical Theorists**" for an undergraduate course on rhetorical theory; "**Syllogisms and Fallacies,**" mass lecture for an undergraduate course in public speaking.

SERVICE

Department Service
- Basic Course Web-Workbook Improvement Committee, Graduate University Communication Arts, 2001.
- Intellectual Concerns Officer, Graduate University Communication Arts Graduate Forum, 1999-2000.
- Web-site design and programming, Communication Studies, Small State University, 1996.

University Service
- University Town Allocation Committee, Program Allocation Team, Graduate University, 1998-1999.

Editorial Service
- Reviewed manuscripts for <u>Philosophy and Rhetoric</u>, <u>Journal of Communication,</u> and <u>New Jersey Journal of Communication</u>.

William M. Grosvenor

421 Webber Building
Graduate University
University Town, State ZIP
(555) 234 - 2936
wmg223@univ.edu
www.personal.univ.edu/wmg223

CURRICULUM VITAE

EDUCATION

2002–Ph.D., History, Graduate University, University Town, State.
  Dissertation: "The Liberal Republican Movement: Reformers and Political Parties in Civil War
    Era Political Culture."
  Advisor: Professor Neville Marcus
1994–B.A., History major, Latin minor, Undergraduate University, magna cum laude.

PROFESSIONAL POSITIONS

1997 to present–Lecturer, Graduate University.
2002, Fall–Lecturer, Regional Campus.
2000, Fall–Lecturer, Nearby College.
1995-1997–Teaching Assistant, Graduate University.

PUBLICATIONS

"The Chicago Fire of 1871 and Federal Power in the North during Reconstruction," *Civil War History*, 47
  (June 2001): 146-63.
"The Won Lost Cause: The Reconstruction of History in the Redemption of South Carolina," *The
  Historian*, 63 (Summer 2001): 769-86.

PAPERS

"'A bombshell to blow up both the parties': Third Party Movements in the Early Gilded Age," at the
  American Historical Association, Chicago, IL, January 2003.
"Defending a Republic: Liberal Reformers and Republican Ideology," at the American Religious History
  Workshop, Yale University, New Haven, CT, March 1999.
"The Won Lost Cause: South Carolina's 1876 Election Violence in the Context of the Lost Cause," at the
  American Culture Association, Orlando, FL, April 1998.

FELLOWSHIPS and GRANTS

West Point Summer Seminar in Military History Fellowship (Summer 2002)
John Port Fellowship in History, Graduate University (Fall 1999)
Research Office Dissertation Support Grant, Graduate University (Summer 1999)
Hall Dissertation Fellowship, Graduate University (Fall 1998)
Sellars Travel Fellowship, Graduate University (Spring 1995)
Graduate School Fellowship, Graduate University (1994)

COURSES TAUGHT

Graduate University
 American Civilization to 1877
 American Civilization since 1865
 American Civil War and Reconstruction
 Western Heritage I

Regional Campus
 American Civil War and Reconstruction

Nearby College
 American Civilization to 1877

Helen Deer
734 S. Atheling St. #394
University Town, State ZIP, USA
Tel: (555) 867-2039
E-mail: hed@univ.edu

Education:

1997-   Graduate University,
             Ph.D. Candidate in Art History
             (A.B.D. Fall 2000).

1991-1996   British University,
             MA (Hons.) Fine Art.
             First Class Distinction in Art History.

Fields of Concentration:

British Modernism
Early Medieval Art in Northern Europe
20th-Century Critical Theory
Modernism and British Literature

Dissertation Topic:

"Representing Britishness": Landscape, Identity and Geography in the Cold War Era.
Advisor, Dr. Sandra M. Gold

Awards and Fellowships:

05/2002-   Graduate University, Arts Institute, Graduate Summer Residency.
08/2002

02/2002   Graduate University, Wendell Bellows Graduate Fellowship.

01/2002-   Junior Fellowship, Centre for British Art, London.
04/2002

04/2000   Graduate University, College of Arts, Creative Achievement Award.

04/2000   Graduate University, Graduate Outstanding Teaching Award.

06/1999   Graduate University, Department of Art History, Art History Donors Travel Grant
            (to research materials in London for Spring 2000, "English Art" Lecture Course).

08/1997   Graduate University, Department of Art History, Grissom Award; a fellowship
            given to an incoming Ph.D. student.

08/1994   British University, Department of Art History Travel Award;
            funding for five weeks' research travel in Spain and Morocco.

Papers Delivered:

03/2001   The Philadelphia Symposium on the History of Art,
            The Philadelphia Museum of Art, Philadelphia, PA.
            "Exhibiting Britishness at the Festival of Britain and the Greenwich Millennium
            Dome."
            This paper was also delivered 11/2000 at The Graduate University, Department of
            Art History, 6th Annual Graduate Symposium in the History of Art.

10/1999   Public Lecture, The Graduate University Catholic Community, "The House
            Church at Dura Europos and Early Christian Imagery."

05/1999   29th Annual Middle Atlantic Symposium in Art History,
            The National Gallery of Art, Washington D.C.
            "Wyndham Lewis: Portrait of a Tyro."
            This paper was also delivered 11/1998 at The Graduate University, Department of
            Art History, 4th Annual Graduate Symposium in the History of Art.

Teaching Experience:

Fall 2001   Instructor of Record for lecture course AH306, "English Art,"
            Graduate University (taught as "British Art in the Twentieth Century").

Summer 2001 Instructor of Record for lecture course AH100, "Introduction to Art,"
            Graduate University. This course was a survey of the history of Western and
            Non-Western Art.

Spring 2001 Teaching Assistant for Professor Sally Welsh, AH320, "Chinese Art."
            I delivered a lecture for this class, "The Lyric Style: Painting in China
            During the Southern Song Dynasty."

Spring 2001 Teaching Assistant for Professor Sandra M. Gold, AH397a, "Art after
            1940." I delivered a lecture for this class, "Pop in England: Fantasies
            of American Consumer Culture in a Subsistence Economy."

Fall 2000   Teaching Assistant for Professor Curt Bellor, AH405, "Pioneers
                 Of Modern Architecture."

Fall 2000   Teaching Assistant for Professor Sandra M. Gold, AH100, "Introduction
                 To Art."

Summer 2000 Instructor of Record for lecture course AH100, "Introduction to Art,"
                 Graduate University.

Spring 2000   Instructor of Record for lecture course AH306, "English Art,"
                 Graduate University. This was a topic-based course examining English Art and
                 notions of "Englishness" in art dating from Stonehenge to the 1997/1999
                 "Sensation" exhibition of work by young British artists from the Saatchi
                 collection.

Fall 1999   Teaching Assistant for Professor Sally Welsh, AH120, "Introduction to
                 Asian Art."

Fall 1999   Teaching Assistant for Professor Calla Duke, AH100, "Introduction to Western
                 Art." I delivered two lectures for this class, "Early Christian and
                 Byzantine Art: Rome and Constantinople," and "Early Christian Art and
                 Architecture in Ravenna."

Spring 1999   Instructor of Record for lecture course AH302, "Art of the Early Middle Ages,"
                 Graduate University.

Fall 1998,   Teaching Assistant for Professor Beth Streams, AH297A,
                 "Ancient to Medieval Architecture." I delivered a lecture for this class,
                 "Viking Architecture: Jarlshof, Hedeby, Stöng and Jorvik."

Fall 1998   Section leader for two sections of 25 students for AH111, "Survey of Western Art
                 I."

Spring 1998   Section leader for two sections of 25 students for AH112, "Survey of Western Art
                 II."

Fall 1997   Teaching Assistant for Mr. Duncan Glimmer, AH305, "European Art, c. 1780-
                 1860."

01/1997-   Community Artist and Educator, "Youth and Arts Project," Art Starts
06/1997   Cultural Center, Canadian City.

10/1996-   Assistant Sculpture Tutor and Printmaking Technician (Voluntary Work),
06/1997   Firtree Gallery School, Art Gallery of Canadian City, Canada.

Professional Activities:

05/2002-   The Graduate University, Department of Art History, Slide
12/2002   Photographer.

05/2002-   The Graduate University, Freshman Advisor for the Department
08/2002   of Art History (Freshman Testing, Counselling and Advising Program).

Fall 2000   Publications Assistant, *Graduate University Papers*, edited by Professor Sally
            Welsh.

09/2000   Graduate Good Offices Committee Member. A committee of graduate students
            and professors from the College of Arts were chosen to sit on a panel at the
            hearing of a Ph.D. student who was disputing a grade.

08/1999   The Graduate University, Department of Art History, Organizer and Facilitator of
            a Graduate Teaching Assistant Workshop on Ethics and Resources.

03/1999   Poster: "Wyndham Lewis: Tyros and Portraits," Graduate
            University, 14th Annual Graduate Research Exhibition.

Professional Affiliations:

College Art Association
Association of Art Historians
Historians of British Art

Languages:

French (excellent reading comprehension, moderate writing and speaking skills)
German (moderate reading comprehension, basic speaking skills)

Michael Ichthus Bensen

245 Scintilla Avenue
Apartment #5
University Town, State ZIP
(555) 232-2039

mib213@univ.edu

240 Dustie Building
Graduate University
University Town, State, ZIP
(555) 862-3918

Education

Ph.D. Hermeneutics, Graduate University   May 2002
(Interdisciplinary Doctoral Majors Program)

Specialities: Classical Philosophy, Classical Rhetoric,
Existential Hermeneutics, Historiography, Rhetorical Theory

M.A.   Speech Communication, Graduate University   Jan. 1980
B.S.   Communication Arts, Undergraduate University   Jan. 1976

Dissertation: *Why Plato Hid the Peloponnesian War* – Defended February 8, 2002

Thucydides and Xenophon, the two historians of the Peloponnesian War, tell us that in the years 431–403 B.C.E.
Athens suffered through a plague, summer raids on its crops and groves, a political panic, two oligarchic
revolutions, a final siege, a civil war, and a deep economic depression. These events do not appear in the dialogues
of Plato, even though Socrates, who does, lived and taught in Athens throughout this period (with the brief
exceptions of his military service abroad). This study asks how and why Plato has hidden the Peloponnesian War. It
proceeds, first, by developing a concise history of the Peloponnesian War from which is derived a short list of the
ways the war directly affected daily life in Athens. This list is then brought to readings of Aristophanes' comedies
and Xenophon's Socratic writings with the aim of obtaining confirmation for these home-front experiences. Next,
the dialogues of Plato are reviewed for direct references and indirect allusions to the Peloponnesian War. The results
thus gathered are then explained by plotting the dramatic dates of Plato's dialogues across a timeline of the war.
This study concludes that Plato conceals the war, even as he reminds us of it, by staging his dialogues in the periods
of peace that punctuate the conflict, often just before some fateful event. Plato follows this strategy, it is suggested,
in order to shame the imperial arrogance of Periclean Athens, the public memory of which supported fourth century
aspirations for a second empire.

Committee: George Wendell (Chair, Speech Communication),
Andrew Angell (Thesis Co-Advisor, Classics)   James Russell (Thesis Co-Advisor, Phil.)
Hans Knoepfl (Philosophy, Emeritus)   Mitchell Coal (Special Member, Phil.)

Coursework

Argumentation	Kant	Speech Criticism
Dialectics	Vico & Cassirer	History of Rhetoric
Hermeneutics	Husserl	Seminar in Rhetorical Criticism
Phenomenology	Heidegger	Speech Theory & Criticism -Ancient
Philosophy of Science	Gadamer	Speech Theory & Criticism - Modern
Structuralism	Tillich	Speech Theory & Cricitism – Cont.
Plato & Parmenides		Problems in Speech Education
Plato	Historical Methods	Communication Probs. & Principles
Aristotle	Historiography	Research Problems – The Sophists

Academic Publications

Review Essay, "The Amnesty of 403 B.C.E.," on *The Divided City: On Memory & Forgetting in Ancient Athens* by Nicole Loraux, and *Remembering Defeat: Civil War and Civic Memory in Ancient Athens* by Andrew Wolpert, forthcoming in *Review of Communication*.

Review Essay on *Plato's First Interpreters* by Harold Tarrant, and *Who Speaks for Plato? Studies in Platonic Anonymity* edited by Gerald Press, Forthcoming in *Philosophy and Rhetoric*.

Review Essay, "Four Recent Studies of Platonic Rhetoric," *Rhetoric Society Quarterly*, 22.13, Spring 2000.

Review Essay, "Empire and Rhetoric: Recent Books on Classical Rhetoric," *Rhetoric Review*, 15.3, Winter 1999.

Review Article, "Constructing Cancer: Five Recent Books on Science, Medicine and Society," *Bul. Science, Technology and Society,* (28.2) 1999.

"A Response to Paul Durbin after *After Virtue* by Alasdair MacIntyre." *Res. in Philosophy & Technology,* (32) 1998.

Papers Presented

"Between The Deaths of Two Pericles: Plato's *Gorgias*, Rhetoric and the Poetics of Consequence." Graduate University Communication Arts & Sciences Colloquium, November 2002.

"Poets, Whores, and Prophets: A Critique of the Rushdie Affair Through An Interpretation of *The Satanic Verses*." Speech Communication Association, Chicago, February 1990.

"McEthics: MacIntyre, Morality, and Modernity." Philosophy Graduate Colloquium. Graduate University, May 1987.

"Plato's Rite of Speech." Graduate University Conference on Rhetoric & Composition, University Town, July 1981.

"Allusions to the Historical Gorgias in Plato's *Gorgias*." National Doctoral Honors Seminar on the History of Rhetoric. Bloomington, April 1979.

Honors and Awards

Dustie Fellowship, Graduate University, 1982 – 1983
Graduate Interdisciplinary Fellowship, 1980 – 1981
Graduate Interdisciplinary Fellowship, 1979 – 1980
Second Year Dustie Fellowship, Graduate University, 1978 – 1979
Participant in the National Doctoral Honors Seminar sponsored by

The Speech Communication Association of America, April 1979.

Teaching Experience

Introduction to Ethics (Philosophy 103 – S, 2003). Meeting college breadth requirements while offering considerable latitude to the instructor, this course introduces students to ethical thought through a sequence of ancient Greek texts: Homer, Herodotus, Hippocrates, Gorgias & Protagoras, Thucydides, Aristophanes, Plato, and Aristotle.

Rhetoric and Composition (English 15 – 2002-03). This option for the first year writing course at Graduate University introduces students to college composition through the rhetorical-situation model.

Effective Group Communication (CAS 100B – F, 2002). This second option for the basic communication skills course presents the fundamental principles and techniques of small group communication and project management in the context of communications theory.

Science and Human Values (Humanities 101). This lower-division course, offered as part of the breadth requirement, examined the evolving relationship between science and culture as represented in novels, extended critical essays, and general histories.

Public Speaking (Speech Communication 200A). A previous incarnation of the primary option for the basic communication skills course, 200A introduced students to the principles and practices of public speaking through the rhetorical-situation model.

Small Group Communication (Speech Communication 200B). (Prev. version of CAS 100B)

Professional Development

Information Technology Services Seminar – ANGEL: Syllabus, Calendar, & File Mngt
January 9, 2003
Information Technology Services Seminar – ANGEL: System Overview
January 6, 2003
Course in College Teaching   October-November 2002.

Other Employment/Professional Experiences

Operations/Resident Manager, The Janice Rickover House, August 1998 – October 2001
Responsible for all daily operations (staff (10) and office supervision, receipts, maintenance, housekeeping, and guest relations) (00-01), and for weeknight security and oversight in The Janice Rickover and Heller-Kranz Houses, two cancer-patient residential facilities on a Maryland university's Medical Institutes campus (98-01). *Dissertation was written during this period.*

Pres./Manager, Libri, Inc. *d/b/a* Michael's Bookshelf (*University Town*)*, 1989 – 1998*
Under the name of *Libri, Inc.* and in conjunction with interested members of the community, in July of 1989 I incorporated *Michael's Bookshelf,* the store I had opened as a sole proprietorship in 1983. Over the next year I raised ~ $250,000 from investors, leased 3000 sq. ft. in a new building just one block west of my original location, designed the layout of the new store and all

its shelves and fixtures, and supervised the store's move. Annual sales increased rapidly—from $350,000 in 1989, to $850,000 in 1994, the year the first superstore opened in University Town. In July 1998, I withdrew from daily management of the store. Early in 2000, faced with the prospect of renewing the lease for a marginally profitable operation, the shareholders voted to close the store.

Producer/Host, Libri, The Radio Book Revue, *WGU, Nov., 1991 – June, 1998.*
In 1991, working with WGU, the National Public Radio affiliate owned by Graduate University, I created a weekly radio program on new and noteworthy books. What began as "live" tapings of informal campus book discussions eventually became a series of professionally produced author interviews, often conducted with the aid of studio-to-studio digital phone-links. Over the six years I produced and hosted *Libri,* handling all the bookings myself, I interviewed some 200 authors and co-reviewed, with Graduate University faculty, another 100 plus titles.

Owner/Manager, Michael's Bookshelf, *July, 1983 – July, 1989.* In July of 1983, I rented a 450 sq. ft. storefront in downtown University Town, one block from the Graduate University campus. I then designed and built all the fixtures, arranged the necessary loans with a local bank, opened accounts with the relevant publishers, and first handled and then supervised all daily operations. The store specialized in literary and academic titles. Its peak annual sales were $350,000, or nearly $800/sq.ft.

Freelance Multi-Media Production (Undergraduate University), 1973 – 1976. Created five multi-media presentations for five different non-profit organizations. Each presentation consisted of 240 slides shown on three projectors synchronized with a 12-18 minute soundtrack. Story-lines were written in consultation with the client, I did all the rest alone.

Community Activities and Service

Participated in the "Environmental Lobby Night" sponsored by, among other organizations, The Chesapeake Bay Foundation, in Annapolis on February 18th, 2003.

Served on the Diversity Action Council, Comprehensive Cancer Center, A Medical Institute, East Coast City, 2001.

Wrote a series of six review essays, on "The American Identity," for the University Town newspaper in the summer of 1998.

Presented, twice, under the auspices of Graduate University's Continuing Education, a faculty seminar on academic publishing/bookselling, *Choosing the Right Publisher—* spring 1998.

Produced and hosted a television program, "The Civil War: Historians Respond," broadcast by WGX-TV (University Town) in the summer of 1996. The one-hour round-table discussion of a recently published collection of essays (Toplin, ed., Oxford) on the history-making Ken Burns series featured four Graduate University historians.

Served on the task force established by the Borough of University Town to create a new partnership for the downtown, 1990-1991. I wrote the first draft of the articles and by-laws for the organization that emerged from these meetings.

Served as a "community columnist" for the University Town newspaper, in 1990, following a "Letter to the Editor" I had submitted during the Salman Rushdie affair. (My bookstore had hosted a cover-to-cover reading of *Satanic Verses*, an event protested by the local Muslim community and covered by local media.)

Co-authored, with science fiction writer James Morrow, a review of *Time Wars* by Jeremy Rifkin for *The Philadelphia Inquirer*, August 23, 1987.

References

George Wendell
> Edgar Dustie Professor of Rhetoric
> 287 Dustie Building
> Graduate University
> University Town, State ZIP
> (555) 862-3029, g8w@univ.edu

Lily Avon
> Associate Professor of Communication Arts and English
> 223 Dustie Building
> Graduate University
> University Town, State ZIP
> (555) 862-2957, lxa23@univ.edu

Mitchell Coal
> Associate Professor of Liberal Arts and International Studies
> A Colorado University
> Mountain City, CO ZIP
> (555) 203-3746, mcoal@colouniv.edu

James Russell
> Associate Professor of Philosophy
> 124 Dustie Building
> Graduate University
> University Town, State ZIP
> (555) 862-3840, jmr39@univ.edu

Owen Welsh
> Interim Head and Professor of Philosophy
> 229 Dustie Building
> Graduate University
> University Town, State ZIP
> (555) 862-1194

Ivy Johnson Taylor

Comparative Literature Department
Graduate University
424 Barrow Building
University Town, State ZIP
(555) 862-0885

737 N. Fox Street
Baxter, State ZIP
(555) 344-0537
Email: ijt7@univ.edu

Education

Spring 2000	Ph.D. expected, Graduate University (Comparative Literature)
1994	M.A., Graduate University (Comparative Literature)
1992	B.A., Undergraduate University (English)
1989	Another Undergraduate University (Thematic Option Honors Program)

Dissertation   "Political Desire in Late Medieval Literature"
Written under the direction of Henry M. Jones (Chair), Catherine Allery, Giuliana Bellagio, and Nancy Sorrel. The dissertation argues for a revised understanding of conventional love language within a social and political context. Included are chapters on Jean de Meun, Brunetto Latini, and Chaucer. Defense scheduled for February 2000.

Grants and Awards

1999	Woodrow Wilson Practicum Grant
1998	Liberal Arts Scholar Teaching Fellow
1998	Research and Graduate School Travel Grant
1997	University Graduate Assistant Teaching Award
1997	Graduate Student Research Exhibition Second Place
1996	Liberal Arts Dissertation Support Grant
1994	Research and Graduate School Travel Grant

Publications

"Governance and Consensual Desire in Usk's *Testament of Love*." *Studies in Philology* 94.2 (Winter 1998): 42-61.

"The Future of Comparative Literature." ACLA Bulletin, *Comparative Literature* 40.2 (Summer 1998).

In Progress:

Educating the Lover in Pre-Modern Literature. (Co-editor) Circulating. A collection of ten scholarly essays and an introduction on desire in the literature of the early periods. The essays cover works from multiple language traditions and contain new approaches to literature and culture.

"Citizens and Lovers: Brunetto Latini's *Tesoretto* and Book 7 of Gower's *Confessio Amantis*." A twenty-five page essay to appear in *Educating the Lover in Pre-Modern Literature*.

Professional Papers and Presentations

1999	"The Lover as Citizen in Brunetto Latini's *Tesoretto*." American Comparative Literature Association Annual Conference, Montreal.
1998	"Dante's Invention of an Amorous Poetics? The Case of the *Detto d'Amore*." Dante Society session, 11th Biennial New College Conference on Medieval-Renaissance Studies, University of South Florida.

1998   "Mutual Discourse and Negotiating Identity in Andreas Capellanus' *De Amore*." International Medieval Congress, Medieval Institute, Western Michigan University.

1997   "Usk without the Anecdote: The Subject of History in the *Testament*." Brown Bag Luncheon Series, Graduate University.

1994   "Memory in Thomas's *Roman de Tristan: La Salle Aux Images* and the *Rhetorica Ad Herennium*." International Medieval Congress, Medieval Institute, Western Michigan University.

Academic Appointments at Graduate University

1998-9   Liberal Arts Scholar Teaching Fellow
Instructor for 100-student Comparative Literature course on Arthurian Literature as part of an undergraduate education improvement grant. Implemented collaborative-learning and technology-in-the-classroom practices, and introduced a more extensive writing format.

1996-8, 1999-00   Editorial Assistant, *Comparative Literature Review*
Responsible for day to day management of correspondence and routing of submissions as well as editing and production duties for each issue. Supervised development of website and training of interns and work-study students.

1993-6, 1999-00   Teaching Assistant, Comparative Literature and English
For all courses I was the sole instructor and responsible for syllabi construction, book selection, individual class instruction, administration of exams and evaluation of student performance.

Arthurian Literature (Comp Lit 106): course for 75-100 non-majors organized around a thematic view of Arthurian matter from Geoffrey of Monmouth to Soseki. (Taught 3 times.)

Occult Literature (Comp Lit 120): discussion based course for 50 non-majors which explored world literature that challenged orthodox belief systems and cultural institutions.

Genres of World Literature (Comp Lit 10): multicultural course for 45 non-majors which explored literature in genre-based groupings ranging from ancient epic to postmodern novel.

World Mythology (Comp Lit 108): multicultural course which taught methods of literary analysis and cultural interpretation. (Taught twice for continuing and distance education program and twice for resident students.)

Rhetoric and Composition (English 15): required course for 24 students which focused on writing as a process and which introduced principles of argumentation and basic style; it also incorporated a research methods unit. (Taught four times.)

1994-5   Research Assistant, Comparative Literature Department
Aided in preparation of departmental benchmarking plan and undergraduate major recruitment and advising, including the development of recruitment brochure and materials.

Other Professional Activities

1999   Panel Organizer/Moderator, "Translating Desire in Medieval and Early Modern Literature." Annual American Comparative Literature Association Conference, Montreal.

1998-00   Listmaster for ACLA-G, national Comparative Literature graduate student listserv.

1997-99   Elected to the American Comparative Literature Association Advisory Board.

1996   Session Moderator, "Gender and Resistance," 10th Annual Midwest/MidAtlantic Feminist Graduate Student Conference, Graduate University.

1995   Organizing Committee, "Cultures in Crisis in 19th- and 20th-Century Literature and Art," English Department Graduate Student Conference.

Departmental/University Service

1998-99	Participated in Faculty in Residence for Student in Transition (FIRST) program
1996-00	Co-chair, Graduate Univ. Group Alliance for Parent-Students (GAPs) Organization
1995-96	Member, Graduate University, Child Care Advisory Committee
1994-95	Student Representative, Undergraduate Studies Committee
1994-95	Elected Member, Graduate Studies Council
1993-94	Student Representative, Graduate Faculty Committee
1993-94	Officer, Comparative Literature, Graduate Student Organization

Medieval Languages

Old and Middle English
Old French
Latin
Italian (reading)

Other Relevant Skills

Internship in academic development and alumni relations.
2 ½ years professional experience in public relations and political consulting.
Computer literate in both PC and Mac platforms, Microsoft products, and basic html skills.

Associations

Modern Language Association
American Comparative Literature Association
Dante Society of America
Medieval Academy of America

Henry M. Jones, Distinguished Professor of English and Comparative Literature, and Director of the
Humanities Institute, Graduate University
(555) 862-9540   email: hmj1@univ.edu

Catherine Allery, Professor of Comparative Literature and English, and Head of the Comparative
Literature Department, Graduate University
(555) 862-8905   email: cla20@univ.edu

Nancy Sorrel, Assistant Professor of English and Comparative Literature,
Graduate University
(555) 862-1626   email: nxs62@univ.edu

Giuliana Bellagio, Director of Italian American Studies, Arthur Connelly University
(555) 793-9434   email: gbellagio@acu.edu

James Farben, Class of 1928 Professor of English and Comparative Literature, and Chair of the
Comparative Literature Department, Ivied University
(555) 522-8006 (*on sabbatical*) email: jmf27@ivieduniv.edu

Dossier available through Graduate University Career Services.

GAIL TUCKERMAN

Graduate University
Department of Romance Languages
342 Furness Building
University Town, State ZIP
(555) 862-0529

411 Wakeport Drive, A-226
University Town, State ZIP
(555) 238-4993
GailTuck@univ.edu
www.personal.psu.edu/gxt121

EDUCATION

Ph.D. in Spanish Applied Linguistics (expected August 2001)
Graduate University
Dissertation: Spanish Stress and Second Language Learning
Co-Advisors: Henrietta Ochs and Robert Alfrith
M.A. in Spanish Literature, May 1997
East Coast University
B.S. in Spanish and English, May 1993
Southern University
Semester Abroad, Spring 1992
Universidad Complutense de Madrid, Madrid, Spain

WORK EXPERIENCE

Graduate University – Department of Romance Languages

Teaching Assistant, Fall 1997 – present
Spanish courses taught: basic, intermediate and advanced language; intermediate and advanced composition; intermediate and advanced conversation; phonology
Materials Developer, Basic Language Program, Fall 1999 – present
Assistant Director and Instructor, Study Abroad Program, Continuing and Distance Education, Puebla, Mexico, Summer 1999
Research Assistant, Professor Roberto Rodriguez, Fall 1998 – Spring 1999

East Coast University – Department of Romance Languages

Teaching Assistant, Fall 1994, Fall 1995 – Summer 1997
Spanish courses taught: basic language
Course Supervisor, Fall 1996 – Spring 1997
Assistant Director and Instructor, Study Abroad Program, Madrid, Spain, Summer 1997
Research Assistant, Professors Robert Medina and Juana Valencia, Fall 1995 – Spring 1997
Spanish Tutor, Academic Athletic Tutoring Center, Fall 1995 – Spring 1997

HONORS AND AWARDS

Graduate University

Dissertation Support Grant, *Research and Graduate Studies Office, College of the Liberal Arts*, for Spring 2001

Juan Riviera **Prize for Spanish** (for citizenship, scholarship and commitment to teaching),
   Department of Romance Languages, April 2000
Graduate Student Scholar Fellowship, *Graduate School of Arts and Sciences with College of
   Liberal Arts*, Fall 1997 – Spring 2000
Travel Grants
   Research and Graduate Studies Office, September 2000, April 2000
   Department of Romance Lnaguages, September 2000, April 2000, October 1999,
      September 1998
   Center for Language Acquisition, September 2000, October 1999

East Coast University

Outstanding Graduate Teaching Assistant Award, *Department of Romance Languages*, May
   1997
DuPont Fellowship, *Department of Romance Languages*, Fall 1996 – Spring 1997

Ministerio de Educiación y Ciencia de España

Diploma de Español como Lengua Extranjera (DELE), *Superior*, February 1995

RESEARCH

Publications

Montoya-Pérez, Juana, Gail Tuckerman, Estrella Malaga-Cortazar and Seana O'Brien. (2000).
   "The acquisition of second language syntax." In *University of Pittsburgh Working Papers
   in Linguistics: Proceedings from GASLA V* (231-141).
Montoya-Pérez, Juana, Gail Tuckerman, Seana O'Brien and Estrella Malaga-Cortazar. "Second
   Language acquisition and the interaction of lexical and syntactical features." In Pérez and
   Limon (Eds.), *The acquisition of Spanish morphosyntax*. Dordrecht: Kluwer Academic
   (forthcoming).

In progress

"Possession in the Spanish Interlanguage: doubling, multiple numerations, and the developmental
   perspective on the projection problem."
"The combined benefits of instruction and study abroad on native English speakers' acquisition
   of the Spanish fricative/occlusive contrast."

CONFERENCES AND PRESENTATIONS

"How do foreign language learners know how to pronounce new words?" Poster presentation at
   the **Graduate Research Exhibit**, *Graduate University*, March 2001. Awarded First Place
   in Arts and Humanities Division.
"The second language acquisition of Spanish stress patterns." **Language Acquisition Graduate
   Organization Speaker Series**, *Graduate University*, January 2001.
"Spanish stress and second language acquisition." Poster presentation at the **Second Language
   Research Forum 2000**, *University of Wisconsin at Madison*, September 2000.
"The combined effects of instruction and study abroad on native English-speakers' acquisition of
   the Spanish fricative/occlusive contrast." **Texas Foreign Language Education**

Conference, *University of Texas at Austin*, April 2000.

"The effects of instruction and study abroad on the acquisition of second language pronunciation," **Foreign Language Acquisition Discussion Group**, *Graduate University*, March 2000.

"Possession in the Spanish Interlanguage: doubling, multiple numerations, and the developmental perspective on the projection problem." **The 1999 Conference on L1 and L2 Acquisition of Spanish and Portuguese**, *Georgetown University*, Washington, D.C., October 1999 (with Estrella Malaga-Cortazar).

"Implementing Video in the Foreign Language Classroom." **Department of Romance Languages**, *Graduate University*, Fall 1999.

"Foreign Language Testing: How to Make 'Good' Tests." **Department of Romance Languages**, *Graduate University*, Fall 1999.

"Writing your dissertation: thoughts on the Ph.D. process." **Foreign Language Acquisition Discussion Group**, *Graduate University*, November 1998.

"Washing the faces: the acquisition of possessor raising in L2 Spanish." **The Conference on Generative Approaches to Second Language Acquisition**, *University of Pittsburgh*, PA, September 1998 (Juana Montoya-Pérez, Estrella Malaga-Cortazar and Seana O'Brien).

ACADEMIC SERVICE

Graduate University

Graduate Student Representative, *Search Committee for Professor of Spanish Applied Linguistics*, Department of Romance Languages, September 2000 – present

Secretary and Founding Member, *Romance Language Graduate Student Organization*, Fall 1999 – Spring 2000; **President**, Spring 2000 – present

Founding Member, *Language Acquisition Graduate Organization*, Fall 1999 – Spring 2000; **President**, Spring 2000 – present

Advisor, *Spanish Club*, Fall 1999 – present

Student Representative, *Graduate Committee*, Department of Romance Languages, Fall 1998 – Spring 2000

Member, *Basic Language Advisory Committee*, Fall 1998 – Spring 1999

Reviewer, *ALPHA Journal*, Department of Romance Languages, 1998 – 1999

East Coast University

Member, *Graduate Students' Library Committee*, Department of Romance Languages, Fall 1996 – Spring 1997

Member, *Graduate Student Organization*, Department of Romance Languages, Fall 1995 – Spring 1997

PROFESSIONAL AFFILIATIONS

Member, *Modern Language Association*, 1999 – present
Member, *American Council on the Teaching of Foreign Languages*, 2000 – present
Member, *American Association of Teachers of Spanish and Portuguese*, 1999 – present

REFERENCES

Conchita Alvarez de Moya
Director, Language Studies Program
School of Advanced International Studies
1619 Massachusetts Avenue, NW
Washington DC Zip
(555) 334-8896
e-mail: conchita_alvarez_de_moya@yahoo.com

Robert Alfrith
Professor, Department of Romance Languages
Graduate University
109 Scintilla Building
University Town, State Zip
(555) 864-3277
e-mail: rxa7@univ.edu

Sanford Pallan
Head, Department of Romance Languages
Graduate University
354 Furness Building
University Town, State Zip
(555) 864-3049
e-mail: spallan@univ.edu

Juana Montoya-Pérez
Associate Professor, Department of Romance Languages
Canadian University
City, Province, Code
CANADA
(555) 861-4857
e-mail: jmperez@canaduniv.ca

Graduate University Letterhead

Search REN   October 17, 2000
Flagship State University
Department of English
New England City, State, Zip

Dear Search Committee Members:

I wish to apply for the Assistant Professorship in Shakespeare/Renaissance literature, which you advertised in the online edition of the *MLA Job Information List*. On December 4, I will defend my dissertation—*Sport, Literature, and Politics in the English Renaissance*—to complete the requirements for my Ph.D. in Renaissance literature at Graduate University. I will receive my degree on time in May of 2001 and believe I am well qualified for the position you describe.

My dissertation argues that sport mediated the poles of excess and control in the Early Modern imagination. Despite contemporary polemical and even modern scholarly representations of sport as disorderly or carnivalesque phenomena, sport also figured at the center of Early Modern conceptions of order. In fact, many of the greatest contemporary prose writers—Elyot, Ascham, and Mulcaster, among others—contended that sport was vital to the health of the nation. In the opening chapter, I demonstrate the influence of Galen and other authorities on Early Modern proponents of sport, who claimed that sport was physiologically beneficial to the practitioner, militarily beneficial to the commonwealth, and socially beneficial to the maintenance of the reigning class system. Over the next five chapters, I explore the manner in which major Renaissance authors—including Shakespeare, Jonson, Drayton, Walton, and Milton—and a host of minor ones employed sporting imagery, metaphor, and allegory to defend or critique the social order that sport was believed to uphold. In its broad coverage of works published between Elyot's *Governor* in 1531 and Milton's *Samson Agonistes* in 1671, the dissertation considers the significance of sport in texts ranging from prose conduct manuals and sabbatarian pamphlets to drama, lyric poetry, and pastoral. Much of my dissertation has already been accepted for publication. An early version of Chapter One, "The 'Two Guises of Game': Anti-Play Polemics in Renaissance Prose" will appear in a forthcoming volume of *Prose Studies*. Part of the final chapter, "John Milton and the Poetics of Restoration Sport," has been tentatively accepted by *SEL*, and the second chapter has been revised and resubmitted to *Renaissance Quarterly*. As I prepare the manuscript for book publication, I plan to add a chapter exploring how Early Modern gender relations were influenced by the developing science we now call "exercise physiology."

By graduation, I will have taught 20 sections of 6 different courses at Graduate University, mainly in our highly regarded Rhetoric and Composition program. In freshman and upper-level composition courses, I have capitalized on the small-classroom environment to emphasize critical reasoning and argument through a student-centered, dialogic approach. Due to my success in the program, the department has granted me the freedom to design and implement several of my own courses within the existing system. These advanced rhetoric courses, such as "Relativism and Absolutism" and "The Problem of Historical Interpretation," have helped students to become more critical readers and more articulate contributors to extremely complex discourses.

As a teacher in the Literature program, I have worked to bring the same focus on critical pedagogy into courses that often enroll more than sixty students. In Introduction to Shakespeare, for example, I highlight the concept of "textual indeterminacy" as a means of encouraging students to be more active and confident readers. This approach helps them to deconstruct the intimidating myth of Shakespeare as the conveyor of an eternal body of knowledge and frees them to interpret each play we study. In British Literature Survey to 1798, two students are required at the beginning of each class to present opposing arguments on a controversial aspect of the text due that day, and their arguments form the foundation from which each class conversation emerges. When combined with small group work, detailed feedback on written work, and frequent office conferences, such methods help to create the sort of small-class atmosphere that allows students to be more active learners.

Last spring, I received Graduate University's most prestigious award for graduate instructors—the Teaching Assistant Award for Outstanding Teaching—along with only four other graduate assistants in the university. Based on the courses I have taught, my average "Quality of Instructor" ranking is a 6.27 on a 7.0 scale, and my highest scores (6.83 in Shakespeare, 6.65 in Freshman Composition, and 6.55 in the Literature survey) have well exceeded departmental averages. Next semester, I will become the first graduate instructor to teach a 400-level Shakespeare course. My serious commitment to teaching is also reflected in the various teaching-related projects I've undertaken, which include publishing a short piece in *Shakespeare and the Classroom*, chairing a conference session entitled "Teaching Shakespeare and Film," and participating in a teaching workshop at last year's Shakespeare Association Conference.

Beyond the dissertation and the classroom, I have pursued numerous other professional interests. In 1996, I earned a research grant from the Folger Shakespeare Library to participate in a seminar taught by the president of the Shakespeare Institute, Peter Holland, on the growing field of Shakespeare and film. More recently, I was awarded a Mellon Foundation grant to attend a four-week seminar focused on the question of traditional versus revisionist criticism in Early Modern studies. I have also taken on several leadership roles at the university. Last year, I was elected president of the English Graduate Organization, an honor that afforded me the opportunity to represent more than 120 colleagues. My experiences as president, and my role as the departmental delegate in the university's Graduate Student Association, have taught me the significant value of departmental service.

I would like to bring my commitment to service, research, and teaching to the Department of English at New England Flagship State University. Enclosed you will find my curriculum vitae, dissertation abstract, and a writing sample. I have requested that Graduate University forward you a copy of my dossier. I can also supply a teaching portfolio at your request. Please contact me at (555) 236-1847 or jxc49@univ.edu if you would like to arrange an interview at the MLA Convention in December. Thank you for your consideration.

Sincerely,

Jorge Colón

Enclosures

Graduate University Letterhead

October 12, 2000

Dr. Jeffrey Smart, Chair
Box 222
Department of English
Southern University
Town, State ZIP

Dear Dr. Smart:

I am writing to apply for the position of Assistant Professor of English in Composition and Rhetoric advertised in the September *MLA Job Information List*. My graduate training--through research as well as extensive administrative and teaching experience--has prepared me well to contribute to a program, such as Southern University's, that is devoted to both teaching and research.

My dissertation, *Women Teach the Soldiers: Volunteer Writing Instructors in the World War I Era*, combines my interests in composition theory, critical pedagogy, literacy studies, and feminist historiography. In it, I study the pedagogical methods of a large cadre of American women who volunteered to teach writing to illiterate American soldiers during the late 1910's. I have drafted three full chapters and an introduction. With the assistance of a year-long dissertation fellowship from the Spencer Foundation, I foresee no difficulty completing the remaining substantive chapter and conclusion in time to defend the dissertation in May of 2001. Please see the enclosed dissertation and research summary for further information about the project.

As the enclosed research agenda and statement of teaching philosophy suggest, my research and my pedagogy inform one another. In addition to the Business Writing course I describe in my statement of teaching philosophy, my extensive classroom experience has prepared me to teach a variety of both lower- and upper-division courses in composition and rhetoric, including Introductory and Advanced Composition and interdisciplinary courses such as Writing in the Social Sciences. Thanks to the pedagogical commitments of the programs at Graduate University and Central State University, I have had numerous opportunities to design my own courses, focusing on themes related to communication, citizenship, and higher education. Themes of courses I have designed include "American Rhetoric of Opportunity," "The Rhetoric of Community," and "Exploring Literacy and Learning Across the Disciplines." Prior to receiving the Spencer Dissertation Fellowship, I designed courses in Advanced Expository Writing and Honors Composition, both with a focus on mass media in American culture and politics. I look forward to the possibility of teaching this material as part of Southern University's program.

My graduate training has also familiarized me with administrative responsibilities in a composition program. As Composition Assistant in the program at Graduate University, I worked with our Director of Composition to mentor teaching assistants through their introductory training sessions and through the "Brown Bag Lunch" series of discussions addressing the pedagogical concerns of both new and experienced teachers. Topics around which I organized these discussions included service learning, computers and composition pedagogy, and classroom diversity. This position also provided me with the opportunity to plan several "Rhetoric Reading Group" meetings, which brought together faculty and graduate students to discuss recent scholarship in composition and rhetoric. Additionally, as Assistant Director of the Conference on Composition and Pedagogy, I helped plan and organize a productive gathering of scholars from various institutions. Most recently, as Web Coordinator for Graduate University's Writing Lab, I have acquired web-authoring skills and become familiar with the complex issues involved in establishing a pedagogically effective presence on the World Wide Web. During the remainder of my time as Web Coordinator, I will be working with the Director of the Lab to enhance the Lab's presence within the Graduate University web site and to develop on-line tutoring venues.

My publications also reflect my interest in rhetorical education, particularly as that education informs democratic citizenship and political discourse. My article, "The Heroine as Teacher in Early 19th-Century American Literature," explores the relationship between nineteenth-century rhetorical education (based largely on the work of Hugh Blair and George Campbell) and the construction of female teachers of English in nineteenth-century novels. Similarly, "Bakhtin and Composition Instruction among Volunteer Literacy Teachers, 1910" uses a Bakhtinian framework to explore the presence of centripetal (dominant) and centrifugal (subversive) discourses in the work of women literacy teachers early in the twentieth century. While these women worked to empower recent immigrants, they simultaneously worked to ensure that those immigrants were steeped in the discourses of American patriotism. Even my study of archival research involves my concerns with pedagogy and research. "Using Archives, Saving the Past" explores the criteria most commonly used by collecting facilities in determining what material to preserve and argues that much rich material relating to the history of rhetorical education is at risk given those criteria. I anticipate that my future publications will continue to connect teaching and research.

My dossier, containing letters of recommendation, will be sent to you under separate cover from Graduate University's Career Center. I would welcome the opportunity to meet with you at MLA to discuss how I can contribute to your program. Please contact me at (555) 235-4487 or petersonj@univ.edu should you require further information or materials.

Sincerely,

Julie C. Peterson
encl.

Graduate University Letterhead

Charles Garrett
Director, Communication Program
Southern State University
123 University Street
Big City, State Zip

Dear Professor Garrett:

Please accept my application for the Assistant Professor position in Communication that your department advertised in the October, 2002 CRTNet. I believe that my combination of administrative experience and demonstrated scholarly potential make me a serious candidate for this position. Enclosed you will find one copy each of my curriculum vitae, my article from last year in *Critical Studies in Media Communication*, and my previous article from *Argumentation and Advocacy*. I have also enclosed one copy of the student evaluations of my teaching. Kenneth Malcom, Eva Moore, and Redmond Innis are sending letters of recommendation separately.

I have taught courses in public speaking, rhetorical theory, argumentation, legal argument, small group communication, and professional communication, as well as a host of guest lectures and special topics related to contemporary rhetorical theory and rhetorical criticism. During my graduate studies I not only taught public speaking mass lectures and labs, but I also completed an internship in directing the basic course. In addition, I gained significant administrative experience during my time at Graduate University by creating a Center for Public Speaking and Civic Engagement, teaching in a grant-funded joint project with the Graduate University Marketing Department, and directing the Graduate University Debate Team.

My scholarship focuses on the politics and ethics of rhetoric. My dissertation was a genealogy of twentieth-century American rhetorical studies, with special attention to the connections between disciplinary politics, communication ethics, and rhetorical theory. The dissertation was motivated by a desire to explore how some of the disciplinary memory that serves to maintain the boundaries of rhetorical studies can be unsettled by the archives of the discipline's own past. By working through the discipline's own history, a space opens for seeing the contemporary interrogations of humanism and rationalism as already integral elements of rhetorical studies, rather than being alien forces that threaten the "core" of the discipline. This project is completed and I will defend in February 2003.

My professional goals are to continue my work on the ethics and politics of contemporary rhetoric in an environment that balances significant research with opportunities to work closely with undergraduate and graduate students who share an interest in rhetorical studies. In addition to revising my dissertation for publication by a university press, I am currently also working on articles related to Jean-Luc Nancy's politics of communication and community, the implications of reductionist fallacies in legal arguments from definition, and the relationship between ethics, justice, and communication in Emmanuel Levinas's writings.

The Communication Program at Southern State University and my interests in rhetorical theory and argumentation seem a very complementary match. The strengths both of the English Department's rhetoric faculty and the Speech Communication program's faculty provide both cohorts and mentors for future work. Likewise, I believe that I can contribute to the program at Southern State by bringing my experience in administration and my strengths in contemporary rhetorical theory, argumentation, and communication ethics, along with my commitment to a caring and generous relationship with students and colleagues.

Please contact me if you should need any additional materials or have any questions regarding this application. I will be attending the National Communication Association Convention in November and would welcome an opportunity to learn more about this position. The best times to reach me at home are Mondays through Fridays from 5:00 PM to 10:00 PM, any time on the weekends, or in my office on Mondays and Wednesdays from 11:00 AM to 3:00 PM.

Sincerely,

Peter Emmett
Communication Arts
Graduate University
123 Dustie Building
University Town, State Zip

p.emmett@univ.edu

555-862-5435 (office)
555-243-5223 (home)
555-397-5557 (cellular)

Graduate University Letterhead

October 12, 2002

Dr. Devin Smythe
Chair, History Search Committee
Regional State University
Box 29384
President City, State Zip

Dear Dr. Smythe:

Please accept this letter as my application for your advertised position of an assistant professor of American history. I completed my dissertation in the summer of 2002 under the direction of Professor Neville Marcus, and graduated from Graduate University in August. I have published two articles and organized a session for the American Historical Association that reflect my focus on a broadly conceived political history. Over the last six years I have designed and taught four different courses, including an upper level Civil War and Reconstruction class, at Regional Campus and Nearby College.

I am ready and willing to teach many different courses. I have already taught both halves of the United States survey, the first half of the Western Civilization survey, and upper-level courses on the Civil War Era. I have experience teaching graduate students, as there are several graduate students taking my Civil War Era course at Branch Campus this semester. In addition to the several courses I have already taught, I can offer courses on slavery, ante-bellum America, the Gilded Age, and United States political, intellectual or military history at both the lower- and upper-division levels. Since much of my dissertation deals with the political responses to economic development during the nineteenth century, I discuss economic history extensively in my courses and would enjoy teaching an economic history course. I am also able to offer some less conventional courses. For example, extensive work in American slavery and slavery in ancient Greece and Rome, both fields in which I took comprehensive exams, enables me to teach classes on slavery and freedom encompassing not only the modern Atlantic world, but also the ancient world. I look forward to continuing to develop classes to reflect the needs of the department, the interests of students, and my current research.

I have begun developing a teaching philosophy during the last six years while designing and running my own courses. My students grapple with questions such as the relationship between slavery and freedom in America, or the changing definitions of citizenship in the twentieth century, for it is important that students see historical events as parts of a larger pattern if the class is to leave a lasting impression. I tell students at the beginning of each semester that if I am successful as a teacher they will view history not as a collection of facts, but as a story, with interconnecting characters, plots, and themes. I have also evolved a teaching style that mixes lecture with discussion, for it is vital to engage students to create an active learning environment. In every class I have students participate in discussions, debates, or role-playing. Students also read works of leading scholars and primary documents. To increase students' writing ability and demonstrate the relevance of history to their lives outside of class, I give students extra-credit if they publish a letter to the editor that uses historical examples from class to discuss a current issue. Students have published letters in the *College Daily* using slavery to enlighten the debate on campus relations and the Era of Good Feelings to call for non-partisanship after the World Trade Center attacks. Under the headline "Inspiration from history," *The Local Newspaper* published the letter of another student, who compared the current fight against terrorism to the American Revolution. Every semester I push myself to continue to grow as a teacher, experimenting with new material and methods.

While a dedicated teacher, I am also committed to scholarship. My dissertation, "The Liberal Republican Movement: Reformers and Political Parties in Civil War Era Political Culture," argues that the failure of the Liberal Republican movement in 1872 marked the end of Civil War Era political culture and the beginning of Gilded Age political culture. I use the term "political culture" because "politics" often refers only to elections and parties, while I am also concerned with questions such as how people conceived of political parties, the role of reform organizations outside of party politics, and the importance of ideology in shaping political actions. During the Civil War Era the Liberal Republicans participated in a political culture in which parties were viewed as temporary organizations and classical republican ideology dominated. Daniel T. Rodgers has demonstrated the complexity of republicanism as a concept, and in analyzing the Liberal Republicans I focus on three major components of republicanism: public virtue, independent citizenship, and vigilance against tyranny. The Liberal Republicans expected that the fragility of political parties and their republican ideology would allow them either to take control of the Republican party or start a new party in 1872.

The Liberal Republican movement, however, coincided with a transition from Civil War Era to Gilded Age political culture, which was to be dominated by a rigid two-party system and classical liberalism. The failure of the Liberal Republicans to perceive the changing political culture caused them to miscalculate their political opportunities. Unsure of the political environment, the Liberal Republicans focused their campaign on President Ulysses S. Grant and Reconstruction, tarnishing the reputation of both for generations. My interpretation of the Liberal Republican movement challenges the paradigms of the New Political History, which have reigned since the 1960s, such as the existence of five distinct, relatively static, party periods and the limited importance of ideology. It also engages the historiographical discussion of when the dominance of republican ideology ended in America, arguing that liberalism replaced republicanism in the early 1870s.

I have talked with Ronald C. Haraway, Social Sciences Editor of the Prestige University Press, several times in the last year about publishing my dissertation and he has asked to see an abstract. With the assistance of Professor Marcus and Professor Hector Mitchell, who served on my dissertation committee, I plan to submit a manuscript by September 1, 2003. I will present some of my findings at a session I organized for the 2003 American Historical Association Conference entitled "New Perspectives on the New Political History: Periodicity vs. Plasticity," in which Mark Augustine and Pamela Baxter have agreed to serve, respectively, as the chair and commentator. My paper is entitled "'A bombshell to blow up both the parties': Third Party Movements in the Early Gilded Age."

I have already published articles on nineteenth-century political culture outside the scope of my dissertation. While the Republican party's constitutional conservatism limited the possibilities of Reconstruction, I assert in *Civil War History* that the Chicago Fire of 1871 demonstrates that the Republican party would abandon its conservatism in some instances. In an article in *The Historian* I argue that after decades of ambivalence toward their Revolutionary heritage, white South Carolinians embraced the tradition of the American Revolution to justify their violence against African-Americans and the federal government in 1876.

I am already doing preliminary work on my next project, a history of the Union Army during Reconstruction. I will use the army as a lens to understand how Reconstruction was actually implemented, what motivated the soldiers who were occupying the South, and the meaning of Reconstruction for the North. The army was the fulcrum of Reconstruction, implementing the political decisions and dealing directly with the freed people. In addition, the political nature of army officers led many to create their own policies. I have made a preliminary search through the numerous collections of army officers' papers at the West Point archives and have identified many other collections at the United States Army War College in Carlisle, the Library of Congress and the Huntington Library. Other important sources for the project include the *Army and Navy Journal* and the Freedmen Papers at the National Archives.

I am attending both the Southern Historical Association meeting at Baltimore in November 2002 and the American Historical Association meeting at Chicago in January 2003 and would be happy to meet for an interview. Please let me know if you would like to see a writing sample, transcripts, or any other information. I can be reached at 555-234-2936. Thank you for your consideration.

Sincerely yours,

William M. Grosvenor

Graduate University Letterhead

January 9, 2003

Luke Wright, Chair
Southern University
Department of Communication
200 Communications Bldg
City, State, ZIP

Dear Professor Wright:

I write to apply for the position of Assistant Professor of Rhetoric advertised in the flyer you distributed at the NCA meeting in Miami last November. I believe I can effectively meet the requirements set forth in that description.

By virtue of my master and doctoral programs at Graduate University (Ph.D. completed May 2002), I am well versed in the theory and history of rhetoric. By virtue of my vocations and avocations I am also practiced in photography, multi-media, and radio. Finally, by virtue of the extensive pedagogical training provided by Graduate University's English Department (2002–03), I have a foundation in rhetoric and composition as well as substantial experience in the classroom. The result is that I now approach questions of rhetorical theory with a broad interdisciplinarity and with a rich understanding of form. And I am learning how to present these questions in meaningful ways, and media, to my students.

Even my dissertation on Plato is inflected by questions of media. When I began my research, Plato's philosophy was interpreted as the product of the transition from orality to literacy in ancient Greece. While I still acknowledge this as a factor, I think the more important contexts for Plato's thought are the dramatic historical events and evolving genres of his time. Thus my dissertation is an attempt to re-embed Plato's philosopher, Socrates, in the Athens of Thucydides' *Peloponnesian War* and Xenophon's *Hellenica*, the two works which together chronicle the final rise and fall of the Athenian empire. Although closely argued, *Plato and the Peloponnesian War* is a wide-ranging work that examines the histories of Thucydides and Xenophon, the Socratic writings of Xenophon and Plato, the comedies of Aristophanes, and the historical anecdotes of Aelian, Aulus Gellius, Apuleius, Athenaeus, Diogenes Laertius, and Plutarch. It is, in short, an exhaustive attempt to reconstruct Plato's engagement with the significant texts and events of his time, a dialogue about democracy and empire, markets and meaning, war and justice.

Despite its density of classical detail, I believe this project has broader, theoretical implications for questions of public memory, political discourse, and the interrelationships among rhetoric, philosophy, and history as disciplined discourses. Thus I foresee the possibility, even probability, of undertaking similar investigations of other eras—late antiquity, the birth of modernity, and the late 19th century and post–WWII Americas—using the techniques of thick, interdisciplinary cultural analysis I have developed in working on ancient Athens. These later projects will rely in no small measure on the "second" education I received in my roles as bookseller and host/producer of a radio book "revue."

For example, through my radio program (see *Libri* lists) I was able to interview figures whose work has articulated the historical background and political implications of race and gender, figures such as Houston Baker, Kathleen Barry, Katie Cannon, Michael Eric Dyson, Henry Giroux, Cheryl Glenn, Peter Hinks, Jacqueline Jones, Gerda Lerner, Manning Marable, Wilson Moses, Mary Beth Norton, Martha

Nussbaum, Lorraine Roses, Londa Schiebinger, Geneva Smitherman, Hortense Spillers, Sterling Stuckey, Nancy Tomes, James Washington, Margaret Wertheim, Virginia Valian, and Margaret Yalom.

These and many other conversations have provided me with a much broader understanding of history and with a richer appreciation for the praxis of scholarship. Thus, I can easily sketch out, as one possible extension of my research on ancient rhetoric, a study of David Walker's use of ancient history in his *Appeal to the Colored Citizens of the World*, a work not usually considered when historians or political scientists discuss the classical influences on revolutionary America. And in the ethics courses I have taught (and am teaching) for philosophy, through ancient sources such as Aristophanes' *Lysistrata* and *Assemblywomen* as well as modern theorists such as Carol Gilligan and Sara Ruddick, I have introduced gender as an important component of our historical and theoretical discussions.

In a similar manner, it was through my bookstore that I was introduced to the work of Edward Tufte, the statistician whose self-published books (*Visual Display of Quantitative Information*, *Envisioning Information*, and *Visual Explanations*) have revolutionized graphic design. After selling his books for many years, I was finally moved, two years ago, to attend one of his seminars in Washington. Since then, I have incorporated his principles, especially his "small and/or scaled multiples," into a lesson on "visual suasions," part of a guidebook to critical reasoning I have just completed for Graduate University's World Campus.

And it was through bookstore conversations, radio interviews, and informal seminars that I was able to observe Ivan Illich's interrogations of our contemporary verities. Annual visitors to Graduate University during the late 80s and early 90s, Illich and his colleagues have shaped my perception of technology, especially technologies of visualization, in ways I am still trying to articulate for myself. I would want to incorporate some portion of their work (e.g. Ivan Illich's *In the Vineyard of the Text*, Barbara Duden's *Disembodying Women*, and/or Wolfgang Sach's *Planet Dialectics*) into any course I might teach on visual rhetoric; I'd want my students to "see" the connective tissues of our seeing.

Making connections was my hallmark as a bookseller, my great pleasure as an interviewer, and my method as a scholar; it is also now what I try to do in the classroom. But connection is not always comfort. One senior, writing afterwards about an introduction to ethics that used readings from Gorgias, Thucydides, Aristophanes, and Plato to question how we rationalize and gender power (this while America waged war in Iraq and warriored Jessica Lynch at home), described our semester-long discussion as one of the most intellectually *and emotionally* challenging courses she had ever taken.

I would like to bring the perspectives and skills learned from both my first and second educations to the role and responsibilities of Assistant Professor of Rhetoric at Southern University. Enclosed you will find my curriculum vitae, an addendum listing selected authors I have interviewed, and a brief description of my projected research program. At your request, I can also instruct our placement office to forward a copy of my dossier, which includes letters of recommendation from the five references listed at the end of my vita. And if you would like to arrange an interview, you can contact me at 555-232-2039 (daytime), or 555-962-3918 (evenings or to leave a message on my answering machine), or mib213@univ.edu. I thank you for considering my application.

Sincerely,

Michael Bensen

Graduate University Letterhead

3 November 1999

Professor Ben Liu
Medieval Search Committee
Western State University
333 Oceanview Road
West Coast City, State Zip

Dear Professor Liu,

I would like to present my credentials for your Assistant Professorship of Medieval Literature. As a Ph.D. candidate in Comparative Literature at Graduate University, I have specialized in English and continental medieval literature. I am scheduled to defend my dissertation in February 2000 and will graduate in May.

My interests in medieval literature are interdisciplinary, focusing on connections between history, culture, and literature. Examining selected courtly texts, my dissertation, *Political Desire in Medieval Literature*, argues for a revised understanding of conventional love language and rhetorical constructions of desire. Specifically, I explore how works ranging from the *Roman de la Rose* to Chaucer's *Troilus and Criseyde* react to social division and factional politics that demand that the subject take responsibility for himself both as a member of a larger group and as an individual. By focusing on two separate cultural moments, the last few decades of the thirteenth century in Florence and the last few decades of the fourteenth century in London, I chart how four texts respond suggestively to competing discourses of desire found in the *Rose* as well as respond to each other. For a more detailed description of my work, please see the enclosed dissertation abstract.

This summer I plan on revising my dissertation as a book and beginning the process of finding an academic publisher. Currently I am trying to find a home for a collection of essays on desire that developed out of a ten-person seminar I organized and led at last year's ACLA conference. I also look forward to continuing work on a long-term project on food, literature, and culture, which is beginning to take shape. For that project, I have found a producer and co-writer and recently won a Woodrow Wilson Practicum Grant to write a script treatment and television pilot.

Along with my investment in scholarly research and writing comes a commitment to teaching. I approach the classroom with enthusiasm and I remain inspired by my work as a teacher. Beyond the scope of the courses I have already taught, I believe the interdisciplinary nature of my coursework and research has prepared me to teach a wide variety of courses at Western State University. I welcome the opportunity to teach early-period literature surveys, Chaucer, and composition. I have taught diverse courses ranging from Arthurian Literature to World Mythologies, and I would be delighted to teach a course like LTWR 300, 410, or even 609 should the opportunity arise. Teaching in the Comparative Literature and English Departments has allowed me to interact with students at all levels and to teach literature, culture, and composition courses to majors and non-majors in both large and small classroom settings.

My accomplishments in teaching were recognized most recently when I received a grant to revise undergraduate General Education offerings in the College of Liberal Arts, and three years ago, when I received the Graduate Assistant Teaching Award from the university. The grant allowed me to develop a multi-media classroom and course structure, and to incorporate web technology and collaborative learning into my pedagogical approach. I invite you to visit my active course website for a survey of Arthurian literature I'm currently teaching, at www.taylor.org/arthur, to see how I combine traditional classroom learning with computer capabilities like cyber chatrooms. Along with these multi-media skills, I have two and a half years of training in language and literature pedagogy and make invited teaching presentations for new teacher training classes. My experience in composition has emphasized argumentation and critical thinking skills in addition to writing across drafts, while my language and literature training has taught me the importance of creating a discussion-centered classroom environment. I would be happy to forward the teaching portfolio I have compiled.

In addition to my teaching duties, I served as Editorial Assistant to the journal *Comparative Literature Review* for two years and recently returned to this position for the 1999-2000 academic year. I also just completed a two-year tenure on the American Comparative Literature Association's national advisory board. My strong record of academic service and teaching skills attest to my commitment to this profession and I look forward to joining a department where I can be a valued teacher and scholar.

I will be attending the MLA convention in Chicago and would be happy to discuss further my interest in this position. I enclose my curriculum vitae, dissertation abstract, and a writing sample. My dossier is being forwarded under separate cover by our Career Services office. Thank you for your consideration.

Sincerely,

Ivy Johnson Taylor

Graduate University Letterhead

Mercedes Alvarez, Chair
Spanish Linguistics Search
Department of Romance Languages and Literatures
Flagship State University
Town, State Zip

27 October 2000

Dear Dr. Alvarez:

Please consider this letter as my formal application for the position of Professor of SLA/Foreign Language Methodology recently posted in the MLA Job List.

I hold a B.S. degree from Southern University and an M.A. degree in Spanish literature from East Coast University. At present, I am a doctoral candidate in Spanish Applied Linguistics at Graduate University and will be graduating in August of 2001.

The opening at your university is of great interest to me because it coincides with my desire to work at an institution that boasts a strong commitment to both teaching and research. During my doctoral studies I have taken courses in various areas of second language acquisition, second language teaching methodology, and theoretical Spanish linguistics, in addition to teaching a variety of classes and participating actively in service to my department and the university. I am particularly well prepared in phonetics and phonological theory, syntactic theory, and multiple aspects of second language acquisition, and I would feel comfortable teaching courses in these areas, as well as a broad range of general language, culture, and linguistics courses.

My primary research interests are the acquisition of Spanish as a second language and theoretical phonetics and phonology. In my dissertation I combine these two areas by first examining the theoretical analyses that have been put forth to explain the system of Spanish stress computation, as the explanations previously proposed have not been entirely satisfactory. Previous accounts attempt to classify the system of stress assignment in Spanish – which syllable of a word receives spoken emphasis—by relying on complicated rules and idiosyncratic markings to explain the arbitrary nature of much of Spanish stress. I ultimately propose another account using Optimality Theory, a model that proposes that all languages contain a set of universal constraints with a particular ranking, dictating which structures are preferred and which are less preferred. In this way, grammaticality is defined in terms of optimization over these constraints. This approach – to language in general and to the Spanish stress system in particular—not only sheds light on the language itself but also invites new research into the process of how this particular aspect of language is learned or acquired. Thus, the second focus of my dissertation is the empirical investigation of the process of acquisition of Spanish stress patterns by native English speakers. My findings will provide insight into the process of learning language from an Optimality Theoretic perspective and will also hold implications for the foreign language classroom, as studies such as these help teachers determine which aspects of pronunciation need special attention. For example, we may determine that a certain constraint exists in English but not in Spanish, and that we must therefore develop exercises or practice for our students in order to make them aware of such differences in their process of learning Spanish. I have written four of seven projected chapters of my dissertation, and am currently incorporating the results of my pilot study into my final data collection design.

During my time at East Coast University and at Graduate University, I have had the opportunity to teach a variety of courses in basic language, conversation and composition. In addition, I have had experience teaching upper-division specialized courses, such as the phonology class I am teaching this semester, a course that is required of all majors and is also taught by tenure-track senior faculty. This assignment has provided me with valuable experience in the designing and teaching of this type of course. I also have extensive experience in supervising basic language courses, a task whose duties prepare me well for future responsibilities such as syllabus design, materials development and T.A. coordination, training and evaluation. My ongoing role as a teacher will benefit from my expertise in designing and implementing new materials and incorporating technology and multimedia resources in the foreign language classroom. I have a genuine commitment to my students, which has enabled me to develop my own philosophy of foreign language teaching, and has won me the recognition of an Outstanding Graduate Teaching Assistant Award. In addition, my students have rewarded me for the past seven years with consistently above-average course evaluations.

I am also involved in various organizations in service to my department and to the university. I have helped establish two new graduate organizations, one for students in my department and another for students throughout the university who are interested in issues of language acquisition. Both organizations serve to unite students and to provide a forum for their concerns to be heard and effectively addressed. I currently serve as president-elect of both of these organizations. In addition, I have served as advisor for the undergraduate Spanish Club for the past two years, helping to organize and coordinate activities such as our bi-weekly conversation hours and cultural trips. This rewarding experience has allowed me to be closely involved with the undergraduate students and to help them further their knowledge of the Spanish language and of Spanish and Hispanic cultures.

Enclosed please find a copy of my *curriculum vitae*. Letters of recommendation and transcripts will be forwarded to you separately. If you have any questions or would like any additional information or materials, please feel free to contact me. I can be reached by calling or leaving a message at (555) 238-4993 at any time, and I can also always be contacted via e-mail (GailTuck@univ.edu). I will be available for an interview at the MLA conference on December 28, 29, and 30.

I look forward to hearing from you in the near future.

Sincerely,

Gail Tuckerman

HELEN DEER

Dissertation Abstract

"Representing Britishness": Landscape, Identity and Geography in the Cold War Era

My dissertation investigates how the production and discussion of landscape art in Britain during the period 1951-1956 can be related to the larger issue of nationalism during the Cold War era. This five-year duration represented a transitional period in British social and political history; a term announced by the post-war civic optimism of the Festival of Britain and concluded by the governmental instability resulting from the Suez Crisis. Throughout the Second World War, and immediately afterwards, the Neo-Romantic landscape art of artists such as John Minton, Paul Nash, and John Piper was celebrated as an established symbol of Britishness, while the national topography itself was viewed nostalgically as the hallowed ground of Shakespeare's "sceptre'd isle." By the middle of the 1950s, however, atomic testing had raised doubts as to even the probability of a future, and the old narratives of a timeless and inviolable land were shaken in a very physical sense. At the same time, the influence of American art and culture, the expanding global media and the new frontiers of science opened up fresh possibilities that challenged the isolationist preservation of an indigenous culture.

The arguments for considering art made in Britain as part of an international achievement, rather than the products of national genius, are even more applicable in our own times, yet even today British critics, curators and historians of British art still insist on essentializing national identity, frequently to locate it in landscape art. Rather than presuming landscape art to bear the indexical traces of an innate national character, my thesis approaches the notion of Britishness problematically to consider the ways in which, as cultural artifacts, paintings contribute not only to the discourse of collective identity but may also act in the perpetuation of social divisions of race and class. The Marxist critic John Berger has described landscape as "a curtain" behind which the conflicts and aspirations of its inhabitants take place. It is the aim of my dissertation to draw back those screens that were frequently constructed to serve the aims of nostalgia and propaganda, to reveal representations of landscape in the 1950s to be sites of anxiety, rather than security, concerning national, political and regional identity.

Madeleine Maxwell: Dissertation Description
The Rhetorical Construction of Pregnant Behavior in American Discourse

Value of Research Specialization

Science has become an increasingly important part of the daily life of most Americans. Because of this, we require critical and rhetorical accounts of the ways science and culture interact. Such accounts will allow us to respond and intervene in ways that recognize the importance of science while simultaneously challenging the institutionalized power inequities of American society. Rhetorics of health and medicine provide a little-examined site for rhetorical analyses while simultaneously addressing these social issues.

Argument of Dissertation

The rhetoric of prevention, incarceration and blame that surrounds maternal prenatal drinking, smoking and drug use is generated in diverse settings, but through one major set of assumptions: those of the medical profession. The extension of these assumptions into popular discourse and the legal arena through news reports, disability narratives, and medical intervention simultaneously infantilizes and demonizes pregnant women as well as dehumanizes their (potentially) disabled infants. Moreover, these assumptions, which frequently emphasize individual choice and responsibility, obscure any social or structural component to either behavior or health. An effective social response to the problem of maternal behavior would begin by mutually targeting individual women, familial and community structures, and structures of inequality.

Contribution of Dissertation

The rhetoric of science traditionally focuses on internal descriptions of science and scientific practices. By combining this with the critical analyses of feminist science studies, which focus on external accounts of science, I am able to
- expand the rhetoric of science to examine how science and scientific ideas move between the laboratory and the wider social sphere;
- expand the rhetoric of science to examine how science and society are mutually constitutive;
- demonstrate the ways rhetorical analysis of science can intervene in social issues;
- show how rhetoric of science can engage critically and usefully with critical traditions rooted in subjectivity, such as feminist theory and disability studies.

Teaching Applications

This research grounds my teaching in rhetoric and technical writing by offering a model of rhetorical analysis that allows the reader/writer to intervene and critique as well as describe. This allows me to engage my students through making rhetoric and rhetorical analysis relevant to their lives and their projects.

Relevance to Future Research

Focusing on the networks in which science and scientific ideas are embedded and to which they contribute gives me a range of both material and publication options. Future projects include an examination of the recurrent and resurgent importance of science as a theme in popular culture and a critical reexamination of fantasy literature and academic response to it through the lens of alternative sciences.

Dissertation and Research Summary: **Jorge Colón**
Sport, Literature, and Politics in the English Renaissance

Value of Research Specialization	In the Early Modern period, sport was believed to be a highly significant phenomenon: physiologically beneficial to the individual practitioner, vital to the preparedness of the military, and necessary to the maintenance of the traditional class hierarchy. Sport's significance in the period is perhaps best registered by its literal and metaphorical centrality in numerous works of literature, including Shakespeare's *Henry VI*, Walton's *Compleat Angler*, and Milton's *Samson Agonistes*, among others. By reconstructing a cultural history of sport and investigating representations of it in contemporary prose, poetry, and drama, I demonstrate its pivotal position in the interlocking spheres of Early Modern science, politics, and art.
Argument of Dissertation	Early Modern scholars have long assumed sport to be synonymous with holiday mirth, drinking, and other such carnivalesque activities. I argue instead that sport mediated the poles of excess and order in the Early Modern imagination. While Bakhtin's influential definition of carnival as a "temporary liberation from the established order" would appear to describe unruly sports such as wrestling, these sports were just as often praised for contributing to the physical, mental, and social stability of the English people. The unusual ability of sport to navigate the extremes of order and chaos, morality and sin, function and superfluity made it an extremely effective vehicle for social commentary in practically every written form available to the Early Modern author.
Contribution of Dissertation	My dissertation expands and changes our current understanding of sport in Early Modern culture and literature. In my research I • Recover a conception of sport as a functional phenomenon. • Challenge the dominant view that sport was primarily associated with carnivalesque or subversive activities. • Establish the manner in which authors commented on or attempted to subvert the status quo through the use of sporting imagery, metaphor, and allegory. • Clarify the need for a more thorough scholarly excavation of the many texts and contexts within which sport figures so prominently. • Suggest that our modern ambivalence about sport is the offspring of conflicting Early Modern conceptions of sports and pastimes.
Teaching Applications	The dissertation's wide coverage of culture and literature—between the publication of Elyot's *Governour* (1531) and Milton's *Samson* (1671)—has prepared me to teach both highly specialized courses on Early Modern culture and much broader surveys. My treatment of several major writers (including Shakespeare and Milton) and genres (prose, poetry, drama) insures a range of expertise in the classroom. In rhetoric and composition courses, my dissertation can be used to encourage students to think more critically about the social significance of phenomena often perceived to be apolitical or trivial.
Relevance to Future Research	I deliberately chose a dissertation topic that would provide a good deal of new material and a range of publication options. We currently lack a comprehensive study of sport in the period. My dissertation, once turned into a book, will begin to fill this gap in our scholarship. I also plan to produce a scholarly edition of a little-known manuscript in the Folger holdings, entitled *The Compleat Swimmer*. Finally, I have begun to research the influence of what we now call "exercise physiology" on Early Modern gender relations.

Chapter Breakdown: Jorge Colón
Sport, Literature, and Politics in the English Renaissance

Chapter 1	"The Legacy of the Anti-Sports Polemic" charts the sixteenth-century construction of sport as a disorderly phenomenon. Moving from an in-depth discussion of the traditionally functional role of sport in England—as described by humanist prose writers (Elyot, Ascham, Mulcaster, etc.)—the chapter considers how the convergence of various social, economic, and intellectual factors enhanced the persuasiveness of the godly, anti-sports polemic.
Chapter 2	"Sport, War, and Contest in Shakespeare's *Henry VI*" continues the first chapter's consideration of the factors that contributed to sport's demise, focusing on innovations in military science. Whereas sport had been justified since antiquity for preparing soldiers for war, its function waned with the military's gradual adaptation of firearms. As a result, sport was increasingly condemned as a superfluous phenomenon. In *Henry VI*, sport figures as a metaphor for war, also condemnable as a result of the shift from the politics of chivalric idealism to the "politics of reality." Throughout the trilogy, Shakespeare indicts warfare as mere sport for ambitious nobles.
Chapter 3	"The Literary Context of the *Book of Sports* Controversy" demonstrates the mutually constitutive relationship between literary and political commentaries on sport. Investigating closely several anti-court satires written in the 1610s—including *Eastward Ho* and *The Isle of Gulls*—the chapter elucidates the manner in which sport was used by dramatists to critique or defend the political policies of James I. The primary focus of the chapter, however, is on James's *Book of Sports* as a reaction to such dramatic commentaries. In short, James's defense of lawful pastimes is a deliberate attempt to counter his popular reputation as an unlawful king.
Chapter 4	"The Burden of the Present" explores a relatively unknown collection of poems entitled *Annalia Dubrensia*, which featured work by Jonson and Drayton, among others. The poems celebrated the Cotswold Games, an English version of the ancient Olympics. The origins of sport, like those of poetry, trace back to Pagan societies, of course. To the degree that poetic identity depended upon a successful imitation of a pre-Christian society, the godliness of the 1630s threatened poetry as well as sport. By collapsing poetic and athletic competition, the *Annalia* defends the lawfulness of poetry at the same time that it defends sports.
Chapter 5	The chapter argues that Walton's *Compleat Angler* is an indictment of the governmental proscription of communal recreations in the 1650s. The anti-sport legislation of the Interregnum is the culmination of the Early Modern reconstruction of sport as a disorderly phenomenon, the process that I begin to chart in the first chapter. In Walton's pastoral world, the orderliness of society and, to a degree, of Nature, revolves around the ability of sport to bring people together.
Chapter 6	"*Samson Agonistes* and the Politics of Restoration Sport," brings us full circle by considering the resurrection of sport by Charles II and, more specifically, Milton's treatment of sport as a phenomenon mediating the poles of functionality and superfluity during the Restoration. Milton expands the meaning of the term "sport," which only implied "jest" in the *Judges* version of Samson's trials, to include athletic games and pastimes; he also employs the epithet "Agonistes"—a term used originally to describe ancient athletic contests—to characterize his protagonist. The deliberate contrast between Samson's functional athleticism, which serves both God and nation, and the Philistines' riotous sport at the Temple of Dagon allegorizes the massive gulf between the defenders of the good old cause and the corrupt new regime.

A Statement of Teaching Philosophy: Lana Lasera

"Great teachers give us a sense not only of who they are, but more important, of who we are, and who we might become."
—Dr. Thomas E. Cronin, A Celebration of Excellence in Teaching

I believe that language studies assist students in better understanding themselves and their world-view; they promote cultural awareness, offer differing perspectives, and encourage intellectual activity. As a language teacher, I aim to prepare students to become critical learners and thinkers, to be excellent communicators in a variety of contexts, and to consider ideas other than their own. In the French conversation and reading course that I currently teach, students engage in a variety of activities that demonstrate these values. In studying issues related to technology, relationships and families, and education, students frequently prepare questionnaires that are used in comparing and contrasting ideas related to a specific topic; they also undertake collective projects, such as debates and news reports, based on these topics. Guest speakers, who hold differing viewpoints, are invited to participate in class discussions; these exchanges serve as a forum to compare and contrast ideas, perspectives, and cultural differences. At the end of September, I initiated a *partenaires de conversation* project to enhance opportunities for communication both in and out of class. Twice a week, partners spend 10-15 minutes of class time in self-directed discussion (based on thematic questions); students are also required to schedule one 30 minute out-of-class meeting. As a result of this project, students have developed confidence in their speaking skills and in their capacity to engage in meaningful conversation with others. Once a week students meet in a computer-equipped classroom where they participate in real-time discussions using a synchronous conferencing client. In the online environment, tasks are reading-based (taken from current articles found in magazines, books, newspapers, and the Internet), and require that students think critically about issues in the thematic unit. During the 50-minute chat sessions, I work individually with 4 to 6 students. This arrangement allows time for discussion of issues related to pronunciation and opportunities for focused dialogue.

I see the classroom as a place of mutual learning and as an environment that facilitates communication; I endeavor to create a friendly atmosphere in which each student has a voice. This type of environment engages students to take an active role in the course and encourages activities that focus on learning. I plan to implement a class correspondence project between classes that I teach and classes in a French-speaking country. This project would help students make connections, draw comparisons, see other cultures, and can assist in developing intercultural awareness, higher-order skills, and communicative competence. I believe that it is crucial to link content in ways that encourage students to pursue their own interests and that allow them to put forth their own voice. My pedagogical framework is one that promotes student autonomy and responsibility, engagement in intellectual and analytical tasks, and creativity in language use; it also shows respect for student ideas and interests.

Language learning is a personal and intellectual journey that can continue throughout a lifetime. While my profession is that of a teacher, I am also a life long learner, as teaching and learning are inextricably linked. To conclude, I believe that students should be challenged and inspired as they continue to gain knowledge of the French language and as they learn to communicate. In providing personal attention to all students, I teach them to understand themselves better, to reflect on the people they are becoming, and to develop a new appreciation for the world in which they live.

Ciena Cornielle   Rigor: A Teaching Philosophy

In "The Rise and Fall of Literature," (*New York Review of Books*, November 1999) Andrew Delbanco discusses the decline of literary studies. He ultimately suggests academia is becoming a center for credentials, not education. Having taught Composition, ESL, Literature, and Technical Writing in preparation for a literary studies career, I find Delbanco's questions significant, but I resist "justifying" teaching. Education is a process, not a product. I require considerable reading amounts, weekly quizzes, several writing assignments, and mandatory conferences—but—I do not award a percentage for participation! Several colleagues have said, **"I would drop your class if I was an undergrad!"** Why set such high standards? Largely, because I was educated in Catholic and Jesuit institutions, and I believe the learning process has value in and of itself. I also do so because my experiences as a student and teacher at a small college and at two research universities have affirmed that requiring *and* modeling educational rigor fosters quality education.

Student evaluations of my courses reflect the courses' rigor; students often assert that my course was harder than any other section of the course, that it took more time than any of their other courses, and that my expectations exceeded their other instructors'. I am particularly proud that my most recent course experiences and evaluations also assert that my courses are intellectually satisfying, the assignments help students succeed in other courses and that they thought my preparation and subject knowledge was extensive. Rigor is relative, and it ought to match the goals of the course. I taught English 140/ Contemporary American Literature as a historical survey course, linking authors such as T.S. Eliot and Adrienne Rich, Joyce Carol Oates and Flannery O'Connor, Thomas Pynchon and Theresa Cha. We began the course by reading St. Jean de Crèvecoeur's "What is an American?" (1782). Some students questioned why I assigned this piece of 18th century literature, written by a Frenchman. Yet, in an evaluation, one of those same students commented, **"I wouldn't really get Adrienne Rich, Allen Ginsburg, and Ishmael Reed if we hadn't read Crèvecoeur."**

One must not only require educational rigor, but one must also model it. I comment on all assignments, vary my texts, trace parallel cultural movements, and use multiple media. In English & Women's Studies 194/ U.S. Latina and Chicana Literature, my students were unfamiliar with the historical relationship between the United States and Latin America. Thus, I prepared additional course content from history, sociology, and ethnography, so we could contextualize the literatures. I paired this content background with what I call the "Short Writing" (SW): a critical thinking tool. Students typically complete ten of these condensed (1-2pp), yet complete, essays. In Composition and ESL, the SW helps students practice definitions, analyses, and evaluations. In Literature, the SW challenges students to apply these analytical tools to texts. The SWs reaped unexpected benefits: students made better use of course materials and viewed my rigor as a catalyst for their own intellectual sweat. As a student in

English & Women's Studies 194 commented, **"The SWs were <u>very</u> important to me this semester. I made certain to read everything carefully so that I could produce a good piece of writing. My writing improved over the semester because of your demanding standards and relentless confidence that I could do better."**

In English 436/American Literature Since 1945, my approach was slightly different. In addition to the reading and writing tasks required in the lower level course, I challenged students to find and report on "lit bits": pieces of history, biography, or current events that linked our literature to extant culture. These "lit bits" help students discover the significant events and cultural climate our readings were produced in. I originally assigned one student to report per day, but by the end of the second week, several students were volunteering a "lit bit" each day. Thus, what initially seemed an instructive task became an entertaining challenge to provide the class with the coolest and most useful "lit bit" of the day. Since this was an advanced course taught during a six week summer session, I also felt it important to introduce theoretical concepts to supplement the students' developing sense of literary history. I drew several concepts from my own research in post-colonial, feminist, ethical, rhetorical, and narrative theories to help students understand the cultural work writing can accomplish. As one student in the course commented, **"I appreciated her cultural studies approach to the material — and her goals to link history with the fiction she selected to represent this particular time period. As a graduate student, I was impressed with Ciena's syllabus and assignments because they (e.g. annotated bibliography) give students a better understanding of how both research and writing occur in the English field."**

Because I have financed my own higher education, I know that it is truly hard to balance work, study, and play. As Delbanco's comments on the "corporatization" of universities suggest, validating literary study is not easy; it might not even be possible. I prefer to articulate my purpose and help students exceed their self-expectations. I encourage students to see how course objectives function as part of a broad educational experience for them, as well as for me. Even when composition students hope they will never need to consider audience again, or when literature students risk lacking "breadth" as they seek "depth," I endeavor to show them that rigorous learning has a purpose all its own: the garnering of education, not just its commonly sought after paper representation, a degree.

Jennifer Oakes: Teaching Philosophy

Through my research and writing, I have investigated the ways that nineteenth- and early twentieth-century female teachers argued for educational opportunities that allowed their students to become active participants in American society. In so doing, I have found that these educators' arguments speak directly to my own primary pedagogical goal—to create a classroom environment in which students gain critical literacy skills so that they, too, can actively participate in the classroom, university, and community. My focus, then, is to formulate classroom practices that enable students to engage in conversations pertinent to their lives, to examine the kinds of messages they receive everyday, and to invent ideas that could shape the world around them.

My daily classroom practices and course assignments illustrate my emphasis on students' active engagement with each other as well as the world inside and outside the classroom. I have designed entire courses so that students spend the semester reflecting on and engaging in particular social and political discussions. In my "What is Citizenship?" course (Rhetoric and Composition), for example, students analyzed readings on citizenship by writers like Malcolm X and Zitkala Ša; students wrote about their membership in certain *cultural* citizenships; and they read about and then joined conversations concerning post-September 11th citizenship. This semester-long endeavor gave students the opportunity to think critically about a topic that affects their lives and then engage in it, as the final course assignment, "Defining Citizenship," allowed students to use class discussions, readings, and writings to define what citizenship meant to them.

Although critical analysis of texts is a major component of my courses, I also stress, in Paulo Freire's words, that students learn to "read the world" as they read the word. One way students have worked to read their worlds was through my "Cultural Literacies" assignment (Honors English). This assignment asks students to analyze the beliefs, values, and worldviews that construct their particular cultures, while they also examine how language functions to constitute and re-constitute cultural cohesion. As this particular assignment enables students to fine-tune their analytical skills, it also introduces them to the idea that understanding their own cultures serves a critical function in their active participation inside these cultures and the larger world around them.

My third pedagogical focus involves providing a space for students' creativity. In my courses, the response-paper assignment, which asks students to submit nine single-spaced pages of writing throughout the term, allows students to respond freely to readings, class discussions, and communal, university, and national issues. These response papers often become spaces where students invent arguments for their essays or take course discussions in innovative directions. Furthermore, assignments such as "Proposing Your Education" (Basic Writing) continue to stress the importance of creativity. This particular assignment asks students to reflect on their educational pasts and imagine (and plan) their future educations as a means to "claim," in the words of Adrienne Rich, the education they want and need. Along with active engagement and critical analysis, creativity completes the three central components of my pedagogical goal, which aims to enable students to participate critically in their worlds.

Eliza Prince: Evidence of Teaching Effectiveness

Student Ratings of Teacher Effectiveness (SRTE)

		Quality of Instructor	Quality of Course
Fa02	English 404	6.14	5.52
Fa02	AM ST 105	6.17	5.88
Fa02	WMNST 001	6.12	5.77
Su02	English 435	6.37	6.06
Sp02	WMNST 003	6.21	5.86
Sp02	English 202A	6.33	5.83
Sp02	English 202A	6.80	6.15
Fa01	English 134	6.2	5.86
Fa01	English 202D	6.25	5.9
Fa01	English 202D	6.18	5.71
Su01	AM ST 100	6.44	5.72
Su00	English 202A	5.89	5.68
Sp00	English 232	6.57	6.43
Fa99	English 30	6.63	6.18
Fa99	AM ST 105	5.85	5.62
Su99	English 202B	(SRTEs unavailable due to computer processing problems)	
Sp99	English 202B	6.59	5.35
Fa98	English 202B	6.45	4.85
Fa98	English 202B	6.56	4.94
Su98	English 202D	5.84	5.68
Sp98	English 202D	5.81	5.43
Fa97	English 202D	5.44	5.13
Su97	English 202D	6.06	5.59
Sp97	English 15	6.22	5.77
Sp97	English 15	5.29	4.81
Fa96	English 15	6.13	5.61
Su96	English 15	5.86	5.33
Sp96	English 15	5.95	5.25
Fa95	English 15	6.50	5.92

Average Rating of Teacher Effectiveness: 6.17/7.0
(The Department considers scores of 6.0 and higher an indicator of exceptional teaching, and ratings of 5.0 and above an indicator of above average teaching).

Eliza Prince: Representative Student Comments

American Studies 100 (SU '01)
"It was informative and I learned a lot about our culture. Eliza was a terrific instructor—really down-to-earth and she cared about us."

"I would recommend this course to anyone with even the slightest interest in American culture. A lot of that has to do with Eliza the instructor."

"The course was fun. The teacher really allowed us to take in the subject and form our own views."

English 202A (SU '00)
"Eliza is excellent at explaining and giving examples. Everything about her teaching is excellent."

"[Eliza] cares about what we're doing and why we're doing it. She doesn't just go through the motions."

"Eliza was very understanding when I had a personal emergency come up. It made dealing with the emergency that much easier."

"Eliza seemed to really take her time when grading the papers. This helped me improve."

English 232 (SP '00)
"[Eliza] has a vast knowledge of the material. She encouraged our comments and thoughts. She was always willing to answer questions, clarify something, or discuss problems. She is a great teacher."

"Eliza was one of the most enthusiastic teachers I have had. She was able to spark my interest in a lot of areas of literature that I wasn't very familiar with."

"[Eliza] encouraged class discussion but also made sure the points she wanted us to get from the work were contributed. I really enjoy her teaching style."

"[Eliza] was outstanding. She stimulated thinking and 'the want for learning.' She is a great professor."

English 030 (FA '99)
"[Eliza is the] best English instructor I have ever had! Compared to the other non-science courses I have taken . . . Eliza is by far and away the best. She knows her stuff and can teach efficiently and effectively."

"Eliza was the best English teacher I've had in a long time."

"This course had the most (and most helpful) student-teacher interaction out of all the courses I took this semester."

American Studies 105 (FA '99)
"[Eliza] went to great lengths to find outside information on the course subjects. She seemed interested in getting the students involved and provided great supplemental examples like movies and videos."

"[Eliza] was a very cool teacher . . . in touch with society and what is going on within it."

"Eliza brought lots of different conversations to class which made the subject come to life."

English 202B (FA '98–SP '99)
"The quality of instruction was superior. She has shown more concern for my education than any other instructor."

"I had started 202B twice beforehand and dropped it. Eliza far outshined other instructors I previously had. She was interesting, funny, and eager to help."

"Eliza was very helpful. She was one of my favorite teachers throughout my four years of school. I liked the small class and being able to openly discuss. Her abundance of comments on each paper was very helpful."

"The quality of instruction in this course was considerably higher in this course as opposed to others. The student was not just a number in this class. Discussion was encouraged and [Eliza] offered insightful comments in her lectures."

"[Eliza] was very well prepared and enthusiastic about our learning. She brought a great knowledge base and personal experiences to her examples to help our understanding."

English 202D (SU '97–SU '98)
"[Eliza] seemed to care about the class and the students to a higher degree than any of my other elective courses."

"Eliza upheld very high standards throughout the course. Other professors/instructors usually do not do so because it is too time consuming. That is very respectable (of her)."

"The things that I learned from Eliza will stick with me. I'm keeping my notes as a reference for [my] job."

"I think she is an excellent instructor (although she is a little harsh with grading)."

English 015 (FA '95–SP '97)
" . . . I thought the instructor was great. Informal yet informative."

"I think going to office hours really helped me a lot. Not only did my grades on my papers show the improvement, but I was much more confident in my writing."

"Eliza was always willing to make us think, become better writers . . ."

Appendix II

Job Market Checklist

School Name_____

Job Description_____

1. Teaching school CV_____   Research school CV_____

2. Teaching school Cover Letter_____   Research school cover letter_____

3. Dissertation Description_____

4. SAS Post Card for acknowledgement of receipt_____

5. Post card received on_____

6. Abridged Teaching Portfolio_____   Longer Teaching Portfolio_____

7. Dossier_____   Requested on____ _____

8. Writing Sample A _____   Writing Sample B ___   Requested on_____

9. Conference Interview Scheduled for_____

10. Campus Interview scheduled for_____

NOTES:

Appendix III

Useful Resources

Boice, Robert. *Advice for New Faculty Members: Nihil Nimus*. Needham Heights, MA: Allyn and Bacon, 2000. An unusual set of suggestions for moderation in work and attitudes, with advice for reducing negative thoughts and unproductive behaviors, written by a professor of psychology who appears to be familiar with meditational or eastern modes of mindfulness. For some personalities, a helpful antidote to panic and paranoia. Applicable to any field.

Boufis, Christina and Victoria C. Olsen, eds. *On the Market: Surviving the Academic Job Search*. New York: Riverhead Books, 1997. A collection of personal accounts and anecdotes about the academic job market. Both successes and failures are described. An unusual focus on the job hunt as psychological experience.

Deneef, A. Leigh, and Craufurd D. Goodwin. *The Academic's Handbook*. 2nd ed. Durham, NC: Duke University Press, 1995. Most original for the discussion of getting grants, publishing research, and learning about academic communities and administration, but useful on job hunting, getting tenure, and academic salaries. Usable for a "professionalism" class.

Formo, Dawn M. and Cheryl Reed. *Job Search in Academe: Strategic Rhetorics for Faculty Job Candidates*. Sterling, VA: Stylus, 1999. Thought-provoking interview scenarios with questions and possible answers. Everything is cast in terms of suitable rhetorics. Has a list of the places where job announcements can be found for all sorts of fields: sciences, business, and such areas as dance and theatre as well as humanities.

Goldsmith, John A., John Komlos, and Penny Schine Gold. *The Chicago Guide to Your Academic Career: A Portable Mentor for Scholars from Graduate School through Tenure*. Chicago: University of Chicago Press, 2001. Chicago is publishing a series of books on professionalism. This volume is quite comprehensive: going to grad school, getting a mentor, writing a dissertation, hunting for a job, teaching and research, getting tenure, and such matters as the effects of gender and of starting a family on your career. The scope is impressive. They extract what is common to fields, so that this can be used by people in biology, psychology, economics, and humanities. Such general coverage prevents their being specific to a field.

Hall, Donald E. *The Academic Self: An Owner's Manual*. Columbus, OH: Ohio State University Press, 2002. A good discussion of how to recognize your own strengths and weaknesses and train yourself to succeed in the academic milieu. Hall stresses the interrelationship between yourself and the community around you.

Heiberger, Mary Morris and Julia Miller Vick. *The Academic Job Search Handbook*, 2nd ed. Philadelphia: University of Pennsylvania Press, 1996. A very good general source, with lots of sound advice, but it covers all fields, so must of necessity scant details on any one. This seems to me the best of these books for the job hunt itself.

Menges, Robert J. et al. *Faculty in New Jobs: A Guide to Settling In, Becoming Established, and Building Institutional Support*. San Francisco: Jossey-Bass, 1999. This will help you once you have a job; it helps you understand how academe works, and helps you learn how to get grants and network within your institution. Each chapter ends with a summary or conclusion, so you can check out the chapter's overall argument before plowing through it.

Moore, David Chioni. "Timing a First Entry onto the Academic Job Market: Guidelines for Graduate Students Soon to Complete the PhD." *Profession* 1999: 268–274. A balanced assessment of the pros and cons of doing a limited, preliminary search.

Schoenfeld, A. Clay and Robert Magnan. *Mentor in a Manual: Climbing the Academic Ladder to Tenure*. Madison, WI: Atwood, 1994. Humanities students have probably taught enough to know the pedagogical material, though reviewing it never hurts. This introduces you to teaching, research, service and to the basics of getting promoted. Perhaps the most original chapter is what to do if you don't get tenure, with a useful bibliography on changing careers.

Showalter, English, et al. *The MLA Guide to the Job Search: A Handbook for Departments and for PhDs and PhD Candidates in English and Foreign Languages*. New York: Modern Language Association of America, 1996. This covers the job hunt for people in literature and languages and offers lots of statistics on the job market (now dated). The style is dryly academic and the point of view rather abstract. Not as helpful as Heiberger and Vick, but the advice is field-specific.

Sowers-Hoag, Karen and Dianne F. Harrison. *Finding an Academic Job*. Thousand Oaks, CA: Sage, 1998. This covers all academic fields, and assumes conditions in which you only apply to jobs that interest you. It offers sound advice, but is not down-to-earth enough and hands-on enough to help the job hunter who has been given little training in professionalism.

Stivale, Charles J. "The Loneliness of the Long-Distance Interviewer." *Profession* 2003: 132–143. Stivale articulates the structure of academic interviews.

Toth, Emily. *Ms. Mentor's Impeccable Advice for Women in Academia*. Philadelphia: University of Pennsylvania Press, 1997. Only this volume addresses the scandals and the often hidden problems of academic politics. Toth gives good advice on how to protect yourself. The gender orientation does somewhat limit the range of problems discussed, though since many problems relate to gendered subordination, and assistant professors in general are in subordinate positions, the advice can be applied by men as well as women.

For a variety of analyses of the job market and the problems of hunting, you can consult the archive of miscellaneous articles at http://chronicle.com/jobs/, site of the *Chronicle of Higher Education*. To gain access to some materials, you need to be a subscriber, but during your job hunting year, you should definitely subscribe so you can look at their job lists. The Modern Language Association's annual series called *Profession* is also a good source of advice on job hunting.

Index